INHERITANCE HIJACKERS

INHERITANCE HIJACKERS

Who Wants to
Steal Your
Inheritance
and **How** to
Protect It

ROBERT C. ADAMSKI, JD

Inheritance Hijackers: Who Wants to Steal Your Inheritance and How to Protect It
Published by Ovation Books in cooperation with Sun Book Publishers, Inc.
P.O. Box 80107
Austin, TX 78758

For more information about our books, please write to us, call 512.478.2028, or visit our web site at www.ovationbooks.net.

Distributed to the trade by National Book Network, Inc.

Publisher's Cataloging-in-Publication
(Provided by Quality Books, Inc.)

Adamski, Robert C.
    Inheritance hijackers : who wants to steal your
inheritance and how to protect it / Robert C. Adamski.
    p. cm.
    LCCN 2008931563
    ISBN-13: 978-0-9814534-4-6
    ISBN-10: 0-9814534-4-9
    1. Estate planning--United States--Popular works.
2. Inheritance and succession--United States--Popular
works. 3. Wills--United States--Popular works.
I. Title

KF750.Z9A33 2009   346.7305'2
                              QBI08-600189

Front cover design by Kristy Buchanan

10 9 8 7 6 5 4 3 2 1

DEDICATION

This book is dedicated to all lawyers who assist their fellow man through diligence and dedication to the highest professional standards. They are all unsung heroes.

and

My family, friends and clients who made this book possible.

TABLE OF CONTENTS

INTRODUCTION

Inheritance Hijackers is the first book to examine and explain the who, why, and how of inheritance theft and how to protect yourself. Three decades of research, observation, trial experience, and analysis in the realm of inheritance disputes have gone into its production.

Thirty years ago, as an enthusiastic law school student eager to make my mark on the world, my interest focused on estate planning. Coming from a working-class home with little in the way of wealth, I was fascinated with acquiring and handling money. Learning what rich people do with their money would be exciting, I thought, and perhaps a little would fall my way.

Soon I was able to create bulletproof wills and trusts (or so I thought) and save gobs of estate taxes for my clients. I admitted to myself that this is not the most exciting area of law, but I decided to trade excitement for a stable income.

In the late 1970s, I relocated from New England to south Florida to escape the harsh winters and help wealthy clients who had also moved from the north to find excitement in their later years. At that time, thousands of retirees were moving to Florida every day with truckloads of money to buy cheap real estate, play golf, do some fishing, and relax. In south Florida, all sorts of northern transplants search for and find his or her place in the sun. Northern transplants were, and still are, overwhelming the local population in numbers and changing Florida forever. As a fellow transplant, I fit right in.

In the Sunshine State, entire cities are created for and populated by transplants who have left their extended families and friends in the snowy north to search for a new start in life. At first, their ties to their past are strong. They travel back home on holidays and host friends from the north during the winter months. Gradually, those urges to visit "back home" dwindle as life in their "new home" becomes more fulfilling. I too came around to the popular transplant conclusion about traveling up north for the winter holidays: "So what if there is no snow for Christmas? We can always go to the beach."

My plan was working superbly. My law practice thrived. I helped clients

> This is the first book to examine and explain the who, why, and how of inheritance theft and how to protect yourself.

plan to pass their wealth to their beneficiaries while saving tons of taxes to provide a more affluent lifestyle for those beneficiaries, and this gave my clients peace of mind. Although I loved the clients and the interaction, regrettably my work became repetitive. I needed more excitement.

One day a lawyer in New York telephoned me. He told me he represented the son of one of my clients, a well-off retiree from New York. I had prepared a trust, will, and power of attorney for my client, who was perfectly competent and lucid at the time. My work was well done. My client had named his three children as the sole beneficiaries of his estate. The client chose to give his son a power of attorney, and a second power of attorney to his "best friend," who lived in Florida. As it turned out, his best friend was his new girlfriend he had met soon after moving to Florida. I had never met her, but my client trusted her and needed someone in Florida to help if he became disabled. My client said she was loving and attentive to my client's wishes and was, in his mind at the time, the logical choice. I warned my client about the potential dangers in giving anyone, except the most trusted persons, a power of attorney. My client acknowledged that a power of attorney might be abused by some people, but assured me that I need not be concerned with his choice.

Not long after our meeting, my client experienced serious health problems. Unable to handle his finances, he soon turned control of his finances to his "best friend." She took that opportunity to use the power of attorney I had prepared to convert my client's bank accounts to joint ownership accounts with herself. This was done "for convenience," she later testified under oath. The legal proceeding that followed revealed she was systematically draining those accounts and transferring assets to her personal account, and also to her adult child's personal account. Only after expensive and lengthy litigation did my client's children recover some of what the girlfriend had stolen.

Had I overlooked something while counseling my client? After reflecting, I knew I would not have been able to dissuade my client from naming his "best friend" as his power of attorney. He was convinced he was making the right decision. I concluded that my client was an isolated victim of a rare occurrence: theft by a loved one. I soon learned how very naïve my conclusion was.

The temptation to steal an inheritance has a powerful pull. In my short life, I had not experienced temptation strong enough to overwhelm better judgment and cause an otherwise honest and generous person to act as they never imagined they would. Under ordinary circumstances, my client's "best friend" was an average person and honest in her everyday dealings with her fellow man. Yet the opportunity to take advantage of my client with little perceived risk resulted in her making a dishonest woman of herself. During the trial she revealed justifications she fabricated to ease her guilt over her theft. It was fascinating to see how she had crossed the line from honest to dishonest in tiny, easy-to-rationalize steps.

Soon after, another client retained me to investigate whether his elderly mother's new will, signed two months before her death, was valid. The will disinherited my client. After a lengthy investigation and trial, the court overturned the new will, finding that my client's brother had exerted undue influence on his mother in an attempt to steal the estate for himself.

At the same time I defended the girlfriend of a man who willed his estate to her, thereby disinheriting his children who all but ignored him in his old age. The girlfriend cared for the man for an extended period of time during his last illness. As a reward, he made a will giving her his modest estate. This was done without her knowledge. The court ruled my client did not cause her boyfriend to unlawfully disinherit his children and upheld the will.

A door had opened for me. I was hooked on the intrigue found in inheritance litigation. It soon grew to be a large part of my practice. A good inheritance lawyer must be a student of human nature, psychology, and the darker side of family dynamics. Litigating estate disputes, particularly among family members, reveals the human condition at its raw core. I became a psychoanalyst as well as a legal analyst, and became acquainted with facets of the human condition that surprised, repulsed, and encouraged me. Within a few years I realized that practicing inheritance law and litigation is as exciting as any John Grisham legal thriller. Since that first case, I have handled disputes in hundreds of estates valued from a few thousand dollars up to an estimated hundred million dollars. I am still learning and still excited about the work. Every new case is a new look inside the human experience.

I still believe that most people are honest and want to do the right thing for their fellow man. However, everyone has their tipping point into dishonest behavior. This is especially true in the realm of inheritances, where family dynamics, old grudges, and jealousies play a powerful role. These factors impact the relationships and lower the tipping point in an amount equal to the intensity of the grudge or jealousy. In family inheritance disputes, the tipping point is often very low and easily reached. In such disputes, the pain inflicted by and upon all parties is usually enough to permanently damage lifelong relationships. This was a hard lesson I came to learn from experience, not from books.

I can tell you that no family is immune from hijacking. Money is only paper or a number on a bank statement unless it is used for some purpose. In many family inheritance situations, the purpose may be to bring revenge on a family member using the stolen inheritance as the tool. Inheritance disputes mix family money with family history. Often, the result is close family relationships being destroyed forever.

Family money may appear to be the center of the inheritance dispute, but the money alone is rarely the cause of the problems that led to the dispute. Dysfunctional family dynamics, perhaps unrecognized for decades, are the root cause. In my experience, a perfectly functioning family unit does not exist. Any family claiming to have such a perfectly functioning unit is blind to the true facts and the potential dangers they face. This does not mean that there will be inheritance disputes in all families. It is a warning that inheritance disputes can arise in any family. Wise family members will guard against inheritance conflicts.

Families can be dysfunctional in many ways. The opportunities increase with the number of siblings, number of marriages and divorces, physical distance between family members, and the difficulty or infrequency of communication and oversight among family members.

Although theft of money is the weapon used to seek revenge, the amount of money involved is often not important. A small inheritance is coveted in the same way a large inheritance is coveted. Money is the convenient weapon in this forum. Often the situation is perceived to be the last opportunity to seek revenge on another, and the hijacker's actions are the desperate work of a tormented person.

The revenge may be sought for some insult or wrong done years ago. Perhaps mom or dad seemed to favor one child over another, and the deprived child desires to compensate for that loss by taking his sibling's rightful inheritance. How often is a sister unable to tell her sister that she is suffering emotionally from something the sister did or did not do? If the offended sister cannot forget and forgive, the situation festers, causing resentment over time. If the sisters cannot talk it out, the dispute is usually settled in another way. Perhaps an insult will do. Perhaps the opportunity to deprive the offending sister of part or all of her inheritance will present itself. Perhaps the only way a hurting person can seek revenge on a deceased rival sibling is to deprive the deceased sibling's child.

The possibilities are as numerous and complex as the human mind. Many motivators are irrational and founded in half-truths or distorted perceptions of an incident. Powerful motivators may be hidden or suppressed for decades until the opportunity to right the wrong presents itself.

While the amount of money involved is not important, the impact that money has on the other party is crucial. If mom dies with ten thousand dollars in the bank and your brother desperately wants his share of the ten thousand dollars, you can inflict real pain on your brother by depriving him of that money. If mom dies with one million dollars in the bank and your brother has ten million dollars of his own, he will fight for his share because the gift represents love from his mother.

In most cases the inheritance thief is seen as stealing the dignity of the victims, as well as the love attached to every inheritance, in addition to the material assets. There is no greater crime, especially between family members.

Experience has proven that this principle is cast in stone. In disputes between family members, the hijacker's motivation is never the cash and nothing but the cash. There is always an underlying psychological factor that compels the hijacker to take advantage of his or her family members. There are exceptions to every rule, but I have yet to find one in family relationships. The victims may not see beyond greed as the motivation for the theft. However, close and objective scrutiny of the relationship between the thief and the victim will reveal other motivations buried within the psyches of the parties.

Although most perpetrators are family members, there is a second class of thief that is related to the victim. Anyone in a confidential or close relationship with another can attempt to steal an estate. This includes caregivers, housekeepers, accountants, business advisors, lovers, bankers, lawyers, friends, and business associates. This class of thief is motivated more by the money than emotional needs and calculates more in cold blood, with little emotional investment in the relationships.

A person in good physical and mental health is capable of protecting himself from a greedy, scheming thief. The exceptions are when love and passion get in the way of good sense. As old age and physical and mental infirmities set in, once robust and capable people become dependent on others and more likely to become a victim. This is not to say that theft of an inheritance will occur at every opportunity. Many people are honest to a fault. However, trusting your inheritance to chance is not wise. It is better to be vigilant and safe than overly trusting and sorry.

HOW TO USE THIS BOOK

Although inheritance disputes are common there is little written on this fascinating subject. This book is the first thorough analysis of why inheritances are stolen, who the victims and the thieves are, and long-term consequences of inheritance theft.

There are two parts to this book. Part one, comprised of chapters 1 through 7, explains in plain English the laws governing inheritances, why and how a hijacking is accomplished, the psychology motivating the hijacker and the victims, and how you can protect yourself.

The subject matter progresses from the simple to the complex. Chapter 1 is a walk inside the world of inheritance theft. Chapter 2 is a primer on estate planning, which explains the basic laws and how assets are transferred through inheritance. Chapter 3 discusses the many possible victims of a hijacking and how many of them make themselves attractive targets for the hijacker. Chapters 4 and 5 outline inheritance laws and the legitimate ways a victim can recover their hijacked inheritance under the law. Chapter 6 lays out the anatomy of an inheritance suit from start to finish, giving the reader an idea of what victims face when recovering a hijacked inheritance. Chapter 7 summarizes the information in the earlier chapters and discusses how you can protect yourself from inheritance theft.

> This book is the first thorough analysis of why inheritances are stolen, who the victims and the thieves are, and long-term consequences of inheritance theft.

After reading part 1, the reader will have a practical working knowledge of inheritance law, how and why inheritances are hijacked, and how the victims can right the wrong. This working knowledge is the first step to truly understanding the subject.

Part 2 contains eight case studies illustrating how the working knowledge in part 1 is applied in real-life situations. These case studies are based on actual hijackings and resolutions. While entertaining, the case studies educate the reader on some of the many different ways inheritances are actually hijacked and how the law treats those different situations. The reader will see themselves and others within the characters in some of these stories, either as victim or potential hijacker. While the names, places, and other details of the cases have been changed to save the parties from embarrassment, the underlying facts are real. These cases are happening somewhere as you read this and will happen again in the future. For better or worse, these case studies are timeless because they are rooted in human nature, which will never change.

This format—first explaining the law, and then demonstrating and analyzing the law as applied in actual cases, is how lawyers are trained in law school. At the conclusion of this book, the reader will have a sound understanding of how, when, and where a hijacking can occur.

Understanding and defining the legal terms in this book is important to understanding the material. Consult the Glossary at the end of the book for definitions as you read. Armed with knowledge and understanding, the reader can safeguard their inheritance as well as anyone can. Happy reading, and good luck with your own inheritance, whether you are giving or receiving.

Part I

INHERITANCE HIJACKING

Chapter One

ENTER THE WORLD
OF INHERITANCE HIJACKING

What is hijacking and why is it a problem to us all?

Inheritance theft is similar to hijacking a truck. A person intends to transfer something—in this case wealth—to an intended recipient. However, the hijacker takes control of the wealth while it is on route to the intended recipient via a will, estate, or other means. Then the hijacker intentionally diverts the wealth to an unintended recipient. The unintended recipient of the inheritance may be the hijacker or another person, such as the hijacker's spouse or child.

> Hijackers take control of an inheritance and divert it to an unintended recipient.

The hijacked asset(s) need not be an entire estate. It may be a single bank account, annuity, insurance policy, retirement account, parcel of real estate, antiques, coin collection, jewelry, or other valuable asset. To complicate matters, the intended recipient may never know a hijacking has occurred.

One hundred trillion dollars will pass by inheritance in the next twenty years. It is estimated there are twenty-five trillion dollars in retirement accounts alone. Three to five times that amount is held outside retirement accounts and will pass through inheritance in the same time period.

How much of this vast wealth will be hijacked and diverted to unintended recipients? The amount is impossible to accurately quantify. There are no statistics. Many hijackings are never detected by the victims. These undiscovered crimes alone will total trillions in wrongly diverted inheritances. It is not an exaggeration to say that every family has been

> The hijacked inheritance may be an entire estate or one of many assets of an estate.

1

or will be affected by an attempted or successful inheritance theft. These thefts are widespread and, when they are discovered, seldom revealed to those outside the small group of affected family members.

A fair question is, "How is it possible to hijack trillions of dollars?" and "Who are these people who allow their inheritances to be hijacked?" You may believe that you, an intelligent person with a good education and happy family situation, will never be a victim of a hijacking.

The answer is that a hijacking is easily accomplished and no one is absolutely safe. Rich and poor alike are potential victims. The most robust, intelligent people can easily be victims, as well as the infirm or feebleminded. Hijacking is simply the act of diverting assets from the intended recipient to another person, and the opportunity to divert assets presents itself quite often.

Most people intending to make a gift by inheritance at their death are inexperienced and may have neglected to properly safeguard their intended gift. Likewise, those expecting the inheritance often have little or no experience with death and passing wealth from one generation to the next. The lack of experience leads to lack of awareness, which offers opportunity to the hijacker.

The crime is all the more difficult to detect because hijackers never use physical violence to accomplish their goals. Violence is easily discovered and punished. The hijacker's behavior usually consists of whispered lies, quiet fraud, forgery, or psychological influence. These acts are not easily discovered, difficult to prove, and rarely punished by the criminal courts.

This book reveals the dangers and challenges you face when intending to gift an inheritance or when receiving an inheritance. There are many valuable lessons and surprises.

Recent societal changes have contributed to increasing inheritance theft

American society has changed considerably in the last thirty years in ways that decrease communication, socialization, and supervision among family members. This increases hijacking opportunities. As a whole, our population has become:

1. More transient and mobile. Family members live farther apart than every before and are often scattered throughout the country and the world. This greatly reduces the opportunity for communication, socialization, and supervision. A family member may be alone and unguarded by loved ones when he or she becomes weak and possible prey for a hijacker.

2. More likely to divorce. When married couples divorce, family members are divided. Relationships are strained and sometimes turn hostile. Second marriages and blended families increase tension in relationships. Loyalties shift among family members. Many times people fall prey to lies and deceit.

3. More likely to live longer. Longevity is a blessing and a curse. Living to a ripe old age can be enjoyable. However, old age often brings isolation, depression, loneliness, physical ills, and a decrease in mental ability if not Alzheimer's disease and dementia. These problems accelerate after the death of a spouse. The elderly and infirm are easily victimized, often when close to death.

4. More likely to crave active sexual relationships later in life. New products and medications allow aging adults to enjoy an active sex life almost indefinitely. Older men and women are now seeking out willing partners for the affection and human contact associated with those relationships. Many of these men and women will allow their needs to overwhelm their good sense and fall victim to a hijacker.

5. Wealthier. More people have more money than at any other time in history. Trillions of dollars will be transferred between generations in the next twenty years. This vast wealth provides more opportunities for the hijacker than at any time in the past.

6. More likely to accept bad legal advice, particularly over the Internet. The Internet is flooded with legal advice that is usually incomplete and sometimes erroneous. Often friends give well-meaning but misleading and dangerous advice. What may appear as a simple situation is often complex. It is a fact of life that legal situations require competent legal analysis, which can be provided only by an attorney trained to recognize all possible issues.

These factors increase our vulnerability to thieves and scoundrels as we age. Without sufficient planning and assistance, we all become victims inviting a hijacker and disaster.

Misplaced trust is often the root of the problem, and often impossible to avoid

A wolf in sheep's clothing is the most common threat to an inheritance.

The most important element in the world of inheritances is placing trust in the proper person. Placing trust in the right people can prevent a hijacking. Conversely, misplaced trust gives a hijacker the opportunity he or she is looking for. Therefore, a frank discussion of who a person should and should not trust is very important.

I have asked thousands of clients, "Who will handle your money if you are unable to do so before your death?" and, "Who will administer your estate after your death?" These questions evoke strong feelings in almost every client. I can see they are internalizing the question and weighing the alternatives, deciding who can and cannot be trusted when they are unable to do for themselves.

The decision is often very difficult, even in what we consider to be model families. We all want and need to trust those who are closest to us in our lives. Without trust we would be lonely, isolated individuals dying from lack of human contact. When asked who they will trust, the client is deciding who will care for them if they are weak and vulnerable and unable to care for themselves. They will likely be unable to undo the decision later in life in their weakened state, perhaps being legally incompetent to make any changes, even if made for their own good. They are also deciding who can be trusted to distribute their worldly goods after they are gone, when they have absolutely no control. They ask themselves, "Who will do what's best for me in all situations and honor my intentions? Who will resist all temptation to steal the inheritance, even a small part of it?" These are often hard questions to answer.

Can you easily answer these questions for yourself? Or do you need to weigh the alternatives and pick the best of a weak group of choices? Do not be embarrassed if you cannot trust every one of your children or even your spouse as much as you would like. You are not alone. No family is perfect.

Even if you choose the most trustworthy person you know to handle your affairs, there is a good chance your worldly goods will end up in the wrong hands, even if you do your best to guard against it. I estimate, based on my almost thirty years of experience in this field, that you or someone in your family has been or will be a victim of inheritance theft. And the odds are that the thief is a family member.

Hijacking is a quiet crime flying under the radar

You may suspect I am exaggerating and ask why this widespread problem is not general knowledge. Why are hijacked inheritances not well-publicized events? Why is a hijacking not as newsworthy as a bank robbery? Why are there no classes or seminars on how to avoid a hijacking?

I believe the answer is that a hijacking is not a dramatic sudden event that occurs in the public view. These are crimes committed in secret, behind closed doors, and out of the public view. They are generally family affairs, with the occasional close family friend playing the thief. In addition, as you will learn, the victims may never know they have been victimized.

Those who do realize they have been victimized will have a very difficult task, legally and psychologically, in recovering their lost inheritance. Victims are prone to blame themselves to some degree, or to be embarrassed or ashamed that a family member or close friend would steal from them. Sometimes the clever hijacker convinces the victim there was no theft or conceals the theft and remains undiscovered.

People are reluctant to tell their neighbors that a family member is an alcoholic or drug addict or thief. The victim often endures the theft in silence, not wishing to air their dirty laundry in public. Just as an alcoholic is enabled by those who help them function, the hijacker is enabled by the victim who refuses to punish the crime. This reluctance to confront and punish the hijacker is most common when a hijacking child steals from a parent while the parent is alive. The parent endures the crime, refusing to seek recovery of the lost assets so as not to hurt the child.

Compiling accurate statistics on inheritance theft is impossible. Inheritance theft cannot be summarized in a sound bite and neatly packaged for the evening news. *Inheritance hijackers* cannot be baited and arrested on television as a sexual predator can. Therefore, inheritance theft slips under the radar of the news media.

There have certainly been a few widely publicized inheritance cases. Howard Hughes and Anna Nicole Smith come to mind. These cases drew attention because of the huge size of the estates and the unusual characters involved. The typical inheritance hijacking involves much smaller amounts of money, and the characters are ordinary people leading ordinary lives, which isn't sensational enough to attract big media. Even if the amount hijacked is not newsworthy in the eyes of the news media, it is undoubtedly a great amount to the victim. One man's pocket change is another man's fortune.

Inheritance theft is not an area of the law highlighted in law school, although it should be—I know more than a few lawyers who make a very good living practicing in this area. I learned inheritance law through experience and by closely observing my clients and their family relationships for the past three decades. Saying that every family has been or will be touched by inheritance theft is not an exaggeration, as you will see.

Meet the players

Every hijacking involves five elements.

1. The first victim or target is the "donor," the person who intends to give an inheritance. I call this victim Target A.

2. The inheritance itself, which can be any single asset a person owns or an entire estate.

3. The second victim or target is the intended recipient of the inheritance. This victim may be a single person or a group such as the children of Target A. I call this victim Target B.

4. The hijacker, who is almost always a single person acting alone but in rare cases may be two or three conspirators.

5. The persons benefiting from the hijacking, who may be the hijacker or others, such as the hijacker's children.

In some situations, Target B may be unaware that he or she was to receive an inheritance and that it was diverted by the hijacker. For example, Millie makes a will that gives ten thousand dollars to each of her several nieces and nephews, and the balance of her estate to her only son. Millie does not tell anyone except her lawyer and her only son about the intended gifts to her nieces and nephews. Millie's son decides to cancel the gifts. Instead of asking his mother to change her will, he waits until she dies and destroys the will. Without a will, Millie's entire estate is inherited by her son. The nieces and nephews may grieve at Millie's death, but they will never know that Millie's son has hijacked their inheritances.

In every hijacking, the hijacker steals the assets Target A intended to transfer to Target B. Both victims have a legal claim against the hijacker. The intended recipient, Target B, is almost always the victim bringing suit against the hijacker. Why? Because Target A is deceased in most inheritance cases. It is my feeling that if the courts gave more weight to the wrong done to the donor of the gift, Target A, more cases would be decided against the hijackers.

If the hijacker strikes before Target A dies, the suit to recover the inheritance will be brought by Target A while he or she is alive. Here is an actual real-life example. An elderly aunt intends to give her home to her many nephews and nieces at her death, which is many years in the future. She chooses one nephew to handle her estate at her death. The

hijacker: One who steals an inheritance by diverting it from the intended recipient.

nephew convinces his aunt to deed her house to him before her death to avoid probate after her death. The nephew then sues to evict her from her own house to enable him to sell the house for his own benefit. This is a clear case of elderly abuse and inheritance theft while Target A is alive. The aunt can sue to over- turn the deed and will be successful. However, the lawsuit will be expensive, time consuming, and will tear the family apart.

Like most people, you may believe that hijacking victims are as rare as vic- tims of shark attacks or lightning strikes. Inheritance theft may be something that happens only to other families. Please let me point out the potential vul- nerability of us all. Here is a list of frailties common to victims. These frailties are not unusual characteristics that curse only a few unfortunate souls among us. On the contrary, these frailties are common in every person's life. It is easy to see why everyone, including you and me, will become a potential victim at some time in their life. Anyone may become a victim if they are

- Infirm, physically or mentally, at any age;
- Elderly and declining in physical and mental health;
- Dependent on others, especially those needing constant personal care;
- Subject to the influence of another person, causing them to act against their free will;
- Prone to make assumptions about inheritance law without seeking professional legal advice;
- Unwilling to make an estate plan or listen to professional advice;
- Secretive about assets and intentions;
- Grandiose and prone to making inheritance promises that cannot be fulfilled;
- Making major changes in their life, such as divorcing or remarrying;
- Estranged from family members, especially a parent and child estranged from each other;
- Without a spouse or direct descendants to inherit the estate; hijackers can more easily influence targets who have no close family ties to family members;
- Careless about who they trust with their financial security.

Just as there are two classes of victims, there are two classes of hijackers. The first is the hijacker who emerges from among the family members of the victims. These hijackers are motivated to utilize the hijacking to settle a family dispute or seek revenge against the victims for a past wrong. This is powerful motivation that overcomes family loyalties and destroys relationships. The second class of hijackers is comprised of non-family members, such as caregivers, spouses in a second marriage, friends from church, and interlopers of any sort. Ironically, even though these hijackers are strangers to the inheritance victim, it is often easier to guard against hijacking by a stranger than a family member.

In all hijackings there must be a relationship between the victim and the hijacker. Here is a list of the dozen relationships where you are most likely to discover a hijacker:

1. An overly friendly stranger assisting an elderly or infirm person often influences the elderly or infirm to give an inheritance, loan money, or make a large gift to them

2. Health care workers or others who provide assistance in the home often request loans and steal valuables

3. Extended family members, such as grandchildren and nieces or nephews of elderly persons, often identify an aging relation as a possible source of an inheritance

4. Family members who move in and take control of the living situation often take control of an inheritance as well

5. New love interests, especially when disparate ages are a factor, may not be in it solely for the love

6. Individual administrators of wills and trusts have great opportunity to plunder. This excludes reputable corporate administrators.

7. Financial planners and advisors who court the senior market can sell financial products detrimental to the customer

8. Those who constantly criticize another person may covet that person's inheritance and be attempting to influence others with their criticism

9. Anyone trusted with handling the money or accounts of another can easily embezzle assets

10. Laymen giving legal advice on inheritance issues often give advice to benefit themselves and harm others

11. A child who moves close to an elderly parent often inherits a disproportionate share of the estate, leaving the other children with less of an inheritance

12. Anyone with a power of attorney to act for another has the power to help themselves to the assets

This is not an exhaustive list of possible hijacker and victim relationships. Just as the characteristics of the victims we reviewed above are common to us all at some time in our lives, these dozen relationships are common in our society. It is easy to see why hijacking inheritances is widespread if not well-known.

How does the law treat a hijacking?

Hijacking an inheritance is clearly a theft and a crime. However, it is ignored by most agencies that prosecute criminal theft. These agencies are busy prosecuting easily identified crimes, such as armed robbery and burglary or property theft.

Theft of an inheritance is a white-collar crime, which is more difficult to prove than a violent act, such as a mugging. Often it is difficult to determine if a theft occurred at all. Theft of an inheritance is often accomplished using psychological influence over the victim, and it is difficult, if not impossible, to prove criminal intent. As a result, hijackers can act without fear of criminal prosecution for the most part. The worst fear the typical hijacker faces is the threat of a civil court suit, where he is forced to repay what he has stolen.

Once the hijacking is complete, victims must go to great lengths to recover their hijacked inheritance. Court battles are expensive and lengthy. Victims must finance their legal battle against the hijacker while the hijacker has access to the hijacked assets to defend himself.

Protecting against a hijacking

It is an unavoidable fact of life that we all must assume the risk that our inheritance may be hijacked. As a practical matter, it is impossible to absolutely protect yourself against inheritance theft.

One impractical but effective solution is to gift your wealth immediately and prematurely to your intended heirs. However, no one expecting to live at least a short time longer would immediately give all their assets to their intended beneficiaries and make themselves destitute. The giver would be forced to be dependent on the beneficiaries for their financial support. Even if the beneficiary is now trustworthy, there is no guarantee they will fulfill all of the financial obligations expected by the giver. Another reason not to gift wealth prematurely is the probable change to the family relationships that will cause the person making the gift to change the plan of distribution of the inheritance. Once the premature gift is complete, it will be all but impossible to reverse.

It is not enough to put the safety of an inheritance in the hands of professionals, such as lawyers or financial advisors. These professionals can help, but they cannot protect one from a determined hijacker who seizes on an opportunity unless the professionals are instructed to do every act possible to prevent theft. This instruction is never given to the professional. It is impractical to contract with a professional to take control of the estate and do every act possible to prevent a hijacking.

Trusting professionals may give one a false sense of security and cause one to drop his or her guard at a critical time. And, ironically, sometimes the trusted professional turns out to be the hijacker.

Chapter 7 thoroughly discusses protecting your inheritance, but don't skip ahead. To get the most out of chapter 7, you need to absorb the interesting and entertaining information in chapters 2 through 6.

The most important weapon against inheritance theft is knowledge and understanding how your inheritance may be hijacked. A knowledgeable person is a powerful person. Now, begin the road to knowledge and understanding inheritance hijacking by taking the short course in estate planning in chapter 2.

Chapter Two

ESSENTIAL GUIDE TO ESTATE PLANNING

When it comes to the law, knowledge is always power. I cannot count the times a client has told me that they did something without consulting an attorney and now regret what they did because it damaged them in some way. Sometimes the damage can be easily reversed. However, in the world of inheritance hijacking, the damage is usually not discovered until after a death. Therefore, nowhere is knowledge of the law more important to prevent mishaps and damage than in the world of inheritances.

Laws regulating inheritances are complex and very precise. An entire inheritance can depend on small and seemingly unimportant details. The hijacker's level of knowledge equals his power to hijack an inheritance. Most hijackers will read a self-help book on the law or consult a knowledgeable friend or attorney. However, knowledge of the law will also help avoid a hijacking. There is an old saying that when a man with experience or knowledge meets a man with money, the man with knowledge or experience leaves with the money and the man with the money leaves with experience. This holds true in the world of inheritances as well. However, even the most knowledgeable hijacker will not be successful against an equally knowledgeable opponent.

> Nowhere is knowledge of the law more important to prevent mishaps and damage than in the world of inheritances.

This section is organized in question and answer format for ease of understanding. The subjects will progress from the simple to the complex.

What is a will?

A will is an essential estate-planning tool that states your last wishes. A will can direct distribution of assets, appoint your personal representative or administrator of the estate, appoint a guardian for your minor children, create a trust to manage property or delay distribution, state your funeral or cremation desires, provide for your pet, apportion any estate taxes, direct which assets are used to pay your debts, disinherit people, and state anything else you wish to say at the time.

A person who dies without a will dies "intestate." If a person dies without a will, state law will dictate who inherits the estate and who acts as personal representative or administrator of the estate. These decisions may be contrary to your wishes. This concept is discussed below.

Any person at least eighteen years of age and of sound mind may make a will.

The law is very particular about how a will must be executed or signed. In Florida and most other states, a will must be written rather than oral and must be witnessed by two persons under formal requirements of law. Will signing, known as due execution, is discussed in chapter 4.

What property is controlled by my will?

Your will controls only the real property and personal property that you owned in your name alone at your death. Property you own as a joint tenant with another with the right of survivorship goes to the survivor and is not controlled by your will. Property on which you have made a beneficiary designation goes to the beneficiary and is not controlled by your will. Examples of this property are an insurance policy, annuity, or bank account.

Note that if you die without a will, the same type of property is subject to probate administration in what is known as an intestate proceeding, which is explained below.

May a person dispose of property in any way he or she wishes by a will?

The answer is yes with two major exceptions:

First, a person may not disinherit his or her spouse without a properly executed marital agreement. The law gives a surviving spouse a choice to take either his or her share as provided in a will, or a percentage (30 percent in Florida) of all of the decedent's property.

Second, surviving spouses and children are protected by law with special rights to homestead property in most states. In Florida, a surviving spouse receives a life estate in the homestead, and the owner's children receive the homestead at her death. This arrangement creates many conflicts between the children and the spouse, particularly in second marriages. In many cases, the surviving spouse finds she is obligated to maintain a house she no longer wants or cannot afford. And the children must deal with their parent's surviving spouse for several years before they inherit the asset.

Are wills made in one state valid in other states?

Wills are handled by the courts in the state in which you die. Therefore, a will is valid regardless of where it is prepared if it is valid where you die. If moving to another state, you should investigate whether your will and other estate-planning documents are valid. Even if valid, an out-of-state will can cause delay and expense. The testimony of witnesses in another state who may have moved or died may be required. The will may be outdated or invalid in some way. It is best to make your last will in the state where you reside at your death.

What happens when there is no will or other plan for distribution?

If you die without a will (or die "intestate," as the law calls it) your real and personal property is under the jurisdiction of the probate court and is distributed according to a formula fixed by the law of that state. The state law determines who receives your property, not you. The inheritance statutes contain rigid formulas and make no exception for unusual needs. The court appoints an administrator, who may be someone you would not choose, to manage your estate. The cost of probating an intestate estate can far exceed the costs in a "testate" estate, where a will controls the proceedings.

Destroying a will causes an estate to be distributed according to the laws of intestacy. It is possible that a person may destroy a will to hijack a portion of the estate they would not otherwise inherit.

Let's assume dad's will gives his valuable business to his son, John, who worked in the business and helped dad his entire life. The will states that the other half of the estate is divided equally among dad's four children, including John. If dad dies without a will, the law provides that each of the children inherit one-fourth of the

decedent: The deceased person who leaves the inheritance.

entire estate. (Assuming dad died without leaving a surviving spouse.) If the will is destroyed, each child receives a share of dad's business as well as the other estate assets, and John is partially disinherited. This may provide enough incentive to a child to destroy dad's will.

What is a "will substitute"?

A will substitute transfers title to property at death without the use of a will. Revocable trusts, joint ownership, and accounts with a pay-on-death or beneficiary designation for an insurance policy or annuity are examples of will substitutes. Many of these are important and convenient tools for the hijacker and are discussed below.

Who manages my estate?

The owner of the will nominates an administrator in the will to act on his behalf to carry out his last wishes. In Florida, the administrator is called the "personal representative." In other states the administrator may be called an "executor" or "surrogate." A convicted felon is disqualified to serve as an administrator in most states. Corporations with trust powers, such as banks, can also serve. If there is no will, or the nominated person is unable to serve, state statues dictate who may serve. The administrator has no power to act until a petition to probate the estate is filed in the probate court and the probate judge grants them the power to administer the estate and take control of the estate assets.

administrator: A person who manages a probate estate or a trust, otherwise known as a personal representative, executor, trustee, surrogate, or conservator.

Acting as administrator is a huge advantage to the hijacker. Estate assets can be secreted, manipulated, and used by the hijacker to fight off attacks by others, such as children contesting their parent's will that disinherited them in favor of the hijacker. Inheritance litigation is costly and sometimes decided in favor of the party best able to endure the litigation expense.

What does "probate an estate" mean?

Probate is the administration of your assets after your death. The process requires collection and distribution of the "probate estate" assets. The assets of the probate estate are all the property a decedent owned solely in his or her name at the time of death. This property is subject to the jurisdiction of the probate court. This may consist of full ownership or partial ownership in property, as in a case of tenants in common each owning a share of the whole. Life insurance policy proceeds are sometimes payable to the estate and are administered in the probate proceeding. Many assets are not subject to probate administration, such as assets held in a trust. Insurance proceeds also pass outside the probate administration.

The probate procedures vary depending upon value and type of assets. The most common proceeding is known as a formal proceeding, where an administrator is appointed by the court to handle the assets, debts, creditor claims, and distribution of assets.

Does a will avoid probate?

No. All property disposed of through your will is subject to probate court jurisdiction.

Why is probate necessary?

The probate court system exists to ensure a decedent's last wishes are fulfilled. Because the decedent is not alive to speak for himself, the law attempts to safeguard his last wishes.

The law makes assumptions when a decedent dies without a will, or intestate, or has not addressed a matter in a last will. For example, the law assumes that a person who dies without a will wants to give his or her estate to all of their children in equal shares if their spouse is deceased. Another assumption made by the law is that a decedent wants their spouse to manage their estate if the spouse survives the decedent, even if they are legally separated and on the verge of divorce.

To avoid an unexpected result, it is best to make a will even if the estate is small and your last wishes are simple.

Because probate laws attempt to address any situation that arises in the administration of the deceased person's estate, the laws are complicated and the process can be lengthy. The probate proceeding is conducted under strict court supervision with due process protection built in at every step to protect not only the decedent's last wishes and the beneficiaries but the creditors of the estate.

The system does not eliminate wrongdoing in estate administration. An administrator can gut an estate leaving little or nothing for the beneficiaries.

Beneficiaries must be diligent and oversee the estate administration as best they can. Unfortunately, the courts rarely bring severe punishment upon dishonest estate administrators. Except in the most egregious cases, the courts punish hijackers with civil rather than criminal sanctions. The victims must finance the action against the hijacker and the best the victims can hope for is a money judgment against the administrator.

Is a probate proceeding time consuming?

The type of administration and type of probate assets determine the time involved, which varies from a few months in simple estates up to a year or more in complex estates. If there is inheritance litigation, the time to settle the estate is extended until the litigation is concluded. Inheritance litigation is discussed in a separate chapter.

What fees, costs, and taxes can be expected?

Attorney fees, court costs, accounting fees, administrator fees, and other expenses average approximately 3 to 8 percent of the assets subject to probate. Inheritance litigation greatly increases the costs.

Short anatomy of an uncontested probate proceeding

Probate begins with filing a petition for administration. The person wishing to be administrator is usually the petitioner. The petition asks the court to admit the will to probate, or if there is no will, to open an "intestate" proceeding. If there is no objection from others involved, the court will admit the will to probate or open an intestate estate. The document that gives the administrator the power to act in place of and on behalf of the decedent is called "letters of administration." The administrator has no power to act until the letters are signed. The court may require that the administrator post a bond to ensure he or she acts to faithfully administer the estate. If so, an insurance company acts as surety for the administrator and is paid a fee or premium from the estate.

The administrator must collect the estate assets; publish a notice telling the world any claims against the estate must be filed within a certain time, typically ninety days, or they are forever barred; give notice of the estate to known creditors; pay the legitimate debts of the decedent and claims against the estate; contest illegitimate claims; collect debts due the decedent; deal with property that is exempt from claims by outsiders; maintain and protect property; sell or liquidate assets; abandon worthless property; pay any income and estate taxes; file an inventory; distribute the assets to the beneficiaries; and file accountings with the court.

When all this is accomplished, the administrator is discharged from his or her responsibilities by an order of the court when the court is satisfied that the administrator has satisfied his or her obligations to the probate court, beneficiaries, creditors, and tax collectors.

How do federal estate taxes work?

Federal estate taxes are imposed on all estates beginning with the first dollar. United States citizens are entitled to an exemption from estate taxes for the first two million dollars in 2008 and three and one-half million dollars in 2009. The result is that estates valued at less than the exemption can be transferred free of estate taxes. The estate tax system will change in 2010. Congress is considering abolishing the estate or death tax and replacing it with a different system not yet decided upon. The information offered here may not apply to persons dying after 2009.

Under the present system, estates of any size can be transferred to a surviving spouse without estate tax liability. This is called the unlimited marital deduction, which allows a married couple to postpone, but not avoid, taxation. The tax, if any, is fully assessed at the death of the second spouse, usually resulting in a higher tax burden.

Federal estate taxes start at 35 percent on the amount above the exempted amounts and can claim up to 55 percent of the value of an estate. Because estate taxes are progressive, the larger the taxable estate, the higher the tax rate.

There is an additional tax called the generation-skipping tax (GST), which taxes transfers in excess of $1,060,000 to persons in a "skip generation," usually the grandchildren and great-grandchildren of the decedent. This tax is designed to discourage transfers to the skip generation by wealthy individuals whose children are also wealthy. The government wishes to tax every generation. Assets subject to the GST are taxed at approximately 70 percent.

As an estate grows larger, the loss in value becomes increasingly significant to the beneficiaries. Keep in mind that estate settlement often includes additional costs—such as state death taxes, debts, and administration and personal expenses—which further reduce assets passed along to heirs.

What about state estate taxes?

States commonly impose estate or inheritance taxes in addition to the federal estate tax. States that do impose taxes at death typically do so on even the smallest estates. As a practical matter, bona fide Florida residents are not subjected to a state estate or death tax in addition to the federal tax. Florida assesses a tax equal to a credit the federal government gives for state estate taxes paid. The end result is that the federal government pays the Florida tax. Many other states generate much of their revenue through estate taxation.

Florida residency: Is it a real tax benefit?

If estate taxation was the only consideration in determining one's home, everyone should live in Florida. As well as the tax advantages discussed above, tax questions are easily cleared in Florida. Problems can arise when one relocates to Florida and leaves a connection, however weak, with another state. Something as innocent as a club membership, small bank account, or stock held by a broker can cause a state to vigorously pursue taxation. For example, New York and other states employ tax examiners to pursue former residents who retire outside of the state but leave accounts or connections behind. Any connection means New York estate taxation may be imposed on assets outside New York.

What is a "trust"?

A trust is a written document that an individual, called a "settlor" or "grantor," creates to provide for management of property held in the trust. In estate planning, the property is typically owned by the settlor before the trust is created and transferred directly to the trust. The settlor appoints an administrator, called a "trustee," to manage the trust. The trust and property in the trust are managed for the benefit of the beneficiary of the trust, who receives the income and other benefits. The terms of the trust control management of the trust property. The settlor creating the trust can be very creative in trust management and distribution to the beneficiary.

> The **settlor** or **grantor** creates the trust. The **trustee** manages the trust. The **beneficiary** reaps the benefits from the trust.

The most common trust is the revocable living trust created by a single person or a married couple. In these trusts, the settlor, trustee, and beneficiary are the same person(s) until the death of the settlor. At the settlor's death, the trust property is distributed as the settlor dictates in the trust. This trust is a substitute for a will, although a "pour-over" will accompanies the trust to complete the estate-planning documents.

pour-over will: A will used in conjunction with a trust in estate planning to ensure all the assets of the maker of the trust are placed under the authority of the administrator of the trust.

A trust is a form of private asset administration. You create your own set of rules that suit you. At death, this private administration replaces the public probate procedures, although a trust may not reduce the cost of administration. When used properly, the trust effectively and efficiently transfers assets to the next generation.

Trusts offer many opportunities for the hijacker. The dangerous features of trusts are discussed in later chapters and case studies.

The most common trust forms and their purposes are the following:

The revocable living trust is created during your life to hold and manage assets during your life and to manage or distribute those assets after your death. During the last decade, the revocable living trust has replaced the will as the most common estate-planning tool.

An irrevocable trust is created during your life to manage assets and is similar to a revocable living trust, but the terms of the trust cannot be changed.

An irrevocable insurance trust, a type of irrevocable trust, owns and holds a policy insuring the decedent. The proceeds are not taxable at the decedent's death (a big exception to the general rule) and are used primarily to provide liquidity and pay estate taxes.

Testamentary trusts are created in your will and are not effective until your death and only if the will is declared to be valid by the probate court. This form of trust will *not* avoid the probate process.

The credit shelter or bypass trust is a tax-saving device that allows a married couple to take advantage of twin estate tax exemptions, doubling the exemption to a total of four million dollars in 2008 and seven million dollars in 2009.

Specialized estate-planning tools, such as QTIP trusts, charitable remainder trusts, family limited partnerships, and several other tax saving devices, are available but do not warrant discussion here.

What about income taxes before death?
How are trusts taxed?

In the case of a revocable trust, if the settlor is the trustee, the Department of the Treasury imposes income tax as if the trust does not exist and therefore does not require a separate income tax return. When a successor trustee assumes control (usually at the settlor's death), a separate income tax return for the trust is required. Other types of trusts, such as irrevocable trusts, require their own federal tax identification number and annual income tax return.

What is a fiduciary relationship?

A fiduciary relationship exists when a person has trust in and relies upon a second person, called the "fiduciary," who has a legal duty to the first person. The fiduciary is relied upon and has an obligation to be fair and honest in his dealings. Should the fiduciary breach the duty he owes by being unfair or dishonest, the fiduciary is liable for damages resulting from the breach of duty.

The trustee of a trust is one type of fiduciary. He owes a duty to administer the trust and must be fair and honest with the settlor and the beneficiaries of the trust. The administrator of a probate estate is a fiduciary who owes a duty to administer the estate and to be fair and honest with the beneficiaries and creditors of the estate.

What are the potential risks in having a trust?

The predominate risk lies with the administrator or trustee of the trust.

In private trusts, the potential for hijacking a trust by a dishonest trustee is great. In my experience, four out of five of the beneficiaries of trusts will have disputes with the trustee over the management of the trust estate. The trustee is often tempted to breach their fiduciary duty of fairness and honesty, even for surprisingly small sums of money. Often the ability to settle a long-running family dispute provides the rationale to bend to the temptation.

fiduciary: One who owes a legal duty to another and who must be fair and honest.

Trustees of private trusts are given wide latitude to deal with trust property without being concerned with direct oversight from beneficiaries of the trust. In the ordinary course of business, beneficiaries have little power to obtain or demand timely information from a reluctant trustee. In most states, trustees of private trusts are obligated by the law to give accountings to the beneficiaries only on an annual basis. A dishonest trustee will often refuse to give any sort of accounting of the trust. This forces the beneficiary to file a civil lawsuit to obtain the information he is entitled to receive and attempt to punish the dishonest trustee. When the beneficiary does discover wrongdoing, there is not a quick and easy remedy. The beneficiary must seek relief in the court system, which brings on expense and delay.

Criminal prosecution of dishonest trustees of private trusts is all but unknown. Criminal cases must be proven beyond a reasonable doubt. Dishonest trustees may be guilty beyond a reasonable doubt in the eyes of the wronged beneficiaries, but prosecutors often find it impossible to prosecute. The dishonest trustee always has a story to tell about why their acts were not dishonest. Prosecutors do not want to be caught up in family squabbles and prefer to treat these cases as private family matters to be settled by the civil courts. There are laws against abuse of the elderly and disabled that may prompt prosecutors to go after some of the worst examples of dishonest trustees, but these laws have little teeth without aggressive prosecution. We'll discuss this at length in chapter 5.

Corporate trustees are almost always honest and not a hijacking threat. If, however, the corporate trustee uses a money manager, the beneficiaries should keep close watch. Money managers earn fees by managing money. They buy and sell stocks and bonds and other financial products. If the money manager is making excessive transactions and generating large fees, the beneficiaries are losing that part of their inheritance to the money manager.

> **private trust:** A trust created by an individual or couple to manage their assets during life and transfer the assets to their beneficiaries at death.

What is a power of attorney?

A power of attorney is a very powerful document that gives another the power to act on one's behalf. The person giving the power is called the "donor." The recipient is the "donee." Examples of the powers typically given by the donor are the ability to write checks on the donor's checking account or to sign a deed to complete a real estate transaction. The powers granted can be general in nature, meaning that the donee can do most legal acts the donor can do. Or the powers may be limited, such as completing a specific real estate transaction. When the donor gives a power of attorney to the donee, he also retains the power to do the same acts for himself. The result is that both the donor and the donee have the power to do the same act at the same time.

Typically, a general rather than limited power of attorney is given by the donor. The reason is because the donor trusts the donee to "do the right thing." No one would knowingly give such power to an untrustworthy person. Giving a power of attorney is equal to giving the donee all your personal information and the power to sign your name on any document. Donees have used powers of attorney to hijack estates by draining bank accounts, transferring real estate, and stealing all types of other assets.

How is a life insurance policy, IRA, 401(k) retirement plan, annuity, or pay-on-death account inherited?

We are all familiar with the typical life insurance policy, which pays proceeds at the death of a person. The most common annuity is an insurance policy providing for monthly payments to begin on a fixed date and continue until death or a fixed number of years. Almost everyone owns an individual retirement account (IRA) or 401(k). A pay-on-death account is held at a bank or brokerage house.

These policies and accounts allow an owner to designate a beneficiary of the policy or account. At death, the account assets go directly to the beneficiary outside of probate. Often, these accounts are unknown to other beneficiaries or family members. Hijacking these accounts is often undetected and below anyone's radar.

However, if the estate is large and subject to estate tax, the account must be reported on the estate tax return. Estate tax may be due on the inheritance. The estate will look to the recipient of the funds to pay the tax due on the asset. A taxable estate demands the services of highly trained professionals who will closely scrutinize a hijacker's entitlement to the accounts, and perhaps contest that entitlement.

How do joint ownership and beneficiary designated accounts assist hijackers?

Assets held in joint ownership between two or more persons are held with what is known as the "rights of survivorship." These survivorship rights mean that if one of the joint owners dies, the survivor(s) take the decedent's share by operation of law. This differs from ownership as "tenants in common," where each owner's share becomes part of their estate and does not automatically go to the co-owners of the property.

The shrewd hijacker will look for every opportunity to become a joint owner on assets of another. A successful tactic is to convince the account owner that joint ownership will help the account owner and others.

For example, an elderly mother owns a bank account and her home. One of five children tells mom that she must avoid probate of her estate at all cost. The child convinces mom that a will is not useful because it does not avoid probate of the estate. The child convinces mom to make that child a joint owner of the bank account and home, promising to distribute the assets equally to the five children at mom's death. When mom dies, the joint owner is the sole owner of the home and the account and refuses to share the wealth. The inheritances of the other siblings have been hijacked.

> An advantage of hijacking by joint ownership or beneficiary designation is that the transaction is always undetected.

This tactic is also successfully used by hijackers in situations where beneficiary designations are made on insurance policies, retirement accounts, annuities, and other like accounts. If the hijacker can convince the account holder to name them as the sole beneficiary to exclude others, the hijacking is complete.

An advantage of hijacking by joint ownership or beneficiary designation is that the transaction is always undetected by the first victim, the decedent, and is almost always undetected by the second victim, the intended beneficiary. The asset passes after death directly to the hijacker. No one else is involved.

How does marriage, the hijacker's silver bullet, affect an inheritance?

Just as a hijacker can inherit more money in five minutes than they can earn in a lifetime, a hijacker can marry more money than they can earn in a lifetime. Marriage and hijacking inheritances often go hand in hand. Hijacking by marriage is the "silver bullet" because it is always successful.

Consider these tremendous advantages. A hijacker who marries a target is entitled to the following benefits:

If the deceased spouse dies without a will, the surviving spouse receives all of the estate if the deceased spouse has no children from a previous marriage.

If there are children from a previous marriage, the surviving hijacker receives at least one half of the estate.

If there is a will, the surviving hijacker receives what the will provides for them. If the hijacker is not satisfied with the provisions in the will, they can elect to disregard the will and take a share of their spouse's entire estate including any assets in trusts and other places. The share allowed is usually one-third of the estate. In Florida it is 30 percent.

In addition, the surviving hijacker is entitled to use the decedent's homestead for life (called a "life estate") if the hijacker does not acquire the homestead by other means, such as joint ownership with the deceased spouse. At the hijacker's death, the homestead goes to the decedent's children, if he has any, called the "remaindermen" or "remainder beneficiaries." During the hijacker's life, he or she can live in the homestead or use it as a rental for income purposes. If the hijacker does not wish to use the homestead, he or she can work out a deal with the remainder beneficiaries to sell the homestead and divide the proceeds.

> Hijacking by marriage is the "silver bullet" because it is always successful.

Consider this wonderful and superior advantage. A marriage is rarely if ever challenged in a court of law. A marriage cannot be challenged by a third party, such as a beneficiary or estate administrator. The sole exception to this general rule is a decedent who was previously declared to be mentally incompetent in a court of law and prevented by the court from contracting to marry. Once the marriage ceremony is completed, the hijacker is guaranteed a large portion of their spouse's estate. It is as easy as falling off a log.

As an addition advantage, a surviving spouse has preference over all others in appointment to act as estate administrator if the decedent did not leave a will appointing someone else. This is a huge advantage. The hijacker can manipulate the estate, control the administration, hijack more assets, and use the estate assets to thwart any attacks on the hijacking.

If the hijacker can convince their spouse victim to make a will giving his or her entire estate to the hijacker, the hijacker is then almost always successful in stealing the whole estate. Spouses are presumed not to have exerted undue influence over their spouse to manipulate the gift of the estate. The presumption can be overcome, but it is a very difficult task.

What is the counterattack to the silver bullet of hijacking by marriage? The prenuptial agreement is the answer.

The prenuptial agreement—avoided by hijackers at all cost, with one notable exception.

Marital agreements are used by many individuals, wealthy or not, usually in their senior years, to protect their assets from would-be hijackers. Marital agreements address the consequences of divorce and death on the spouses and their estates. The marital agreement is usually made before the marriage, but can be made after the marriage ceremony. Hijackers never consider a marital agreement that does not benefit the hijacker.

remainderman: One who succeeds to ownership at the end of a life estate.

The most common misconception about prenuptial agreements is that they are used only in marriages where one spouse is wealthy and the other is poor. On the contrary, most wealthy people use prenuptial agreements whether they marry a rich or poor spouse. A second misconception is that the rich spouse always totally disinherits the poor spouse. This is rarely the case. Most marital agreements provide benefits for the poorer spouse in the event of divorce or death.

Hijackers can use these agreements to their advantage. A divorce after a short-term marriage will not yield much in the way of assets from the wealthy spouse if there is no agreement benefiting the hijacking spouse. A prenuptial agreement addressing the terms of divorce can provide much more for the hijacker than a divorce court would grant. An agreement may provide that the hijacker is entitled to a lifetime income or a lump-sum settlement in case of divorce. This advance agreement benefits both spouses by avoiding expensive, lengthy litigation and uncertainty in the event of divorce. In the worst case, the hijacker who is divorced after a short-term marriage will receive financial benefits and need not wait until the death of their spouse.

An agreement may yield other benefits. A marital agreement is valuable if the victim develops long-term illness or becomes impossible to live with. It is the hijacker's safety net. The prospect of a divorce and payment of a large agreed to sum to the hijacker may also discourage a victim from divorcing a hijacker who is no longer wanted as a spouse, preferring to wait until death to part with their spouse rather than part with a sizeable sum during life. This situation benefits a hijacker who prefers to remain married.

While prospective spouses are experiencing the bliss of new love, they often overlook the economics of the planned union. Everyone desires and expects their marriage to last forever. Discussing a marital agreement can be very difficult for prospective spouses. This gives the hijacker an advantage. Their prospective spouse and victim will concede more assets while in the blissful pre-marriage state than they would be willing to give once the marriage sours.

The variations in terms of settlement in the event of divorce or death are limited only by the prospective spouses' imaginations. The final terms are the result of the leverage the prospective spouses have over each other in the negotiations. A savvy hijacker can easily manipulate a gullible prospective spouse who is blinded by love and lets their guard down momentarily. Everyone needs love and affection. Even a very capable person can be so smitten with their new love interest that their good judgment leaves them. Only later, when the shine is off the relationship, do they realize they may have made a mistake in allowing their hijacking spouse to steal their wealth.

Although full financial disclosure is not required to make a valid agreement before marriage, the savvy hijacker will insist on full disclosure. Only through full disclosure can a hijacker properly assess the victim's assets and take full advantage. If the victim is reluctant to make full disclosure, the smart hijacker will convincingly explain that full disclosure ensures the agreement is bulletproof to protect the victim.

Are there penalties for hijacking?

Although hijacking an inheritance is theft under any definition, the legal system does not impose criminal penalties except in the most extreme cases of abuse of an elderly or disabled person. Law enforcement agencies and prosecutors prefer to view inheritance cases as civil disputes among family members rather than criminal matters. As a practical matter, the criminal justice system offers virtually no relief to typical hijacking victims.

The victims must look to the civil court system and struggle to bring the hijacker to justice. Here is an example illustrating the difficulty encountered in punishing a hijacker.

Hijackers do not use physical force to commit their crimes of theft. Careful hijackers rarely do any act in plain view of others and rarely leave a paper trail, such as an embezzler might do. Hijackers operate by quietly misleading and slyly manipulating, all under a veil of secrecy. Consequently, their crimes are very difficult to reconstruct. The only evidence is circumstantial.

Suppose dad disinherits four of his children on his deathbed by making a new will giving all of his property to his fifth child. The four disinherited children know they have been cheated out of their inheritance. What can be done? Unless the fifth child held a gun to dad's head to force him to sign the will, and it can be proved, or some other overt act occurred that voids the will, the disinherited children must rely on purely circumstantial evidence and go to the civil courts for justice.

What is the circumstantial evidence in this case? Dad signed the will on his deathbed disinheriting four of his children, whom he loved and cared for throughout his life. Did dad have a change of heart toward his children during the last days of his life? Was he incompetent to sign his last will? Was dad somehow under the undue influence of the favored child? Who was in the room when dad signed his last will? What did he say? All this and much more is relevant to whether dad's last will is valid.

Who prevails in any particular inheritance suit is subject to the limitations of human understanding. These cases are decided by ordinary people sitting as judge or jury in a courtroom. They have no ability to revisit the past to determine the hard facts. These ordinary folks carry with them their own personal history and prejudices. Their decision is made on the basis of the circumstances, which must be reconstructed in the courtroom. Memories fade. Lies are manufactured. These cases are always complicated and convoluted. The outcome is never a certainty. One side is always disappointed. If the accused hijacker prevails, he or she leaves exonerated. What are the penalties imposed on the hijacker if the victim prevails? First, the hijacker must pay his or her own attorney fees. Next, they are shown and proven to be a thief and, in a perfect world, the fruits of their wrongdoing are returned to the rightful owner. Is this enough for the wrong done to the victim and his or her family? It is difficult to make a blanket statement on the issue.

Hijackers have a great advantage if the hijacking is complete before the lawsuits are filed. At that point they have little to lose. Once the hijacking is complete, the hijacker possesses the fruits of his or her labor, usually in the form of cash. If a suit is filed against the hijacker, they can use those assets to defend their case. The victim, on the other hand, must use their own money to pursue the hijacker with no guarantee of a victory.

Even if the victim is victorious, it may be a hollow victory. A sly hijacker will have put the assets beyond the victim's grasp by the time the court case is concluded. Recovering the assets is difficult at best and often impossible. In such a case, there is no real penalty imposed on the hijacker.

Are taxes paid on a hijacked inheritance?

Hijacking an inheritance has a large advantage over working for the money. There are absolutely no income taxes imposed on inherited money, hijacked or otherwise. The only exception is that an inherited individual retirement account (IRA) may carry an income tax liability. There are no capital gains taxes on inherited money. In most cases, there are no estate or death taxes on the inherited money.

How much has the hijacker saved in income tax? Income is taxed by the federal government at a rate of 10 to 35 percent. Some states also tax income. The hijacker legally avoids both the federal and state income tax.

Estate tax is not imposed on inherited money except in larger estates subject to federal and state estate or death taxes. The threshold in 2009 is three and one-half million dollars. The end result is that inherited money, except in larger estates, is tax-free money.

This carries with it another important advantage for the hijacker. There is little or no requirement that the hijacked money be reported to governmental taxing agencies. Therefore, the paper trail that is always important in proving a hijacking case based on circumstantial evidence is reduced and may not exist at all. No income tax return must be filed. Unless there is an estate tax due, an inheritance need not be reported to any governmental agency. There may be scant record of the transactions involving the inheritance. The lack of required reporting and paper trail greatly assists hijackers in concealing their activities and thwarts victims in recovering their inheritance.

. . .

The savvy hijacker, armed with a good working knowledge of estate-planning law and estate administration, is a formidable operative and foe to those with assets and their intended beneficiaries. Only a vigilant prospective victim armed with knowledge can defeat a determined, well-armed hijacker.

Chapter Three

TARGETS AND HIJACKERS

A successful hijacker once told me, "You can inherit more money in five minutes than you can earn in your lifetime." The hijacker would have more accurately described his situation if he had said, "You can *hijack* more money in five minutes than you can earn in a lifetime." As we all know, both statements are true.

Money is a motivating factor when an inheritance is hijacked, but it is rarely the only major motivation. Psychological factors are strong and may be the prime motivation in all family and near-family inheritance disputes.

As discussed earlier, hijacking an inheritance occurs when a person intends to transfer wealth to an intended recipient, but the wealth is diverted by the hijacker to an unintended recipient. The hijacker's behavior causing the diversion is rarely an overt act of physical violence, which is easily discovered and punished. The hijacker's behavior is a combination of silent fraud, forgery, psychological duress, and constant but secretive undue influence. These acts are not easily discovered, difficult to prove, and rarely punished.

Targets and hijackers

This discussion expands on what we first introduced in chapter 1. Remember, there are two classes of hijacking victims. The first class of victim or target is the person who possesses the wealth: Target A. This target is the person the hijacker interacts with in most cases. Target A rarely learns he or she has been victimized by the hijacker. Target A is often elderly or ill and unable to recognize or fight off a hijacker's clever maneuvers. The hijacking is rarely discovered before this class of victims dies. Examples of these victims are elderly parents, persons with no children and no close family, and lonely persons desperate for a connection with another human being.

The second class of target is the person who should inherit the wealth, but who loses out to a hijacker: Target B. Target B may expect an inheritance from Target A, or may be utterly unaware of the intended gift.

Target B victims sometimes choose not to become deeply involved in the lives of Target A victims, fearing they will be thought of as meddlers or greedy people. The distance Target B puts between him or herself and Target A is the advantage the hijacker exploits for success. In some instances Target B may never learn of the hijacking. The hijacker may have convinced Target A to title an account in joint names with the hijacker, promising to fulfill Target A's last wishes after death. At death, the account is closed and secreted by the hijacker, never to be discovered. Target B may never meet the hijacker and may never know the hijacker's identity. Target B may never realize they have been cheated out of a portion of their inheritance.

Target B victims may be weak or strong in other aspects of their lives, but they have one thing in common as a class of victims: They did not protect their inheritance. Either out of ignorance or neglect they were simply not paying enough attention to their inheritance.

Now that we have identified the two classes of targets or victims necessary to a successful hijacking, let's discuss the interaction between the two targets.

The relationship between Target A and Target B is extremely important. A vulnerable Target A is not an attractive target without an equally vulnerable Target B. A strong and resistant Target A is never an attractive target even if there is a very vulnerable Target B. Likewise, a vulnerable Target A is no use to a hijacker if Target B is strong and watchful. A successful hijacker must find a vulnerable Target A who intends to transfer his or her wealth to a vulnerable Target B.

> Successful hijackers choose their victims based on the chance of succeeding with that particular victim.

Successful hijackers choose their victims based on the chance of succeeding with that particular victim. Just as a mugger would not choose a large athletic man as his victim, a hijacker chooses a victim who cannot easily defend against the hijacker.

Attractive Target A victims are generally the elderly, infirm, lonely, trusting, neglected, and those suffering from drug addiction or alcoholism or diminished mental capacity and/or illness, as well as those who are unsupervised in their financial dealings. Those dependent on others are likely targets, as are those who are vulnerable or susceptible to influence for any number of reasons.

Attractive Target B victims are those who are not carefully watching the activities of the Target A victims. They are sitting on their hands waiting to collect the inheritance. These are usually the children or other relatives of Target A victims who are neglectful, not in touch, disconnected, unconcerned, uncaring of the Target A victim, and perhaps abusive toward the Target A victim. Target B victims who are ignorant of the law of inheritances make many assumptions about the law that are not correct and damaging to their position. The best thing any potential victim can do for him or herself is to learn the basic laws regarding inheritances. Knowledge is power and strength. Hijackers arm themselves with knowledge of the law. Potential victims should also be well armed.

Regrettably, the victims often present themselves as being vulnerable. For example, if a hijacker discovers a Target B victim who has verbally or physically abused a Target A victim, the hijacker may feel he or she has hit the jackpot. Abuse and neglect are excellent reasons the hijacker can hold up to the world to justify the hijacking. The hijacker will make the most of the situation. A diligent hijacker will document each incident and involve as many witnesses as possible. Spreading gossip about the abuse will give the incidents credibility among a larger group. Contacting the adult protective agency to file a complaint against the abuser will also increase the credibility of the abuse allegations. If the hijacking must be justified to a court of law, the hijacker has plenty of evidence of Target A's motivation to disinherit Target B.

Arguments between elderly parents and their children are common but are not always cause for the parent to disinherit the child. Abusive behavior is more than arguing with another person. It is inflicting physical or mental suffering on that person. A hijacker will attempt to make a mountain out of molehill and characterize an argument as abuse. The hijacker may appear to attempt to protect the victim as best they can, trying to drive a wedge between the abuser and the abused. This protection will also enhance the argument that the victim genuinely desired to benefit the beneficent hijacker.

When would this complex situation arise in everyday life? It is going on behind closed doors every day in every town. Simply imagine the hijacker as a son or daughter intent on disinheriting their siblings. You may even recognize the people as your family members or neighbors.

Where do hijackers find their targets?

Most targets are discovered close to home, sometimes living in the same house or close by. Targets are often the hijacker's parents or siblings or some other close relative. Sometimes they are the next-door neighbor or employer.

Most hijackers stumble on the opportunity to take advantage of a family member, neighbor, or close companion. These stumblers are surprised to find themselves with an opportunity to divert assets to their advantage. This one incident may be the only hijacking they ever commit in their life. Or, it may provide schooling in the art of hijacking, which they use to hijack other inheritances.

Trust, which the hijacker will later break, is essential in any hijacking. Hijackers rely on the trust others have in them to accomplish their goals. Targets often choose themselves by trusting a hijacker and submitting themselves to the partial or full control of the hijacker. As we age, we rely on others for care and advice as our abilities decline. There are often sharp declines in the last few years before death. This is when we all become more attractive as Target A victims. However, if a potential donor or Target A victim relies on his or her intended beneficiary, who would otherwise be a potential Target B victim, rather than a stranger, there is little room for the hijacker to intervene. If, on the other hand, a Target A victim relies on someone other than his or her intended beneficiary, there may be a good opportunity for a hijacking.

> Trust, which the hijacker will later break, is essential in any hijacking.

Even if the potential victims are close to each other, there may also be a hijacking opportunity if either Target A or B can be manipulated to suit the hijacker.

Who are the hijackers?

Although there are serial hijackers motivated only by greed who prey on many victims, most hijackers are close by and have been given only one opportunity in their lives to hijack an inheritance.

Most hijackers steal from family members, and their motivation comes in two forms. All hijackers are thought of as greedy individuals motivated only by the lust for the dollar. On the contrary, close scrutiny of the hijacker who steals from a family member shows he is motivated by a compelling need for revenge or sense of entitlement, or both.

The need for revenge for past wrongs, real or imagined, is powerful. Often the opportunity to hijack a family member's inheritance is viewed as the last chance to right the wrong and heal the wound. The length of time a person will hold a grudge and hope for revenge is sometimes absolutely amazing. A remark or imagined insult made decades before may be enough to motivate a hijacker years later to seek revenge. I handled one case where a man called his brother-in-law a "boney-ass son of a bitch" while they were having an argument years ago over a dispute long since forgotten. That remark was one of the prime motivators behind the brother-in-law hijacking the man's inheritance. The hijacker just could not forgive the insult.

A sense of entitlement is the second principal powerful motivator. There are two classes of beneficiaries who feel a sense of entitlement. The first class is made up of those beneficiaries who believe, with no basis in reality, that they are entitled to a larger inheritance than was provided for them. Although they cannot rationally explain their reason for being entitled, in their minds it is a fact that cannot be disputed. Resolving issues with this somewhat delusional beneficiary in any amicable way is simply not possible.

The second class of hijackers who feel entitled believe they have provided a service above and beyond the call of duty for which they have not been properly compensated. This often arises in caregiver situations, where the caregiver feels they have not been compensated properly for the care given. The most common cases are child and parent relationships, although a sense of entitlement can arise when a friend or neighbor provides care for another.

At some point, the caregiver feels they are being taken advantage of, or that they are giving too much of themselves without proper emotional or monetary compensation. If the opportunity to steal something arises, the caregiver can easily rationalize the theft as compensation they are entitled to receive.

Caregiver entitlement is a very sensitive subject within many families. If one child makes a personal sacrifice to become a caregiver for an ailing parent while the other children ignore the situation and go about their lives, the family relations become strained. The caregiver may have put their own life on hold to assist the ailing parent in their last years of life. Caregiving is in itself a very stressful position that is often not fully appreciated. If the caregiver is not given sufficient emotional support, recognition, or compensation for their unselfish work by the parent or their siblings, a feeling of resentment may grow into a feeling of entitlement. The other children may honestly not realize the sacrifice made by the caregiver, especially after the parent dies. The long hours spent caring for the ailing parent are soon forgotten by others. When the caregiver asserts his right to a larger share of the estate, the caregiver is met with resentment for her now "selfish" behavior. The typical

> Hijacking from a family member is most often motivated by a need for revenge or sense of entitlement, or both.

comment is, "I know she was being kind to our mother just to get what she could from her." The speaker is always someone who does not want to give a share of their inheritance to the caregiver.

In some cases, the caregiver feels entitled to be compensated long before the parent's death and acts to secure their compensation before the parent dies. The caregiver may seek a change in a will, or seek to become the sole beneficiary of a life insurance policy. The parent may willingly agree and the compensation may be reasonable. The trouble starts when the caregiver extracts more than fair compensation (as judged by other beneficiaries) from their ailing parent, who may be totally dependent on the caregiver. When these changes in the inheritance shares are discovered by the other children, the family conflicts erupt. The caregiver must justify their gift and suffer the pain of being accused of being a hijacker.

These two motivators, revenge and entitlement, often sit dormant for years and then suddenly surface without warning to turn families upside down.

The first-time hijacker is rarely a dishonest person looking for an opportunity to steal assets. He or she is typically a family member and otherwise honest person abruptly confronted with the opportunity to take all or a part of a family member's inheritance. If neither of the principal motivators, revenge and entitlement, are present, the opportunity is usually rejected. If either principal motivator exists, the hijacker will almost always act on the opportunity to hijack the inheritance.

> Nagging motivation often festers for years before surfacing to turn families upside down.

A distinction must be pointed out here. A common thief or embezzler without a conscience who steals from strangers is not likely to be in a position to hijack an inheritance. This brand of criminal rarely, if ever, has the opportunity to hijack an inheritance because those close to him are wise to his thieving ways and are cautious around him. This brand of thief is never given the trust he needs to pull off a hijacking. A successful hijacker, on the other hand, is a trusted friend or member of the family, not a black sheep or outcast who has proven they cannot be trusted with something as important as an inheritance.

Moral issues confront the hijacker

Accepting an opportunity to hijack an inheritance brings about serious moral issues to be resolved by the hijacker. Denying Target A his last wishes and denying Target B his inheritance are both very traumatic events that all involved must live with for the remainder of their lives. If a person cannot resolve these issues, he or she should not think about hijacking an inheritance. The test of conscience and mental strain will destroy even the cleverest hijacker. The closer the hijacker is to any of the victims, the more profoundly the hijacker is affected by his own immoral actions. The hijacker's moral fiber may not allow him or her to commit the hijacking.

A hijacker motivated by a strong need for revenge against the victim may have resolved the issues of conscience and guilt many years earlier. The hijacker may not lose sleep worrying and may sleep better knowing an old score has finally been settled. I'll discuss the guilt issue and other ways hijackers overcome it at length a little later in the chapter.

Intangible assets are more valuable than the tangible assets

Inheritance is less about monetary value than it is about the intangibles represented by the inheritance. Our inheritance may be millions of dollars or it may be a painting, Bible, or other object of little monetary value. Both inheritances have the same intangible value to the donor and the donee. The gift is a material object, a form of vessel, that carries the love the donor has for the donee, and the dignity of the victims.

Inheritances are not just money or real estate or jewelry or other tangible assets. Intangible assets are attached to every tangible asset in an inheritance. The intangible assets are the love and affection the donor intended to show to the beneficiary.

Assets are earned by hard work. Time is sacrificed to earn the assets, and time is the most precious commodity a person has in life. When we devote time to earn assets to pass to the next generation, we are making a great personal sacrifice of the little time God has given us on Earth. We could have used that time to pleasure ourselves in some way. Instead we used it to improve the life of the intended recipient. By making that sacrifice, we are telling the recipient of our assets that we love them. That's how human beings are built. We all want our descendants or other loved ones to live a better life than we have and be more successful than we are. One way to help is to pass on wealth to the worthy ones.

> Inheritance is less about monetary value than it is about the intangibles represented by the inheritance.

We all understand this concept. How often have you heard someone say that their parents worked hard to give them a good education? That hard work and the gift of the good education are expressions of the love the parent has for the child. Inheritances represent love in the same way. Have you ever heard an adult child say that their father did not work all his life just to see his money taken by a woman he met later in life after his long-time spouse died? This is a more pointed comment on how much the child believes the father loves the child, than it is a condemnation of the new relationship between the father and his new lady friend. The child does not want the love represented by the father's assets to be diverted to the new woman. These very strong emotions drive most inheritance disputes.

People involved in an inheritance dispute often fail to recognize the strong drive motivating a person to give an inheritance to a loved one, as well as the psychological needs of the person expecting the inheritance. The donor wishes to express their love for the donee by giving the gift of an inheritance. The donee craves the love of the donor represented by the inheritance. Hijacking an inheritance cheats both donor and donee.

A hijacking diverts and steals much more than material assets. The hijacker is diverting the love the giver of the inheritance intended to show and give to the intended recipient. This is often the essence of the conflict between hijackers and their targets or victims. Many people may not care about the material assets. They feel they have been cheated out of the intangible asset, love.

Just as a divorcing couple will spend thousands in attorney fees fighting over a dinner plate worth twenty dollars, heirs will spend thousands fighting over personal items with little monetary value but great sentimental value. Why? The items symbolize the love the decedent had for them. By acquiring the item they are reassuring themselves that the decedent loved them.

Without exception, a victim of a hijacking will fight much harder to recover their inheritance if the victim wanted love from the decedent. The greater the want, the more likely they are to fight for their inheritance.

The Target B victim who is emotionally detached and distant from the Target A victim is more likely to view litigation over an inheritance as a business decision. These victims are more likely to weigh the litigation expense against the expected gain without a large emotional factor looming over the decision. The hijacker's success rate is much greater with this type of Target B victim than with victims who have a strong emotional investment in their relationship with Target A.

Sadly, the courts cannot resolve inheritance litigation in any better manner than to tell the litigants that one party is entitled to a money judgment and the other is not. Even though an inheritance lawsuit may be all about the expression of love the hijacker has stolen, love cannot be directly recovered in a court of law. If the victim prevails in court, they can recover only a judgment stating the hijacker was wrong and the inheritance must be returned to the hijacker's victim. Nevertheless, the money judgment often has a much different and profound meaning to the warring parties. If the victim defeats the hijacker, the victim feels that he or she was indeed loved and that the love stolen by the hijacker has been recovered. The loving relationship between Target A and Target B is restored by the court order.

A victory means there is also a loss. Loss can be very distressing when the parties are warring family members who both believe in their hearts that they are morally and ethically correct. They are both fighting for the love of the donor, which they both feel entitled to receive. In such cases, the court's decision means that one party was loved by the donor, usually a father or mother, and the other was not loved as much or perhaps not at all. This is an imperfect and inadequate resolution to these disputes. It leaves the parties with unresolved issues for the remainder of their lives.

Successful hijackers must resolve inner conflicts in their favor

Hijackers who successfully resolve guilt issues in their favor must believe in the decency of their actions.

Since hijacking is rarely committed between strangers in absolute cold blood, family members and family history are always important factors that create inner conflicts that both motivate and trouble the hijacker. Stealing from a family member is not an easy thing to do. Remember that the hijacked assets represent love as well as wealth.

Hijackers have a conscience that they must be prepared to deal with, the inner voice that keeps you on the route dictated by your moral compass. Hijackers should be forewarned that if they hijack an estate and later believe it was unethical to do so, they will pay with nagging regret and guilt for the rest of their lives. In extreme cases, the hijacker might believe his soul will go straight to hell the instant he dies, or he might believe the hijacked inheritance is cursed. The next time anything goes wrong in the hijacker's life, he will deem it punishment for what he did.

A guilt-filled hijacker will not enjoy the fruits of the hijacking. He or she may become severely depressed and even suicidal in extreme cases. Literature is filled with tales of unresolved guilt that destroys the protagonist. *Crime and Punishment* is a classic example. These stories are not just figments of the writer's imagination. They are true stories disguised as fiction. Their popularity attests to the truth of the moral of the tale.

The psychological impact of stealing an inheritance on the mind of the hijacker cannot be understated. Once an opportunity presents itself, the hijacker must immediately resolve the question of right and wrong. After all, the hijacker is usually dealing with a family member, employer, or close associate. These people trust and maybe even love the hijacker. They may have protected and nurtured the hijacker earlier in life. The hijacker brings family history into play and often asks these questions at the outset: Is it right to divert to my advantage? Or is it right to just walk away from this opportunity? What is the honest thing to do? What would Jesus do? What would Allah do? What if someone did this to me? How would I react?

The hijacker answers these questions in his favor. He tells himself he needs and deserves the assets more than anyone else in the world at that particular time. He convinces himself that Target A, the donor, is not thinking straight or is deluded or is being selfish toward him. He convinces himself that Target B, the intended donee, is not worthy. Perhaps Target B displayed some signs of laziness or immorality in the past. Has Target B ever insulted anyone? The remoteness of the event is not important. For the hijacker, the past insults are as fresh in his mind as if they occurred this morning. Now is the time to even the score. If Target B is a brother or sister, the issue of sibling rivalry may assist the hijacker, who tells himself that he was the favorite child, and mom and dad would have wanted him to benefit from their hard work and sacrifice. Or it may be that he was not the favorite child. Other brothers or sisters were favored by the parents. In this case, he chooses to get even because this is probably the last chance to prove mom and dad loved him just as well, or even more. The hijacker will take the money, and the love that it represents, to even the score.

A successful hijacker avoids the psychological dilemma by dealing with issues of right and wrong in a more shrewd and delicate fashion, always resolving the issues in his own favor. He weaves the truth and sometimes lies into a scenario that justifies the hijacking. He repeats the scenario to himself and others until he believes his manufactured tale. Only then, when he is convinced he is acting decently, can he be at peace within himself and not succumb to guilt. The ability to convince oneself that wrong is right is enhanced if time is available to complete the task. In cases where the hijacker spends years whispering lies into a victim's ear, the hijacker himself finds the lies easy to believe. If the hijacker has only a few months to complete the hijacking, the hijacker may not have time to learn to believe the scenario justifying the crime. The hijacker who is also a compulsive liar has an advantage in this regard because they believe their lies the moment they are uttered.

When a hijacker gets to the point where he actually believes he is doing the right thing, and believes that God and his own conscience will not punish him, he must not stop believing under any circumstances. He must repeat the reasons for his beliefs like a mantra until they are embedded in his subconscious. Only then, when the hijacker believes in what he is doing, can he convince others he has done the right thing. He will not be dissuaded even though others berate him and label him a thief and scoundrel. He may be dragged into a court of law to explain what he has done, but he will not give one inch in his beliefs.

If the case is tried in a court of law and he loses the case, he does not take this as an indication that he was wrong from the start, that he should not have hijacked the inheritance. He tells himself that he is the victim and judges and juries make mistakes every day. An adverse judgment does not take away his dignity. He was right from the start.

If for some reason the hijacker is overcome by guilt before the hijacking is completed, he may be totally defeated in pursuit of the inheritance. If the hijacker gives in under the pressures of a lawsuit brought by the victims, the result is a twofold disaster for the hijacker. The hijacker is branded as a failed thief and cast out of that family and social circle. In addition, he loses his hijacked inheritance. Therefore, resolving any issues of guilt early in the game is vital to the hijacker.

On the other hand, people who truly think of themselves as "honest" feel that if they hijack an inheritance, they will not be able to live with the guilt. They are afraid of the consequences of the deceitful act, even if they are successful and forever undiscovered. They know they cannot rationalize a hijacking to themselves. This is the motivation that keeps them honest. They know it is wrong. They know they cannot live with themselves if they do wrong. As a result, they do no wrong.

· · ·

You can see that inheritance disputes are a cornucopia of complex, convoluted, and challenging psychological issues defying straightforward resolution.

It is little wonder that so many of these disputes are in litigation. All parties know in their heart that they are right and they demand justice.

The next chapter gives a broad, inside view of inheritance litigation from beginning to end and tells you what it takes to prevail in an inheritance suit.

Chapter Four

INHERITANCE LITIGATION

It is unfortunate but true that no one can be perfectly safe from a hijacking. Avoiding a hijacking is infinitely more desirable than attempting to repair the damage after the deed is done. We will discuss avoidance in chapter 7 and in the case studies, but don't go there yet. You need to understand inheritance law as a prelude to understanding how to protect yourself.

Knowledge is power. Nowhere is this axiom more important than in the law of inheritances. Unfortunately, few laymen have a basic understanding of the laws governing inheritances. This allows a knowledgeable hijacker to more easily exploit his victims. A working knowledge of the law is an important weapon against potential hijacking. Just as a hijacker increases his chances of success as he learns the law, a potential victim can identify and avoid a hijacking opportunity.

> Inheritance disputes are more about the baggage attached to material assets than the asset itself.

Inheritance disputes are about the combined elements of material assets and the emotional baggage attached to the material assets. The two are almost indistinguishable. We discussed the fact that inheritance is as much about love as it is about money in chapter 3. Although inheritance disputes tend to focus on the material aspects of the inheritance, the parties and their lawyers must consider the emotional aspects of the inheritance as well. It is very difficult to win an inheritance suit without giving the emotional issues due consideration in the proceeding. As you read this chapter, try to imagine how emotional issues might combine with the legal issues in your own life situation. This will help you understand the legal concepts and guard against a hijacking.

There are many legal remedies available to the beneficiary whose inheritance has been hijacked. Unfortunately, all of them involve the court system. Court proceedings are expensive, time consuming, and unpredictable. These trials are never cut-and-dried affairs. Hijackers always have a legal argument, truthful or otherwise, supporting their position. A victim must risk his own money on a gamble that the courts will restore his inheritance. From the hijacker's point of view, avoiding a court battle greatly increases a hijacker's net income and reduces the time before a hijacker can fully enjoy the fruits of his or her labors. This is why smart hijackers learn the law and fashion their hijacking to conform to the law as best they can.

As in medicine, the legal remedy depends on the malady. If the hijacker used a will to steal the inheritance, the victim attacks the will. If an amendment to a trust was used to hijack the estate, the victim attacks the amendment. If the hijacker pilfered a bank account, the victim attempts to overturn the transactions and perhaps prosecute the hijacker and put him or her behind bars if criminal sanctions are possible.

Let us begin with the legal grounds available to attack a will or trust. These legal concepts apply to trusts as well as wills because trusts are often used as a substitute for a will in distributing property at a person's death. Amendments to wills, known as codicils, and trust amendments are subject to the same rules.

In chapter 2 we discussed wills and trusts and their uses. A codicil to a will is an amendment to the will. It does not revoke the earlier will as a new will would. It makes minor additions or changes to the earlier will. Amendments to trusts are used the same way.

Codicils to wills and amendments to trusts are convenient hijacking tools. A codicil or amendment can make small changes that may not be challenged by the victims because the cost outweighs the potential gain. For example, in the event Lois, who is Alice's caregiver, covets Alice's automobile, Lois may prepare a handwritten codicil to Alice's will that gives the automobile to Lois. When Alice is in a weakened state, Lois can secure Alice's signature or forge the signature if necessary. Two of Lois's friends can act as witnesses to Alice's signature. With those simple acts, Lois has a valid codicil to Alice's will. When Alice dies, Lois inherits the automobile unless Alice's true intended beneficiaries, the victims of Lois's deceit, contest the codicil. Chances are that the codicil will not be contested. The cost of asking the probate court to overturn the codicil may exceed the value of the automobile. The intended beneficiaries and victims may grudgingly walk away from the fight.

A will can also be used in the same way as Lois used the codicil. Let us assume that Alice had no will or trust. Lois can easily create a will that addresses only the automobile. The remainder of Alice's estate would be distributed to Alice's blood relations dictated by state statutes.

Codicils can be attacked without attacking the will itself. For example, Uncle Jack makes a will ten years before his death leaving his estate to his niece, Madonna. Uncle Jack then signs a codicil to his will ten days before his death giving half of his estate to his housekeeper, Maria. In this case, Madonna attacks the codicil and argues that it is not legal and binding. If Uncle Jack had signed a new will, rather than a codicil, Madonna would have attacked the new will and claimed that the first will is valid.

codicil: An amendment to a will that does not revoke the earlier will but makes minor additions or changes.

How does one launch an attack upon a will or codicil or trust? It is not enough for one to simply state that the document is invalid. One must have "legal grounds" as the basis for the attack. Legal grounds are reasons the law would void a will or codicil or trust. An attack on other than legal grounds is considered frivolous under the law. The legal grounds are explained here.

Although Florida law is the basis for this discussion, the legal principles are used throughout the United States, Canada, and the United Kingdom. The laws of these nations have evolved from the English common law.

Lack of testamentary capacity voids a will but is difficult to determine

Just as in any other legal situation, a person must be "competent" when he or she performs an act they intend to be legally binding. If the person is not competent, the act may be absolutely void when it happens, or it may be voidable.

An example of a voidable act is the making of a contract by an elderly person who is under a court-appointed guardianship because he has been declared legally incompetent to enter into a contract, among other things. If the person under the guardianship goes to his friendly local car dealer and signs a contract to purchase an automobile, the contract is voidable by the court-appointed guardian. The dealer can be forced to rescind the transaction and return the purchase price. If, however, the guardian approves of the transaction, although he was not consulted before the transaction, the contract can remain in place. The choice is his. The contract is voidable by the guardian if he so chooses.

A void transaction, unlike a voidable transaction, is invalid and a nullity when it is done. Let's assume that the incompetent elderly person entered into a contract to do an illegal act, such as pay an illegal gambling debt. The contract is void when made regardless of whether the elderly person is incompetent. Void contracts cannot be enforced in a court of law.

A will or codicil or trust is void when it is signed if the person signing the will is not competent to make the will. This is known as "lack of testamentary capacity."

Evaluating whether a person possesses testamentary capacity is always subjective in a court of law. Psychiatrists and psychologists have developed tests to evaluate a person's legal capacity. These tests are seldom useful in inheritance litigation. No hijacker asks his incompetent victim to undergo a test for testamentary capacity at the time the will is signed. Therefore, any decision as to capacity is made by a judge many months or years after the will was signed. The judge's evaluation is based on circumstantial evidence rather than direct evidence of mental condition at the time. A smart hijacker will do as much as possible to recognize and preserve evidence of their victim's testamentary capacity at the time the will is signed, while destroying evidence of mental incapacity. Evidence of strong testamentary capacity can also help overcome a claim of undue influence discussed later in this chapter.

maker: A person who signs their will or trust.

The legal threshold a person must cross to possess testamentary capacity is low. A person need not possess a normal IQ. Nor must they know how to read and write or sign their name. To execute a valid will, the person making the will, known as the "maker," need only have the ability to understand three things, in a general way:

1. The nature and extent of the property to be disposed of. The maker must simply be aware of his or her assets. If a person is very wealthy and is not capable of assessing the extent of their wealth, they may lack testamentary capacity. On the other hand, if a poor person makes large gifts in their will, they may lack testamentary capacity.

2. His or her relationship to those who would naturally claim a substantial benefit from his or her will (i.e., the "natural objects of his or her bounty"). This requires the maker to have an understanding of his or her family relationships. This does not mean that the maker must give their estate to their spouse or children. It does require that the maker be aware of people who would inherit their estate if they died without a will. These people are, in order of preference under law, the surviving spouse, children, grandchildren, great-grandchildren and other lineal descendants, parents, siblings, cousins, and other distant family members.

A maker may disinherit a spouse or children as the maker wishes, with a few exceptions. It is always good practice to state in the will the maker's intention to disinherit any person. Although this statement may not prevent an attack on the will, it is evidence of the maker's state of mind.

3. A general understanding of the practical effect of the will as executed. The maker need not understand every detail of how the will affects their estate or the beneficiaries. This would require that every maker possess a law degree and be an expert in estate planning. It is enough that the maker realizes the general result of signing their will.

In a probate proceeding there is always a presumption that the maker had testamentary capacity when the will was signed. This presumption is a great help and convenience in the administration of the estate. The presumption allows the court to declare the will is valid without the need for testimony regarding the maker's testamentary capacity.

If someone wishes to attack the will on the grounds that the maker lacked testamentary capacity, the attacker must file a lawsuit within the probate proceeding. In that proceeding, the attacker has the burden of proving the lack of testamentary capacity. The issue is decided by what is known as a "preponderance of the evidence." A preponderance is nothing more than a majority or 51 percent of the evidence. The preponderance or majority is not measured by the number or words spoken or the number of witnesses who testify. It is measured in the mind of the judge or jury, who decide which evidence is most convincing based on their own personal life experience.

What sort of evidence is presented when testamentary capacity is at issue? The maker cannot testify because the maker is deceased. The lawyers must reconstruct the signing of the will and the circumstances surrounding the signing. Almost all this evidence is circumstantial. The list of possible witnesses is long. The lawyer who drafted the will, the witnesses to the will, notary, nurses, doctors, visitors, family members, friends, and neighbors are all possible witnesses.

It may be undeniable in a testamentary capacity trial that the maker lacked a certain degree of mental ability to make a will. The proponent of the will would then argue that the maker made the will in what is called a "lucid moment." A lucid moment occurs when a maker who is incompetent suddenly becomes competent for a short time and then relapses back into incompetency.

I have seen several cases where all agreed that the maker was on her deathbed, seldom conscious, full of drugs to induce sleep and ease her pain, and just hours from death. In spite of this obvious lack of testamentary capacity, a hijacker somehow procures the scribbled signature of the maker on a new will with witnesses present. This new will benefits the hijacker, of course. The hijacker claims the maker miraculously rose to the occasion and signed the will in a "lucid moment" before falling back into her comatose state. The hijacker is seldom successful in these cases.

There are cases where a marginally competent person can legitimately have a lucid moment and make a valid will. If so, the lawyers and others involved should do all possible to preserve proof of the lucid moment in preparation for an attack on the will.

If competency is an obvious question at the time the will is signed, an evaluation by a psychologist or psychiatrist trained in this area is a very good idea. The risk is that the maker may be found to be incompetent and a new will is out of the question. This may pose a significant problem. If the maker is incompetent to make a new will, he or she may also incompetent to void an older will.

For example, assume that an elderly mother, now incompetent to make a will, found that her daughter was stealing large sums of money from her. Rather than criminally prosecute the daughter, the mother decides to change her will to disinherit her daughter, who is also a beneficiary in an earlier will. If the mother is incompetent, she may not be able to disinherit the disloyal daughter by making a new will or revoking the old will. The result is that the daughter will inherit part of the estate.

The same problem may arise if tax laws change to allow a maker to save significant tax dollars with a will change. If the maker is incompetent, he may be precluded from doing so.

A video memorializing the will signing may be very helpful in proving the maker's testamentary capacity. In the typical video, the maker answers pertinent questions posed by the lawyer. The signing, showing the maker and witnesses and notary public present in the same room, is preserved on video in the event it is needed to prove capacity.

The issues of competency to make a will and undue influence over the maker of the will are closely related. A person may have minimum capacity to make a legal will. However, the capacity may diminished by illness or dementia, thereby making that person more susceptible to undue influence by a hijacker.

Undue influence over another is the most fascinating type of inheritance hijacking

Undue influence is one of the most common grounds used in attempting to set aside a last will. This is also the most complex and fascinating issue in inheritance litigation. A will or trust procured by undue influence is void when made.

Undue influence occurs when one person takes control of another such that their acts are not their own free will. The influencer uses deceit, threats, or other means, which cause an impact such that the victim is under the control of the influencer and the victim acts as the influencer wishes against their own free will. The control need not be over all aspects of the person's life. It is enough that they influence will or trust.

The incidents of undue influence are widespread and severely damaging to victims and their families. So much so that the Florida legislature wisely adopted legislation to help protect against undue influence. Florida law declares that it is presumed that undue influence is present if three elements are present in any case. This is strong policy enacted to protect citizens in the face of widespread abuse. Many other states follow Florida's lead.

The presumption of undue influence is raised if the alleged hijacker (1) is a substantial beneficiary under the new will, (2) occupied a confidential relationship with the person making the will, and (3) was active in procuring the will.

A "presumption" in the law is a legal fiction created to reach a conclusion in the absence of hard facts. In other words, it is presumed that a fact is true if certain circumstantial evidence is presented to the court. The law says that if the three elements are present, the circumstances are such that undue influence must be presumed to have occurred. Because almost all evidence in an inheritance trial is circumstantial, presumptions are very important in assisting the judge or jury in reaching a verdict.

> Undue influence occurs when one person takes control of another such that their acts are not their own free will.

As applied to cases of undue influence, upon proof that a substantial beneficiary of a will occupied a confidential relationship with the maker and was active in procuring the execution of the will, it is presumed the ultimate fact is true. That is, that the will was procured as a result of undue influence on the maker by the person who holds the confidential relationship. The consequence of the presumption is that, in the absence of credible evidence contradicting the presumed fact, the court must rule as a matter of law that the presumed fact is true and the will is void.

The presumption, once established, is important in the legal proceeding. The presumption is not proof in and of itself, but it can be the deciding factor if there is a lack of evidence to the contrary. Like most legal presumptions, the presumption of undue influence is "rebuttable." Once the presumption of undue influence arises, the proponent of the will (the hijacker) must rebut the presumption and show that undue influence did not play a role the maker's decision to make the will. If the proponent of the will cannot present convincing evidence, the court must rely on the presumption of undue influence and declare the will to be void.

The alleged hijacker is given ample opportunity to present evidence to overcome the presumption of undue influence. There is almost always some credible evidence supporting the fact that the maker desired to make the will. The lawyer for the proponent of the will is sure to find something, however slim, to support the will presented by the alleged hijacker. Once this evidence is presented, the presumption disappears and the case is decided on the preponderance of the evidence. Whoever weighs in with 51 percent or more of the evidence wins.

Although the presumption disappears, the evidence presented to the court that allowed the presumption of undue influence to be created is not disregarded. It is still an important part of the evidence in the case. To prevail in the trial, the alleged hijacker must present evidence that outweighs the evidence of undue influence on the maker by the hijacker. If the hijacker cannot overcome the evidence that he used undue influence, the hijacker will lose the case.

If this sounds complicated and confusing, it is. Judges wrestle with how all this works during the trials before them. Lawyers wrestle with the issues and argue their client's cases under the cloud of confusion created by legal presumptions. It is my experience that the judge or jury will usually decide the case on what they think is fair and just without regard to the confusion caused by legal presumptions.

Because the important issues in a case of undue influence are always decided on purely circumstantial evidence, these cases are very intriguing. A high degree of skill on the part of the lawyers is required to turn circumstantial evidence into a convincing case. Circumstantial evidence consists of unrelated facts that in themselves may prove nothing in regard to undue influence. The skilled lawyer weaves these facts into a credible story supporting his client's case. Often the same detail or event is used by each opponent to prove their case, each putting a different spin on a detail or event.

Perhaps Aunt Mabel stated five years before her death that she wanted to "change her will to include her sister's children." Aunt Mabel said nothing more on that subject, as far as anyone can recall. As it turns out, one of her sister's children, Suzie, visited elderly and lonely Aunt Mabel just before Aunt Mabel died. During that visit, Aunt Mabel changed her will to give Suzie a substantial gift. The change cost Sam—another of Aunt Mabel's relatives and a beneficiary under an earlier will—tens of thousands of dollars. He sued to throw out the will, claiming that Suzie used undue influence over Aunt Mabel to procure the will. Suzie's lawyer brought three witnesses who heard Aunt Mabel say five years before her death that she wanted to change her will to benefit her sister's children. This was proof, Suzie's lawyer argued strong and long, that the will was not procured by undue influence. Sam's lawyer, on the other hand, argued long and strong that Aunt Mabel did not want to change her will to benefit Suzie. His argument is that Aunt Mabel did nothing for five years to change her will to benefit Suzie until Suzie's visit. He argued that Suzie used undue influence during her visit to cause Aunt Mabel to change her will and give Suzie the pot of gold Sam should have received. Had Suzie not visited, Aunt Mabel would have died with her first will as her true will.

These are two good arguments using the same facts. How would you decide?

Appellate courts have wrestled with appeals of undue influence cases for centuries. Law books are full of reported appeals with different courts reaching contrary decisions on the same facts.

Of the three factors necessary to reach a conclusion that undue influence was used to procure a will, the most perplexing is the question of whether the person was active in procuring the will. The questions of whether the gift was substantial and whether a confidential relationship exists can easily be shown by the will itself and the relationship of the parties. However, the question of whether the beneficiary was "active in procuring the will" is the heart of the issue of undue influence. This is a legal term that has defied strict definition. No one knows precisely what it means, but everyone thinks they know it when they see it. The courts must decide whether the will would have been made if the beneficiary had not been active on a case-by-case basis. You can imagine the vast variety of evidence that may be relevant. Everything from Aunt Mabel's childhood to what she ate on the day she made the will may be important. It all rests in the hands of the creative attorneys drawing a picture of Aunt Mabel and the circumstances surrounding the will for the judge.

The Florida appellate courts have given some guidance and adopted seven factors to aid a trial judge in deciding whether the party was active in "procuring the will." These factors are relevant to cases in any state. If one or more of these factors are found to exist, the judge or jury *may* rule that undue influence was used to procure the will, but the decision is always in the hands of the judge or jury, who may find that undue influence exists even of none of the factors are present. The seven factors are:

1. Presence of the beneficiary at the execution of the will. Was the beneficiary at the maker's bedside when the maker made the will? If so, this is a point against hijacker and the validity of the new will.

2. Presence of the beneficiary on those occasions when the maker expressed a desire to make a will. Was the beneficiary coaching the maker? Did the beneficiary accompany the maker to the attorney's office and sit in on the interview with the attorney? This may be evidence of influence or coercion upon the maker by the beneficiary.

3. Recommendation by the beneficiary of an attorney to draw the will. Did the maker have his or her own attorney to ask for independent advice? Or did the beneficiary suggest an attorney who the beneficiary trusted not to upset her applecart? An independent attorney of the maker's choosing always gives the best advice to protect the maker without regard to any other person.

4. Knowledge of the contents of the will by the beneficiary prior to execution. The maker must be acting of his or her own free will. Knowledge of the contents begs the question whether the beneficiary knew of and approved the contents, and whether the maker's actions were being dictated by the beneficiary.

5. Giving of instructions on preparation of the will by the beneficiary to the attorney drawing the will. This is one of the strongest indicators of undue influence upon a maker. If the beneficiary dictated the terms of the will, the maker may be under the beneficiary's control.

6. Securing witnesses to the will by the beneficiary. This often occurs when a will is signed at a nursing home or the maker's own home. In the typical case the beneficiary has brought a will to the maker for signature. The beneficiary sometimes brings friends to act as witnesses. Or the nursing home staff can be recruited by the beneficiary. The maker may be mentally incompetent or being coerced by the beneficiary. This activity may also indicate a lack of ability on the part of the maker to recruit his own witnesses, as well as a lack of willingness to sign a new will and lack of freedom of choice.

7. Safekeeping of the signed will by the beneficiary. Beneficiaries know the maker cannot destroy the will if the beneficiary has possession. Often a beneficiary will not provide a copy to the maker. This avoids discovery of the will by others, perhaps those who are disinherited by the new will. The beneficiary reveals the new will after the maker's death, when

the maker cannot testify to the maker's competency or willingness to make the new will, or the circumstances surrounding the signing.

There are literally hundreds of additional factors that can be considered by the judge when deciding whether undue influence was used upon the maker. What is the family history? Who did the maker favor during her life? Was the family dysfunctional? Did the maker make any loans that have not been repaid? Is the maker equalizing an inheritance or punishing an ungrateful beneficiary? What was the maker's medical condition? What, if anything, did the maker say about the new will? How often did the persons who were disinherited visit or talk with the maker before the new will was made? How far away did the disinherited beneficiaries, usually the maker's children, live from the maker, and how often did they visit? Who paid the attorney's bill for preparation of the will? Did the beneficiary prepare the will without the help of an attorney? The list is as long as a clever lawyer's imagination.

insane delusion: A form of incapacity resulting from the contention that a person has a diseased mind and has reached a conclusion that has no basis in fact.

The questions are as numerous as the facts of the case. Because undue influence cases are decided on circumstantial evidence, the importance of each scrap of evidence is often blown out of proportion to its true bearing on the case in hopes that it will greatly influence the decision.

Mistake by the maker renders a will void

A will procured by a mistake is void. The mistake necessary to set aside the will must be what is called a "mistake in execution" of the will.

For example, the maker executed a will believing it to be another document. If a hijacker tells the maker the will is a different document, a medical directive perhaps, the will is void. But who will testify that the maker was unaware he was signing a new will? These issues are litigated only after the maker's death. If the maker has signed the document and the witnesses are in on the hoax, there is no one to testify to the contrary.

A mistake in executing a will must be distinguished from a mistake of fact. A maker who believes a fact to be true that is later proven to be untrue is making a valid will. Again, this decision is subjective. However, if the mistake rises to the level of insane delusion, discussed below, the will is invalid.

For example, if the maker believes his summer home is on the side of Mount Snowtop while it is actually on the side of Mount Sunnytop, the mistake of fact is of no consequence. If, however, the maker believes his summer home is on the moon, the will is invalid because this rises to the level of an insane delusion.

An insane delusion voids a will

As discussed above, a mistake of fact is not enough to set aside a will. However, if the mistake of fact arises to the level of insane delusion, the will can be set aside. An insane delusion is a form of incapacity based upon the contention that the testator's will was the product of a diseased mind that caused the testator to reach a mistaken conclusion having no basis in fact. The Florida Supreme Court has defined insane delusion as fixed false belief "without any evidence of any kind to support it, which can be accounted for on no reasonable hypothesis, having no foundation of reality."

If the maker believes his son, James, is a drug addict while James is not a drug addict, and disinherits James, the will is valid because, to the maker, this is a mistake of fact. If, however, the maker disinherits James because the maker believes James has attempted to take over his mind by shooting gamma rays into his brain, the will is void.

Fraud and duress are dangerous hijacking tools

Fraud that voids a will can be either in the execution of the will or in the inducement to make the will itself. "Fraud in the execution" occurs when the maker is told that the document he or she is signing is something other than a will. Such a will is also void on the grounds of mistake in execution.

"Fraud in the inducement" occurs when the maker was intentionally misled by a material fact that caused the maker to make a different will than he would have otherwise made. There must be a causal relationship between the lie and the action taken as a result of the lie.

If a hijacker tells a lie to the maker, stating that the maker's son, Elwood, is actually the biological son of the maker's brother, and the lie causes the maker to disinherit Elwood, the will disinheriting Elwood is void. On the other hand, if the maker disinherited Elwood because the maker gave Elwood many gifts during the maker's life, rather than because Elwood was not his biological son, there is no causal relationship between the lie and the act of the maker. In this case the will is valid.

Duress may involve threat of physical harm or some coercion practiced upon the maker by the hijacker. This is most often practiced in private. You will never see a maker sign a will at a lawyer's office with a gun held to the maker's head. The threat of physical harm in these cases usually occurs at home.

A hijacking son or daughter may threaten their aged and frail parent with some action or inaction if the parent does not comply with their demands. The threat need not be physical harm at all. The threat of placing a parent in a nursing home can be very persuasive. Threatening to stop caring for an aged parent's daily needs can be persuasive. Threatening to not let a grandparent visit with the grandchildren can exert immense pressure. A hijacker may threaten a lonely person with the withdrawal of attention he or she craves.

The possibilities are endless. Hijackers often make the victim or target dependent upon the hijacker for emotional support, physical care, love, or simply friendship. The threat of withdrawing whatever the victim needs can force a victim to give huge inheritances to the hijacker, who is actually their false friend or lover.

Failure to execute with the required formalities renders a will void

A will must be signed, or executed, with particular formalities. These laws in themselves avoid a tremendous amount of fraud. After all, a will is valid only at the death of the maker. There is no opportunity for a maker to testify about the will after his or her death. Without strict rules, all sorts of ingenious frauds would be available to the inventive hijacker.

These are the required formalities in most states:

1. The will must be signed by the maker, or the maker's name must be subscribed by another person in the maker's presence and at the maker's direction. An X mark will suffice as a signature if that is the maker's mark. A paralyzed or infirm person may direct another to sign their name to the will.

2. The will must be signed at the end, not in the middle. This helps ensure that the maker knew all the contents of the will and avoids additions to the will after the maker signs.

3. There must be at least two attesting witnesses to the maker's signature. These should not be people interested in the will, such as a spouse or beneficiaries, although these persons can sign in most cases.

4. The maker must sign in the physical presence of the witnesses.

5. The witnesses must sign the will in the presence of the maker.

6. The witnesses must sign in the presence of each other.

7. The maker must know he or she is signing a will, rather than some other document, and the witnesses must know the maker is signing a will, although the witnesses need not know the contents of the will.

Lawyers follow these rules religiously. Most lawyers develop signing rituals at their offices to avoid breaking the rules and invalidating a will or trust.

Oral wills are not valid in most places, including Florida. You can imagine the opportunities for fraud if they were.

Any will can be made "self-proving." These wills are admitted to probate without the necessity of procuring the testimony of a witness to prove the will is valid. A hijacker with a self-proving will has an advantage because he can ask the court to admit the will to probate without involving other people. On the other hand, a self-proving will is almost always created by a lawyer rather than a layman hijacker operating on the fringes. This helps ensure the will was procured properly if the lawyer is working only for the maker and not the hijacker.

The location of a probate proceeding must be the county where the maker lived when he or she died. This offers hijackers an opportunity to choose in which county the probate proceeding is held. A hijacker may move their elderly parent to their home shortly before death to ensure the probate proceeding is held in their county away from other family members.

Wills created in one state are generally valid in all other states. This allows a will signed in New York to be probated in California. A hijacker may move a victim to another state away from other family members to probate a questionable will.

Here is an example. Madison lived her entire life in Ohio and becomes infirm in her later years. Her son, Matt, realized his mother's will divided her estate among her three children. Matt believed he was entitled to the entire estate because he provided care to her that his siblings did not because they lived in distant states. Matt brought his mother to his own lawyer, who prepared a will giving her entire estate to Matt. Matt threatened to cease caring for his mother and place her in a nursing home if she did not sign the will. Clearly, this will can be overturned by Matt's siblings. With the will in hand, Matt moved himself and his mother to sunny Florida, where Madison died within a year. Matt hired a Florida lawyer to probate Madison's estate. Madison's two other children were beside themselves with anger over their mother's will. However, they chose not to litigate the matter because of expense and uncertainty of result. Matt successfully hijacked Madison's estate for himself, victimizing Madison and his two siblings.

Revoking a will or trust. What are the consequences?

Revoking a will is a simple task. A will can be revoked by a new, validly executed will, by a valid codicil, or by physical act of the maker such as burning, tearing, canceling, defacing, obliterating, or destroying it with the intent and for the purpose of revocation. The maker may direct that another person do these acts for the maker.

A maker cannot revoke a portion of the will by physical act. People sometimes use a pen to cross out one beneficiary's name and add another. This is not legal. An attempted partial revocation by physical act is invalid, and the part the maker attempted to revoke can be admitted to probate if it can be recreated. If a maker desires to revoke part of a will, it must be done in writing with the formalities of law.

Revocation may be presumed by the court, as well. When a will that is known to be in the possession of the maker cannot be found after the maker's death, a presumption arises that the will was destroyed by the maker with the intention of revocation. The presumption may be overcome by proof of the maker's intention not to destroy the will.

In some situations the revocation of a will is all that is needed to complete the hijacking.

Nick and Sophie had two children, Jennifer and Daniel. Daniel was a "taker," as Sophie put it to her lawyer, and Jennifer was a "giver." Nick and Sophie gave and gave to Daniel to keep him from drowning in debt. Jennifer never asked for a thing from her parents. Nick and Sophie decided to give their entire estate to Jennifer to make up for the gifts to Daniel. Nick died before Sophie. When Sophie was ill and close to death, Daniel visited her home and searched through her papers. When he discovered the will giving his mother's estate to Jennifer, he destroyed the will. The result is that Sophie died intestate (without a will) and Daniel and Jennifer equally divide the estate. With one simple act Daniel hijacked half of Jennifer's inheritance.

In the case outlined above, Jennifer would have a good case against Daniel's destruction of the will had she known about the will. Unfortunately, Nick and Sophie were secretive about their personal dealings and never shared the will with Jennifer.

Who has the right to challenge a hijacker in the court system?

A person must have some interest in the estate being litigated to be allowed to ask the court to hear the case. An interested person is defined as any person who may reasonably be expected to be directly affected by the outcome of the particular legal proceeding. An individual who will not be directly affected by the outcome cannot ask the court to right an alleged wrong.

The general rule is that a person has the right to bring the suit if the person has either been disinherited by the will being presented to probate, or the person will benefit if the will is declared to be void. Business entities such as charities and other corporations can also bring suit if they meet these qualifications.

In the case of Nick and Sophie's will, the only two persons directly affected are their children, Jennifer and Daniel. Jennifer's husband cannot bring a suit to reinstate the will even if he knew about the will. Neither can Sophie's brother, who was furious about the outcome.

Florida also allows a person named as an administrator or personal representative in an earlier will to contest a later will. This law elevates a person who may be a stranger to a status similar to a beneficiary in inheritance litigation. This law is unnecessary and allows abuse of the probate system. I was involved in one case where a person named as personal representative in a will that had been revoked by several later wills petitioned the court for the probate of the will. None of the beneficiaries of the estate supported his position. The beneficiaries were forced to pay him a settlement to get him out of the probate proceedings. Many involved thought of the payment as extortion.

When is the time to enforce your rights and litigate?

If you are a hijacker, the answer is never, but if you are forced to litigate, you must delay the matter as much as possible. If you are a victim, the answer is *now*. Delay allows the transfer and secretion of assets, causes witnesses to forget facts, undermines the victim's case, and allows the hijacker to better prepare for a court battle.

A clever hijacker will throw up road blocks and diversions to keep the victims off the scent as long a possible. However, in the end the tenacious victim will bring the matter to court.

An action to test the validity of a will cannot be brought until the maker is deceased. This is because a will can be changed at any time and is not valid until a person is deceased. A person may make a will at any time right up until their death. It makes no sense to tie up the court system while a person is alive litigating the validity of will that has no legal significance.

An action to contest the validity of all or part of a trust may not be commenced until the trust becomes irrevocable. This rule is based on the same logic used in will contests. A trust that is not irrevocable is revocable and can therefore be changed by the maker at any time. A revocable trust usually becomes irrevocable when the person making the trust dies.

If a will is presented to probate, the person presenting the will must give notices to people who are interested in the proceeding. If these notices are given, the people receiving the notices must act quickly if they are to bring a will contest. Often the recipients do not realize the importance of the notice and do not act. This results in a waiver of their right to contest the will in the future. A potential victim may file what is known as a "caveat" with the probate court to ensure they will receive notice of any proceedings. This will enable them to act quickly, even if notice is not provided to the victim by the hijacker.

When other causes of action are not available, a suit for interference with an expected gift may be successful

In some cases, the conventional legal procedures do not provide a cause of action for relief. In such cases, a victim may have a cause of action for "tortious interference with an inheritance." Four elements must be present.

First, the victim must have a reasonable expectation he will inherit assets from someone. It does not matter who. This expectation of an inheritance is known in the law as an "expectancy."

Second, an alleged hijacker intentionally interfered with that expectancy in a wrongful way. For example, the alleged hijacker may have told lies about the victim that caused the victim to be disinherited.

Third, the victim must show that if the alleged hijacker had not acted as he did, the victim would have received his inheritance. In our example, the lies must have caused the victim to be disinherited. If there are other reasons the victim was disinherited, the alleged hijacker's actions are of no consequence and there is no cause of action. If, for instance, the plaintiff murdered a family member, thereby causing the disinheritance regardless of the alleged hijacker's actions, the alleged hijacker is not liable.

Fourth, there must be damages to the plaintiff. The damages are equal to the amount the victim lost to the alleged hijacker.

Under this legal theory, the hijacker need not divert the expectancy to anyone in particular. It is enough that the victim did not receive his expectancy. The hijacker is liable in any event.

This action can be brought only if the victim has no adequate remedy in the probate courts. If the plaintiff could have obtained the relief being sought in a probate proceeding, the plaintiff cannot maintain an action for interference in a separate suit.

The remedies available in an interference action include money damages and/or the imposition of a constructive trust upon the lost inheritance. Damages can include not only the lost gift but past and future mental or emotional distress resulting from interference.

Pre-death transfers are a form of theft that can be overturned

Sometimes a hijacker convinces a victim to transfer assets to another before the victim's death. Such transfers made prior to death are also voidable after death on the grounds of fraud, duress, mistake, undue influence, and lack of capacity. The same standards discussed above apply in these cases. The cause of action to set aside such transfers are brought by the administrator of the decedent's probate estate, who is then acting on behalf of the decedent.

For example, Tom convinces his elderly and frail aunt, Patricia, to deed her home to him by telling her that she will lose it if she goes into a nursing home. Tom tells his aunt that she can live in the house for her lifetime and that at her death he will sell the home and distribute the proceeds to her grandchildren as she wishes. After Patricia's death, Tom claims the home as his own. Patricia's estate can sue Tom to recover the home if they can prove the lies Tom told to obtain the home by deed from Patricia.

Beneficiaries of trusts can enforce their rights and demand an accounting

Beneficiaries' Right to Information

Present and some future beneficiaries of trusts are entitled to a copy of the trust and all relevant information related to the assets of the trust and the details of administration, including an accounting at least annually.

Enforcing a Beneficiary's Rights for Breach of Trust

Trustees have a fiduciary duty to beneficiaries that can be enforced in a court of law. A trustee who breaches his or her fiduciary duty has committed what is known as a "breach of trust."

Unfortunately, a cheated beneficiary usually learns of the breach of trust only after the fiduciary duty has been breached and the hijacking is complete. I cannot exaggerate the importance of diligence on the part of trust beneficiaries. Unscrupulous trust administrators often find ready hijacking victims among unconscientious beneficiaries. In trust administration, an ounce of prevention on the part of a beneficiary is worth a pound of cure. The cure, which comes in the form of a lawsuit against the hijacking trustee, is expensive and time consuming. An example of breach of trust is found in part 2, case study 1, later in this book.

All states have limitations on the amount of time a person has to bring an action against a trustee who hijacks the trust assets. In Florida these rules apply:

- A trustee must adequately disclose trust accounting matters to beneficiaries.
- A beneficiary who has a claim against a trustee must bring suit within six months of receipt of the trust information. After that time, the beneficiary is barred from bringing an action concerning any matter disclosed by the trustee.
- If no information is given by the trustee to the beneficiaries, a beneficiary has only four years to bring a claim against the trustee.

. . .

The legal remedies described in this chapter are the traditional remedies used for centuries to bring hijackers to justice. Recently, because life expectancies have increased greatly, state legislatures noticed the large and vulnerable senior population and enacted laws to better protect us as we age. Chapter 5 describes the protections and discusses whether there is any real value in these new laws.

Chapter Five

A Trap for the Hijacker: Abuse of the Elderly Laws

Abuse and exploitation of the elderly is becoming an epidemic in the United States. The reasons are easily understood. The population is aging and people are living longer. Elderly persons are attractive targets because they become more weak as they age and more dependent on others for their basic needs. Remember, a mugger would not choose a young athletic man as a victim. The mugger would victimize the elderly lady who cannot fight him off or do much to sound an alarm.

Lawmakers throughout the world have recognized the spread of elderly abuse, and have enacted laws to punish the wrongdoers. Florida and many other states allow both civil and criminal penalties. New laws allow triple the money damages. But do they have bite?

Florida statutes define exploitation of an elderly or disabled adult as knowingly, by deception or intimidation, obtaining or using, or endeavoring to obtain or use, an elderly person's or disabled adult's funds, assets, or property with the intent to temporarily or permanently deprive the elderly person of the use, benefit, or possession of the funds, assets, or property, or to benefit someone other than the elderly person or disabled adult by a person who either (1) stands in a position of trust and confidence with the elderly person, or (2) has a business relationship with the elderly person or disabled person.

Another statute provides that exploitation includes cheating or conspiring to cheat an elderly person by a person who knows or reasonably should know that the elderly person lacks the capacity to consent.

In appropriate cases, either criminal or civil penalties or both can be had against the hijacker. The impediment to use of these penalties is the standard of proof needed to prove a case. In the criminal courts, the crime must be proved beyond a reasonable doubt. In the civil courts, the case must be proved by clear and convincing evidence, which is a higher standard than proving a case by a preponderance of the evidence, or 51 percent.

How do these laws affect a hijacker? That depends in large part on how committed the state prosecutors are to enforcing the laws, and how easily the crimes can be prosecuted. To date there is little evidence to show the laws have any teeth. Prosecutors are more concerned with prosecuting violent crimes or clear-cut embezzlement cases, which are easily proven.

If someone is hit over the head with a beer bottle, they are clearly a victim. The beer-bottle-wielding criminal is dragged into court and fined or sent to jail. Case closed.

Prosecuting white-collar crimes is more difficult unless there is a clear paper trail and a victim to assist the prosecutor. If a dishonest employee embezzles money from their employer by writing checks to herself, there is a clear paper trail and a victim to assist in the prosecution. The prosecutor will drag the check-writing thief into court, wave the checks in front of the jury, and easily get a conviction. It is much more difficult to prosecute a dishonest nephew who convinces his frail and elderly uncle to make large gifts to the nephew, thereby impoverishing the uncle. "My uncle signed the checks," the nephew will argue. "How was I to know he couldn't afford to make the gifts?" It is almost impossible to prosecute this type of case without the uncle's testimony in court. The uncle may be unable to testify because he is incompetent or dead by the time the matter gets to trial. Lack of testimony from the victim is one important reason hijacking from the elderly goes largely unpunished.

Hijacking the inheritance of an elderly person by undue influence or other means is clearly exploitation of the elderly. Why is this difficult to prosecute? Again, the answer lies in the evidence or paper trail, or lack thereof. Hijackers operate in the shadows and leave little evidence behind.

For example, many hijackers use lies as their tool to manipulate a victim. The hijacker does not shout out the lie for all to hear. The hijacker whispers the lie a thousand times into the victim's ear until the lie seems to be the truth to the victim. The victim then acts on the lie, and the hijacker has successfully made off with the inheritance.

Another example is a hijacker who uses coercion to force her mother to change her will to give the entire estate to the hijacker and exclude the hijacker's siblings, who were included in the previous will made years earlier and never changed. This is common when one child lives close to the parent while the other children live in distant places. The child who lives close to the mother becomes a caregiver out of necessity. There is no one else to assist the aged parent. The parent becomes dependent on the hijacker for his or her daily needs. Often the parent cannot even obtain food from the store and cook it to feed herself. She may rely entirely on the hijacker. The hijacker may threaten to kick the elderly parent out of the house or to move her to a nursing home. Under these circumstances, the parent is likely to grant any request made by the hijacker. If the hijacker wants to cheat the siblings out of their share of the parent's estate, the parent is likely to make a new will if the hijacker demands she do so. What else can the parent do? The parent relies on the hijacker for daily sustenance and needs. She cannot resist.

The disinherited siblings may recover their inheritance in a civil suit. But how can a prosecutor prove this secret crime in a criminal court where the standard of guilt is beyond a reasonable doubt? Who are the witnesses? The hijacker and the victim are the only witnesses. The victim is dead, and the hijacker will not testify against himself. Prosecutors will not take a second look at this case because it is a loser in the criminal court. This crime goes unpunished.

In civil cases brought under the elderly abuse statutes, the problem facing the victim is again the high standard of proof required by the courts. Some elderly abuse statutes require proof by clear and convincing evidence. This is the equivalent of proof beyond a reasonable doubt required by the criminal courts. This higher standard of proof is probably to protect hijackers against the threat of triple the money damages allowed in these cases. It may be fair of the legislature to demand a higher standard of proof when a person asks for triple the damages. But the system would better serve the elderly if they were allowed to recover what was stolen with a lower standard of proof. The standard of proof in other civil cases is a preponderance of the evidence, or 51 percent, as was discussed earlier. This would allow the elderly to bring their cases to court. Under the present system, the elderly are denied a large part of the justice due them.

If this sounds confusing, it is—even to the lawyers and judges who deal with these issues on a regular basis. The high degree of confusion in applying these different standards of proof, as well as the difficulty in proving these cases, leads to the inevitable result that these white-collar abuse cases are not handled by criminal prosecutors. And they are seldom successful in civil courts. With the increase in inheritance hijacking cases, it is possible that prosecutors will find these cases on their radar and begin to prosecute hijackers, but as of yet a hijacker need not be concerned with criminal penalties.

...

Now that you have an understanding of the people involved in a hijacking and the inheritance laws, you are ready to take an inside look at how the court system really operates.

Chapter Six

ANATOMY OF AN INHERITANCE SUIT

There are two preeminent rules in any inheritance litigation. There are no exceptions to either rule.

The first rule is: The victims are always surprised by the hijacking.

The second rule is: The sole remedy is time-consuming and expensive litigation.

Inheritance litigation involves three parties, a hijacker and the two victims. The first victim is the person intending to give the inheritance, Target A. The second victim is the person or persons expecting the inheritance, Target B. Chapter 3 discusses the relationship between victims and hijackers.

This chapter focuses on what happens when a hijacking is discovered and how an inheritance lawsuit proceeds. I have handled more than a thousand inheritance disputes in my almost thirty years practicing law. Not every hijacking results in a lawsuit, but many inheritance disputes can be resolved only through litigation.

Initial investigation and confronting the hijacker

All victims, without exception, did not see the hijacking coming. Or if they did, they ignored the warning signs. Once the hijacking is discovered, the victim seeks out a lawyer for advice.

During their first interview, each victim tells their lawyer how surprised they are that the hijacker cheated them. Had they seen it coming, they say, they would have done something to stop the hijacking.

These victims are not unintelligent. Many of them are well-educated professionals. Only a fool would allow a thief to steal right in front of his nose. They are not fools.

Nonetheless, they are surprised by the hijacking and furious with the hijacker. "How could (insert hijacker's name here) do this to me?" they ask. "I never expected this to happen."

They want and demand swift justice. They have chosen this particular lawyer because they believe that he or she is a bulldog and will tear the hijacker apart.

The first order of business is a preliminary evaluation of the available facts. Facts are the most important part of every case. Without facts to present to the court, there is no case. But fact gathering can be difficult if a hijacker has attempted to cover up his crime. Gathering information about a deceased person's accounts may be impossible before filing a lawsuit. Financial institutions, brokerage houses, and health care providers have strict limitations on the information they can legally divulge to strangers who do not possess legal authority to demand the information. If the account holder is deceased, a probate estate must be opened or a lawsuit must be filed to obtain that legal authority to demand information. Often the only documents and information available are the decedent's bank statements and records received by the victims by mail after the death. These records may reveal bank accounts that had been hijacked before death, or accounts benefiting the hijacker after death. Many hijackers will rush to a decedent's home soon after death to destroy or hide a decedent's account records in an attempt to cover up their crime.

After gathering and analyzing all available facts, the hijacker is confronted. The hijacker should be approached by the attorney rather than by the client. At this stage, clients have strong feelings against the hijacker, and any personal confrontation may lead to a shouting match or physical violence. The attorney should use a letter to communicate with the hijacker. As well as making demands on behalf of the client, the letter should set out the facts and suspicions in detail to show the hijacker that there is a credible case at hand and that the clients are serious about pursuing their rights.

I would like to say that a demand letter from an attorney always puts the fear of God in the hijacker and leads to an immediate good result for the victim. This is sometimes, but rarely, the result. If there is a true misunderstanding about the facts and the parties genuinely desire to clear up that misunderstanding, a resolution can usually be reached.

In some cases, a review of the facts will cause a victim to walk away from a case even though they feel they have been wronged. The possible reasons for this action by the victim are many. The amount in controversy may be small, the case difficult to prove, the victim lacks the resources to pursue the case, or the victim may even sympathize with the hijacker.

Resolute hijackers, however, are reluctant to give up what they have schemed and worked so hard for simply because they receive a demand letter from an attorney. Unfortunately, the typical response is a letter from the hijacker's attorney denying any wrongdoing, or no response at all. Litigation is then the only route to resolution.

Beginning the litigation: Who has the right to sue?

Although inheritance litigation may be initiated by the person intending to give the inheritance if they discover the hijacking while still alive, the litigation is almost always initiated by those expecting the inheritance after they learn it has been hijacked. These folks may be the children or grandchildren who have been cheated out of their inheritance. They expected to inherit the fruits of their parents' or grandparents' hard work and sacrifice, but it was diverted by the hijacker.

The victim may be the child or sibling of a decedent who was financially abused by a hijacking stranger or family member before their death. The victim may be a spouse who was cheated by a hijacking child or caregiver. The list of possibilities is almost endless.

In all cases, the victim who is now the plaintiff must have what is known as "standing" under the law. Standing to sue in an inheritance case requires the plaintiff to be in a position to benefit if the suit is successful. For example, a widower prepares a will disinheriting his children and giving his entire estate to a friend. The disinherited children have legal standing because they will inherit the estate if the will is challenged and overturned.

How an injured victim asserts their legal rights

Every lawsuit must be brought under a legal theory recognized by the courts as a legal means to remedy the wrong suffered by the victim. It is not enough to simply tell the court your sad story. You must fit your situation into a pigeonhole known as a legal cause of action. For example, if you want to invalidate a will you must make allegations which give you the right to legally invalidate the will. Alleging the maker was incompetent is one legal reason to invalidate a will. In most inheritance cases, all possible legal theories are alleged by the victims in the initial complaint or petition to the court.

Chapters 4 and 5 discussed the elements of the legal causes of action relevant to inheritance suits. This chapter explains how the causes of action are handled in the court system.

Validity of the will is always in question

Wills and their validity are often the focus of litigation. In some cases, a trust or codicil to a will may be in question rather than a will, and the same legal procedures apply. Let's begin with an explanation of how a will is declared to be valid or invalid by the courts.

A will is not recognized as valid under the law until it is declared to be so by the court. Only then can the provisions of the will be fulfilled. When a person desires to ask the court to validate a will, he must file a petition with the court. A petition to the court is a document telling the court why you are entitled to the court's assistance and what you want the court to do for you. The person who presents the petition is called the petitioner. In a probate proceeding the petition explains who the petitioner is and why the will should be declared to be valid by the probate judge.

The petitioner may be the person who wishes to be administrator of the estate or another person on their behalf. The petitioner must give notice of the proceeding to all other persons interested in the proceeding. Anyone whose inheritance is affected by the will is an interested person. If the petitioner wishes to cut off the rights of all persons who may challenge the will, he will give notice to anyone who has the right to challenge the will. If, however, the petitioner wishes to conduct the proceeding with as little attention as possible, he will limit notice to only those absolutely required to receive legal notice.

petition to the court:

A document telling the court why you are entitled to the court's assistance and what the court should do.

For example, let's say that John went to his father as his father was dying and convinced him to make a new will. His father's previous will gave his estate to his three sons in equal shares. The new will disinherits John's two brothers, Paul and Ringo, and gives the entire estate to John. There are many reasons to challenge the will. John's father may have not been competent to make a will. John may have told his father lies to convince his father to make the will. John's father may have not properly signed the will with the requirements of law.

John is allowed by law to present the will to the probate court without giving notice to Paul or Ringo because they are not beneficiaries under the new will. Paul and Ringo live in another state and would not know of the probate proceeding unless they conducted their own inquiry into their father's estate. If Paul and Ringo do not investigate and learn of the probate proceeding,

John can complete the proceeding and claim without their interference. Paul and Ringo will have a very difficult time attempting to recover their hijacked inheritances after the probate proceeding is completed.

Let's assume that Paul and Ringo learned of the proceeding at an early stage and they contest the validity of the will John presented to the probate court. Paul and Ringo will inherit part of the estate if the will is overturned, and therefore they have standing to challenge the will.

Their legal argument to overturn the will is that their father was not competent to make a will, that John may have coerced his father, or he may have defrauded him, and that John used what is known as "undue influence" on their father to cause him to disinherit his sons. This puts the siblings in court to slug it out over the validity of the will.

Suing strangers is sometimes possible to recover an inheritance

The second primary type of inheritance litigation is against a stranger to the will, an outsider. In these cases the will is valid and not in dispute. The will is admitted to probate without question. The personal representative is appointed to administer the estate. The personal representative finds that the decedent was swindled before his death and sues the swindler who hijacked the estate to recover the assets.

In this example, let us assume John was honest and did not convince his father to make a new last will on his deathbed. John, Paul, and Ringo agreed to admit their father's will to probate and divide the estate among them. To their dismay, they soon learned that their father's longtime girlfriend, Lucy, had convinced their father to make her a joint owner of some of his bank accounts. Lucy had actually promised their father to hand over the accounts to John, Paul, and Ringo after their father's death. However, no one else knew of this promise. She explained to John's father that this procedure will avoid probate and the boys would have the money as soon as he died. In addition, Lucy agreed to assist in paying the father's living expenses if necessary. "It is too much to bother those three busy boys with," Lucy explained. "They have their own lives."

As it turned out, Lucy reneged on her promise to John's father. After the father's death, she claimed the bank accounts were a gift to her. She produced a death certificate at the bank and drained the accounts. When John and his brothers asked about the accounts, Lucy claimed they were a gift to her as an expression of John's father's love and affection for her.

In this situation, the personal representative or administrator must bring an action against Lucy to recover the funds. What are the chances of recovery? The answer to that question depends on the proof before the court at the trial. Who is there to testify about the promise Lucy made to John's father? John's father is deceased. Lucy is the only person who can testify to that promise. If she will admit to making the promise, which is very doubtful, the court will enforce the promise. What are the chances of Lucy admitting to the promise she made to John's father? She will never admit the promise if she intends to hijack the inheritance. A written memorandum of Lucy's promise to John's father would refute her claim. However, Lucy saw to it that no written memorandum of her promise existed. The end result is that John, Paul, and Ringo were disinherited by Lucy.

A trustee is often a hijacker who must be brought to justice

The third primary type of inheritance litigation involves trusts. The typical revocable living trust is created by a person during their lifetime to manage their property and avoid the probate court at their death. Most people believe a trust is a foolproof and money-saving means of transferring an inheritance. The person creating the trust is known as a settlor or grantor. The trust states who is to receive the property at the death of the person who made the trust. This is also known as a type of will substitute because it distributes property at death and avoids probate. This type of trust is very popular among people with even modest estates.

Trusts need not be recorded or registered anywhere except in rare cases. Unless contested in a court of law, a trust administration is private and not subject to any court review. Although the trustee owes a fiduciary duty to the beneficiaries, the duty is frequently ignored. Trust administration is fraught with fraud and asset manipulation. A trustee need not hire an attorney to assist in the administration. There may be absolutely no oversight or court supervision of a trustee. The trustee is free to do as he desires unless the beneficiaries can scrutinize the trustee's administration of the trust.

If a trustee hijacks an inheritance, the litigation must be against the trustee for errors in administrating the trust and breach of the trustee's fiduciary duty to the beneficiaries.

For example, let us assume John's father created a revocable living trust to manage his property during his life and distribute it to his three boys at his death. John is named trustee to serve at his father's death. After John's father's death, John learns that there is a million dollars in bank accounts held in the trust. John visits the bank with his father's death certificate and drains the accounts. He then tells his brothers that dad was broke and left only a small amount of cash. He sends them each a check for ten thousand dollars as their share. John has hijacked Paul and Ringo's inheritances.

If Paul and Ringo are to receive their rightful share of their inheritance, the first obstacle Paul and Ringo must overcome is the lack of information. If John avoids giving them information, how are they to learn of the existence of the fat bank accounts? The bank, citing privacy laws, will refuse to give them any information without a subpoena from a court of law.

Unless Paul and Ringo suspect John is a hijacker and are willing to begin a lawsuit against him, they will never learn of the accounts. John will have successfully hijacked their inheritances.

A victimized trustee may sue strangers to recover assets

Now let us assume John is honest, but again Lucy has pilfered John's father's accounts, which were held in the trust. In this case she did not ask John's father to make her a joint owner of the account. She asked him to loan her money from time to time, always with a promise to repay the loan. John's father wrote checks to Lucy and others for hundreds of thousands of dollars. He paid for her new Cadillac and paid off the mortgage on her condominium. Only in one case did he ask her for a promissory note. Lucy asked for a loan to bail her daughter out of a bad marriage and pay for the divorce attorney. John's father made the loan and received a promissory note for twenty thousand dollars from Lucy's daughter.

John assumed the role of trustee upon his father's death. When he reviewed the accounts he discovered the checks to Lucy and her daughter. John's lawyer made a demand on Lucy for repayment of the debts. Lucy explained that the money she received is a gift from John's father. Lucy also claimed that the promissory note from her daughter was voided the previous Christmas as a present to her daughter, whom John's father had never met. Lucy produced a copy of the promissory note with "VOID, Merry Christmas" written across the note in big black letters. Lucy claimed John's father voided the note, although he did not. This was a forgery. Without better proof to the contrary, John and his brothers decided to drop the matter and let God deal with Lucy in his own way. Lucy had successfully hijacked a large portion of the boys' inheritance.

Righting the wrong outside the probate court system

If all else fails, the victim may be able to sue under the legal theory of "tortious interference with an inheritance." This cause of action is allowed only when there is no remedy in the probate courts and an action by or against a trustee is not viable. The case is filed in the regular civil court rather than the probate court. This cause of action is a very powerful tool. However, it is not well known and sometimes misunderstood by lawyers and judges alike.

As explained earlier, the plaintiff must show there was a fixed intention that he receive a gift and that someone wrongfully interfered with that gift, causing the plaintiff to lose the gift.

Under this legal theory, the hijacker need not divert the expectancy to anyone in particular. The hijacker is liable in any event. It is enough that the victim did not receive his expectancy. This cause of action is especially useful in cases where an inheritance is hijacked through use of a trust. For example, let us assume again that John's father made a revocable living trust that gave all of the trust assets to John, Paul, and Ringo at their father's death. Lucy, this time, is not a hijacker but a warm, loving caregiver to John's father. In exchange for the care and devotion Lucy gives to John's father, John's father made a promise to Lucy. He agreed to amend his trust to give her 20 percent of his estate at his death. This, he says, is in exchange for the love and affection she gave to John's father. At the time John's father made the promise, he was competent, and the gift is reasonable. Paul learns of his father's intention to make the large gift to Lucy. Although Paul agrees that the gift is fair in exchange for the love and care John's father received from Lucy, Paul browbeats his father into not making the change to his trust. Paul has interfered with Lucy's inheritance. Had Paul not interfered, Lucy would have received the inheritance. Lucy was damaged in an amount equal to what she would have received. All the elements of the tort are present. Lucy clearly has a cause of action against Paul for her loss.

The intangible assets are often most important and motivate the victim

I described in chapter 3 why victims go to court to recover their inheritances. The fight is not always about the money but about the love the money represents. The hijacking victim typically feels that he or she is a victim of a hijacking, not of money, but of the love the money represents. They know in their heart that they were loved and would never have been disinherited if the hijacker had not stolen their inheritance. Their only means of recovering the love lost to the hijacker is a suit to recover the money the hijacker stole from them. This need to be compensated for stolen or lost love is a powerful motivator and drives may victims to seek court-ordered relief.

The march toward justice is not a sprint

Once the hijacking is suspected and then revealed, the lawsuit is filed with high expectations. Now begins the slow, steady march toward justice. Note that I said "march," not "sprint." The victim's lawyer may well be a bulldog and fight like one for his client. However, the justice system is slow and cumbersome. Having worked within the court system for three decades, I respect that the system must grant every litigant due process of law. This means that everyone is on an even playing field and gets their day in court to seek justice. The last thing any party to a lawsuit wants is a rush to judgment that leaves them without their day in court to plead their case. Unfortunately, giving every litigant due process of law requires a great deal of time.

The result of this need to do justice results in a methodical but sluggish justice system. To do justice and make a decision on the merits of each individual case, the judge or jury must have all the facts presented to them in an orderly fashion. The lawyers must collect the facts. Each party must be given a fair chance to prepare and present their case. The lawyers need to be thoroughly familiar with the facts of the case and apply the facts to the law. In the interest of justice, these things should not be rushed.

Once the lawsuit is filed, the defendant typically has twenty days from the date he or she is served with the summons to file what are known as responsive pleadings. Responsive pleadings can be an "answer," which is a legal pleading admitting or denying each individual allegation made by the plaintiff. If an answer is filed, the defendant typically denies all allegations of liability.

It is at this point, before responsive pleadings are filed, that the defendant's lawyer has the first opportunity to obstruct and delay the plaintiff's lawsuit. Rather than file an answer to the plaintiff's complaint, the defendant can file what is called a "motion to dismiss the complaint" as a delay tactic. A defendant's attorney always seeks to force the plaintiff into a settlement on the defendant's terms. Obstruction and delay stand in the way of the plaintiff's goal, which is always a favorable outcome in a short time. From the defendant's point of view, the possibility of a favorable settlement is greatly enhanced if the defendant's attorney can cause the plaintiff to believe that the probable result of the lawsuit is not worth the trouble and expense the plaintiff is putting himself through in this case. The defendant hopes the plaintiff will tire of the litigation and either drop the case or accept a pittance in settlement of the claim.

A "motion to dismiss the complaint" tells the plaintiff that the defendant thinks the plaintiff has not stated a legal cause of action and the plaintiff has no case. Defendants often file a motion to dismiss even if the complaint does state a valid cause of action. In the rare case where the plaintiff has not stated a cause of action and has no hope of stating a cause of action, the defendant's lawyer will seek an expeditious conclusion to the case. He may file his motion to dismiss immediately rather than waiting the twenty days allowed by law. The judge may dismiss the case, but there will be amended complaints and appeals to higher courts. A case that lacks merit, just as a meritorious case, may not be resolved for years.

Judges, also, are sometimes the cause of delay. Settlement of any case is also in the best interest of the judge sitting on the case. Removing a case from the docket is very important to many judges. Judges receive efficiency ratings for completing cases when compared to their peers.

If a case is settled by the parties, it is final and off the docket with no chance of a retrial or appeal to a higher court. Some judges will take opportunities to discourage both the plaintiff and defendant in hopes of forcing the parties to compromise out of frustration with the legal process. This saves the judge the trouble of conducting the trial and issuing a decision, which may possibly be appealed and reversed by a higher court. Most judges dislike conducting trials because they are time consuming and intellectually demanding. Judges loathe nothing more than being reversed by a higher court.

When a motion to dismiss the complaint is filed, the judge must consider and rule on the motion to dismiss before the case can go forward. This requires a hearing before the judge and an order signed by the judge. Most judges schedule hearings one to three months in advance. Therefore, the case is delayed for those one to three months to hear each motion to dismiss the complaint.

When ruling on the merits of the motion to dismiss, the judge has two options. First, the judge can rule that the motion to dismiss is granted and the case is dismissed with permission for the plaintiff to file an amended complaint that states a legal cause of action. Or the judge may order that the motion to dismiss is denied and the defendant must answer the complaint. In the order either dismissing the complaint or denying the motion to dismiss, the judge states within how many days the parties must comply. For example, a judge may order that the motion to dismiss the complaint is denied and the defendant has twenty days to answer the complaint. Astute lawyers pay close attention to this detail. A lawyer wishing to delay the proceeding will ask for a longer time to comply, thirty rather than twenty days. Opposing counsel should oppose the longer time period.

An astute attorney wishing to expedite the case will insist that the time for compliance run from the date of the hearing. The order is usually signed days or even weeks after the hearing. So, if the order states that the time for compliance runs from the date the order is signed, the matter is delayed that much longer.

Attempting to end a suit by frustrating the opposing party is common. However, a plaintiff will rarely just throw up his hands and walk away from the suit unless continuing will result in financial or emotional ruin. The plaintiff has too much emotion, time, and money invested in the suit. Remember that the plaintiff feels he or she has been cheated out of the love they deserved, not just the money. They need closure.

Discovery, the process used to learn the facts, is cumbersome but effective

The astute lawyer will begin his or her formal fact investigation, known as "discovery" in legal jargon, as soon as the suit is filed. Discovery is the most important, time-consuming, and expensive element in any inheritance lawsuit.

Fact investigation begins before the suit is filed and continues until the day of trial. The lawyer and his clients can never know enough about the facts of the case and the opponent. In all discovery proceedings, the parties are allowed to ask any question or request any document as long as the request *may* lead to admissible evidence. This allows an attorney to go on fishing expeditions into almost any area or subject in hopes of finding relevant evidence. The facts investigated or discovered need not be admissible at the trial, where every piece of evidence must be relevant. An example of unrelated areas the attorney is allowed to explore is the personal life of the defendant or the defendant's family. It may not be important that the defendant's daughter was divorced three times, but it can be investigated. Sometimes discovery is used to embarrass a party, but this tactic rarely does more than give the opposing party the opportunity to gloat over details of the embarrassing moments.

Discovery can be conducted by sending written questions known as interrogatories, by asking oral questions known as a deposition, or by demanding that documents be produced for inspection, known as a notice to produce. All responses to these discovery tools must be made under oath under the penalties of perjury.

Interrogatories are written questions to the parties or others. The respondent must answer the questions under oath. Interrogatories are best used as a prelude to a deposition and to discover additional areas to explore. The party being asked to answer the interrogatories is allowed thirty days to respond, and no sooner than forty-five days from the date the party is served with notice of the suit. This means that the earliest a defendant is expected to give any information to the plaintiff is at least forty-five days after the suit is filed.

Depositions are formal proceedings where the parties, witnesses, and experts are asked oral questions under oath with a court reporter present. A transcript of the deposition is prepared by the court reporter to be used at the trial. Depositions are time consuming and often difficult to schedule because a group of people must be available to meet for the deposition. The attorneys, the clients, and the person being deposed must schedule the event.

A demand for production of documents requires the person served with the request to produce the documents for inspection and copying. This is used to obtain medical records or other printed materials from third parties. Here again, an attorney has the opportunity to delay the proceedings. The attorney desiring the information must send a notice to all other attorneys that he or she is requesting information from someone who is not a party to the suit, such as a doctor, nursing home, or bank. If any attorney objects to the request, the attorney desiring the information must schedule a deposition of the custodian of the documents. This impedes and delays the discovery of the documents. It increases the cost because a deposition must be scheduled with the parties and a court reporter. More delay and expense raises the frustration level.

Should a party refuse to sit for a deposition or provide documentation or otherwise impede discovery, the only solution is to ask the judge for help. Unfortunately, judges expect the attorneys to be reasonable and work out discovery problems. Judges simply do not like to spend their time listening to one attorney complain about the other party's refusal to comply while the other attorney offers some lame excuse for the noncompliance. The judges will order compliance with the discovery request, but rarely will a judge sanction the wrongdoer in any meaningful way. This allows a reluctant defendant to further delay the process, and perhaps altogether avoid producing what the opposition seeks to inspect.

Expert witnesses are necessary to support your legal theories

Expert witnesses are a necessary element in inheritance litigation. Experts are often asked to give their opinion on whether a person was competent at a point in time, when they signed their will for example. Unless the doctor examined the deceased person around the critical time, such as when the will was changed, the opinions are based on medical records. The medical history and physical and mental state are important, as are the medications administered at the time. Most opinions are given by doctors who never met the deceased person. Nevertheless, a good expert can paint a credible picture of a person for the judge to consider at the trial.

Forensic accountants are sometimes used to untangle a financial mess and present an orderly explanation of complex financial transactions to the court.

Handwriting experts may be called in to testify if forgery is an issue.

Experts on any subject are expensive and add to the cost of the suit. Not only must they be paid for reviewing the medical records, but they must sit for a deposition by the opposing attorney and be paid for testifying at the trial. Most psychiatrists and psychologists will give an honest opinion of the deceased person's state of mind. However, there are doctors who will reach the conclusion desired by the attorney regardless of the facts. I recall one particularly disgraceful case where a psychiatrist hired by the opposition testified that the decedent was probably very lucid at the time she signed an amendment to a will. In fact, the decedent was under hospice care and was using a dozen medications to ease her journey into the afterlife, including an intravenous morphine drip. She died within forty-eight hours. Fortunately, the judge saw through this expert's testimony and found the decedent was incompetent at the time.

Witnesses to the facts are essential

Friends and family who witnessed the actions of the decedent or the hijacker must be interviewed and deposed. Often the testimony of one witness will reveal new facts, which must then be investigated. Unless a person has some special expertise, he is not able to give his opinion on any legal issue. The facts and just the facts are all the court is allowed to hear.

Occasionally, witnesses who were once thought to be reliable are reluctant to testify against a family member or friend and will choose not to recall important details.

If the validity of documents is at issue, the attorneys, witnesses, notary, and anyone else with knowledge of the documents may have compelling testimony.

Mediation often leads to resolution of the case

Months pass quickly. Depositions are taken. Documents are reviewed. Attorneys posture. The clients posture. Trial preparation is an interesting piece of showmanship. When the bulk of the discovery is finally completed, a notice is sent to the court requesting a date for the trial. Knowing that the parties are ready for trial, the judge then typically orders them to mediate the case before the judge will schedule a trial.

Mediation is very successful in reaching resolution of many cases. The mediation process is simply a meeting of the parties to determine if they can voluntarily settle the case. The parties are required to sit across a table from each other with their lawyers by their sides and the mediator at the head of the table. The parties have probably not spoken to each other since the lawsuit began. The lawyers communicated with each other throughout preparation for the trial, but the parties were excluded from those communications. That the parties are in the same room with each other with the opportunity to tell their side of the story directly to the opposing party can be a real icebreaker. There is no substitute for face-to-face discussion. The physical proximity helps each party understand that the opposing party is not the devil reincarnate but a human being with flaws and problems just like everyone else.

At the outset, the mediator explains the simple rules. The parties are expected to behave like ladies and gentlemen. Outlandish behavior is forbidden. Everything said at mediation is confidential and cannot be used outside the mediation. If a party violates this rule, the court will impose very harsh sanctions, which may result in losing the case even before the trial. This rule facilitates settlement because the parties and lawyers are free to make offers and say things that cannot later be used at the trial.

The mediator also tells the parties that reaching an agreement at mediation means that they control the outcome. Most lawyers agree that leaving the case in the hands of a judge or jury is like rolling the dice. The outcome is always in doubt because judges and juries are made up of individuals with their own prejudices and personal history that give them a distinct point of view. That point of view may vary greatly from what is expected by the parties.

The plaintiff's attorney then explains the plaintiff's cause of action without interruption. The plaintiff is allowed to speak if he wishes to do so. Then the attorneys for the defendant and other parties tell their side of the story. The important aspect of this arrangement is that for the first time the parties hear the opposing party's story while sitting in the same room with the opposing party. This usually has the effect of putting things in focus for the parties. They may believe the other party is a liar and a hijacker, but they understand them better than ever before.

Just as truth is in the eyes of the beholder, each party tells their side of the story believing their version of the facts is the truth. This is true even if the hijacker knew they were committing theft at the time of the hijacking. As I discussed in earlier chapters, all thieves justify the theft in their own mind. As a consequence, the victim and the perpetrator both believe they are in the right, making compromise that much more difficult.

Following initial discussions, the mediator splits the parties and puts them in different rooms. The parties seldom speak to or see each other again that day. The mediator shuttles back and forth between the rooms. His or her job is to understand the case from the perspective of all parties. The mediator then points out the flaws in each party's case and chips away at the confidence of the parties. This is done without prejudice to either party. The mediator has no dog in the fight. His or her job is to reach a settlement that the parties agree upon. Many mediators feel that a good settlement is reached when neither party is totally happy. This means that neither party walked all over the other and each party compromised to reach settlement.

Mediation is a time for the parties to take a realistic view of their chances in court. Emotions may be boiling over, but the parties must force themselves to be realistic. It is often difficult for a client to accept the fact that their case is not open-and-shut. Emotion should be set aside for the moment in the interest of deciding what is best for all concerned at that particular time. When leaving the mediation office one day, I overheard a party to a mediation tell her attorney, "You witnessed a miracle here today. I never thought we would settle this."

Miracles do happen at mediation. Sometimes one party will agree to settle because he vastly overestimates the strength of the opponent's case. Perhaps there is a reason unrelated to the case and unknown to the opposition that forces a party to give more than they should, illness for instance. Or a party may desperately wish to move to another state and put this incident behind them. Perhaps both parties have pressing reasons to settle the case. The time between the filing of the case and the mediation is often more than a year. Personal circumstances can change considerably in that time.

If the parties reach a settlement, it is written up at the mediation and signed by the parties. The case is then over, and the terms of the settlement agreement are fulfilled by the parties.

Mediation allows all parties to claim they are the winner in the case. Regardless of the terms of settlement, everyone can find reason to claim victory and profess that justice has been done. Claiming victory, even a small victory, soothes the emotional wounds, which are more important than the monetary considerations.

What to expect if the case is tried before a judge or jury, and the aftershock

Should settlement not be possible, the matter proceeds to trial. Within a few months following the failed mediation, the judge holds a docket sounding and assigns a date and time for trial. The docket is simply a list of cases that are ready to be scheduled for trial. There are many cases on each trial-period docket. If a case is far down the list of cases, there is a good chance the trial will be postponed until the next trial period weeks later.

If the hijacker has been delaying the trial because it is clear the result will go against the hijacker, time has run out for the hijacker. Even in the cumbersome legal system, a defendant can run but not hide. The trial will be scheduled for a specific date, and the victims will have their day in court. The witnesses are subpoenaed to ensure their presence at the trial. The lawyers prepare their exhibits. The parties try to calm their nerves.

The parties may still be talking about settlement. The mediation revealed strengths and weaknesses to the opposing parties. The lawyers and parties may be negotiating up to and during the trial itself. There is always a chance to settle until the judge signs the final order.

Inheritance suits are almost always tried before a judge without a jury in Florida. The civil trial courts are informally divided into what is known as "legal side" and the "equity side." Suits on the legal side are only about money damages, such as personal injury or breach of contract actions. The trials are usually before a jury, which awards the winner money damages. Suits on the equity side are all about doing the right thing and righting a wrong. The court is asked to use its equitable powers to render a decision. For example, the court may be asked to rule that a will is invalid because it was forged or procured by undue influence. The only decision that can be rendered is whether the will is valid. If it is valid, it is admitted to probate and the probate proceedings go forward. If it is found to be invalid, the probate proceedings go in a different direction. No decision about money is rendered by the court because no issues about money are before the court.

This ancient system of legal causes of action versus equitable causes of action developed early in the English common law, which is the basis of American jurisprudence. Before the common man was generally well educated, it was decided that juries are unnecessary in these cases and the decisions must be left to a lone, better-educated judge. This is the same reasoning that gave us the antiquated Electoral College. Surprisingly, whether the system should be altered is rarely debated. Lawyers accept the legal-versus-equity court system without question.

Trials are very exciting events conducted in very subdued environs. The atmosphere, although perfectly formal, is charged with adrenaline. The parties and attorneys will remember the trial for the rest of their lives. The parties will remember the testimony and mull it over in their minds years later, wondering how important each particular piece of testimony was to the outcome.

Trial courtrooms are solemn places, soundproof with no distractions from the outside world. Judges insist on formal decorum because it is the only way to maintain order. It has been said that the single greatest step forward in the history of the justice system was enacting the rule that only one person is allowed to speak at a time.

Everyone in the courtroom is riveted to the witness as he or she testifies. The witness's demeanor is very important to the judge and jury, who are trying to determine who is telling the truth and who is lying. Some are hoping the witness delivers the silver-bullet testimony that can carry the day and win the case. Others are hoping the witness delivers the bomb that blows the opponent's case out of the water. Rarely does a lone witness offer such exciting testimony. Rather, the final decision is based on the cumulation of testimony from all the witnesses offered by all involved. The judge or jury then "weighs the testimony" and decides whose case has the most weight. That party is the winner in spite of the losing party's credible arguments.

Surprises are frequent during any trial. Unfortunately, witnesses are unreliable. Often the testimony of a witness at trial is not what a party hoped or expected it to be. In some cases the witnesses reverse earlier testimony. If a party's witnesses do not provide the expected support for a party's case, the party may accept a settlement before the opposition picks up on the disappointing testimony and withdraws the offer.

In all trials, a fact is never proved until it is believed to be true by the judge or jury. Until then the fact is simply a statement that the witness believes to be truthful. Truth, much like beauty, is in the eyes of the beholder. Ten witnesses may testify to a particular fact and the judge or jury may believe the opposite to be true. This is why bringing a case to trial is risky for all concerned. Some lawyers believe bringing a case to trial is no less risky than rolling dice in Las Vegas. This is not because of incompetence or dishonesty in the judge or jury, but because truth is in the eye of the beholder, that is, the eye of the judge or jury.

Following the testimony and final arguments, the judge or jury is charged with making the decision everyone has been anticipating for the past year or more. Judges have the habit of taking the matter under advisement rather than announcing their decision in open court with all the parties present in the courtroom. I am of the opinion that the judges wait to allow the parties a cooling off period between the trial and the decision. If the decision was announced immediately after a highly charged trial, the parties might come to blows or worse in the courtroom.

Customarily, the lawyers receive the decision by letter from the judge. One party is happy and the others are unhappy. The clients are informed and react each in their own way depending on the level of emotional investment they made in the proceeding. The winners are, of course, happy to be validated as the party who is right. They feel justice has been done. Losers, on the other hand may be resigned and/or angry. The parties have a lot to cope with when the decision is finally announced.

If the decision is adverse, the lawyer may file a notice of appeal. The appeal process is longer than the trial process. An initial appeal brief need not be filed for months. The entire trial transcript must be prepared by the court reporter and filed with the appellate court. The expense can be as much as the lawsuit itself. The appellate courts are flooded with appeals and the appellate judges are overworked. It is not uncommon to wait more than a year for a decision.

If the trial court's decision is overturned, the matter goes back to the trial court for a new trial. If the appeal is denied, the case ends unless there is a question to be resolved by a higher court.

In any case, the dispute eventually reaches a final conclusion. Some litigants are happy. Others are saddened, angry, and disheartened with the court system. The aftershock lasts for years.

. . .

Litigating an inheritance dispute is a little like trying to put the horse back in the barn after it has run off. People often try to restore the status quo before the hijacking occurred, but life for the family and others will never quite be the same. The fabric of the family has been torn, and no amount of mending will make it new again.

Now that you have read about all that can go wrong and learned who the good guys and bad guys are, you are probably looking for some good news. The good news is that you can avoid a hijacking. Chapter 7 discusses how you can protect yourself and your loved ones. The case studies in part 2 give practical lessons in how to recognize a dangerous situation and avert a hijacking. Enjoy yourself.

Chapter Seven

HOW TO PROTECT YOUR INHERITANCE

A simple plan or system that avoids all hijackings has not and never will be devised. That our justice system handles hundreds of thousands of inheritance cases each year is proof that even the sharpest of minds in our society cannot provide a universal solution. The variables in our lives are infinite and unpredictable. Relationships, marriage, divorce, health, employment, location, birth, death, and many other factors affect our lives, often without warning. Each event forces us to adapt to a new situation. What may appear to be a perfectly safe state of affairs on one day may be a perfect opportunity for a hijacker the next day.

Protecting an inheritance in a changing world can be very challenging. However, there are several things that can be done to make an estate as hijack-proof as possible. Discussion of the elements in every hijacking will illuminate what you can do to meet the challenge.

As discussed in chapter 1, every hijacking contains five elements:

1. The "donor," who is the person intending to give the inheritance, who is Target A
2. The inheritance itself
3. The proper beneficiary and intended recipient of the inheritance, who is Target B
4. The hijacker
5. The persons benefiting from the hijacking, who may be the hijacker or others, such as the hijacker's children

Now that you have read the earlier chapters and have an understanding of how the five elements interact, we can discuss how to prevent a hijacking.

Element 1: Donor, the first line of defense.

The first line of defense against a potential hijacking is the donor, the person intending to give the inheritance. The donor can do several things to protect the inheritance and avoid becoming a victim we call Target A.

First on the list of to-do items is preparing an estate plan. Without an estate plan, the inheritance is up for grabs. A visit to an experienced estate-planning attorney is essential. It is important to be frank and open in discussions with the attorney. Every family has skeletons in the closet, and the attorney has probably heard about all of them over the years. So there is no reason to be embarrassed if you reveal a few skeletons of your own. Remember that all discussions with your attorney are subject to the attorney-client privilege. The client rather than the attorney owns the privilege. The attorney is duty bound not to reveal to a third party anything he learned from his client.

Choosing the right attorney

There is not a one-size-fits-all estate plan. Every client and every case is different. An estate plan may be as simple as a will or as elaborate as a series of trusts designed to save taxes, protect beneficiaries from themselves, avoid probate, and make large charitable gifts before death to save income and estate taxes.

This makes the choice of an attorney of utmost importance. A good relationship with an attorney allows the client to feel confident that they can seek and receive help at the time they most need help. Reputable attorneys always put the client before their own personal interests. The client should always feel confident that the attorney listens and responds to the client's needs. The client never should feel that the attorney is trying to sell the client a product to benefit the attorney. For example, if the client feels the attorney is trying to sell them an expensive estate plan that is more than what they want or need at that time, the client should find another attorney. Red flags should go up if the attorney is trying to sell insurance or annuities to the client, or even referring the client to a close associate who sells such products.

> The first line of defense is in the donor, the person intending to give the inheritance.

Although good attorney-client relationships last for decades, it is not ethical for the attorney to insist on charging a mandatory recurring annual fee to review the estate plan. The client should be free to consult a different attorney at any time.

The client should expect quality services for a reasonable fee. Prior to engaging the attorney, the client should ask about the range of fees the attorney charges for his services and what is provided in exchange for the fee. Choose an attorney who charges a fee that is fair when compared to the other attorneys in the area. Avoid the price gougers because you will be paying too much for the service provided. Avoid the low-end discount attorneys because they are either inexperienced or tempting you in the door to sell a more expensive product.

Always avoid any attorney who uses salesmen to cultivate new clients. Disreputable attorneys sometimes will send salesmen into senior communities to sell estate plans. These estate plans are always grossly overpriced and the legal services are always inferior.

The best inheritance attorneys are well-rounded and litigate as well. An attorney who litigates understands the issues in inheritance theft cases best of all. The attorney should be competent, not only in the law of estates and trusts, but also in the areas of real estate, small business, banking, estate administration, and certainly estate litigation. In Florida, real estate is big business, and everyone owns real estate. It is important to have an attorney who understands real estate investments and sales when planning an estate. The attorney will see beyond the simple gift of real estate. He will understand how that gift can be handled after your death and advise you on avoiding problems. If you are in the oil-producing business, you want an attorney who understands that business. If you are in the mining business, you want an attorney who understands that business. The broader range of experience and knowledge, beyond simple estate document preparation and tax laws, gives everyone an advantage. You do not want your beneficiaries to be confronted with a problem the attorney should have seen and avoided when designing your estate plan.

How to locate and choose your attorney

Finding and evaluating an attorney is not mysterious or difficult. Search the Internet using www.Lawyers.com or www.Findlaw.com or other search engine to find lawyers in your community. Go to their web sites. There should be information about their personal history and free general information about estate planning on the site. If you are acquainted with a lawyer or receive a recommendation from a friend, you should visit that lawyer's web site to check their estate-planning credentials. The first estate-planning consultation should be free. This is not a sales tool. You and the lawyer should feel comfortable with each other before proceeding with some of the most important decisions you will make in your life. During the first interview, the lawyer should tell you what you will pay for his services. If the fee is too high, you can leave with no obligation to the lawyer.

Your estate-planning attorney should be all of the following:

- Reputable in the community with many years of experience
- Experienced in litigating inheritance disputes as well as preparing documents
- Well-rounded in his practice, with experience in life as well
- A good listener who patiently answers any question and proposes alternatives
- Loyal to you, with no allegiance to others
- Identifies and solves potential inheritance theft issues
- Prompt in responding to the client's everyday needs and available in a crisis
- Reasonable about fees
- Willing to discuss the fee openly and early in your attorney-client relationship
- Enthusiastic to help you
- A gatherer of information who looks at the big picture
- Owner of a modern web site that educates and communicates
- Knowledgeable about modern ways to safeguard your documents, such as digital scanning
- Willing to conduct a free initial consultation in estate planning
- Prompt to inform you if changes in the law affect your estate

Avoid an attorney with any of these flaws:

- Uses a salesman to approach potential clients
- Demands recurring mandatory fees
- Sells products such as insurance or investment products
- Has little time or sympathy for your personal problems
- Has a weak understanding of your personal problems or business
- Has a conflict with representing others who you suspect may covet your assets
- Not enthusiastic about helping you
- Is not in good standing with the state Bar Association
- Might not be available to assist in a crisis or in the long term

- Makes sensational or exaggerated statements, such as claiming to be a super lawyer
- Has limited experience in estate planning or declines to discuss the depth of his experience with you
- Cannot communicate effectively with you and answer your questions to your satisfaction

How to prepare to make an estate plan

The minimum estate plan should consist of the following:

- A will or revocable trust with pour-over will
- A grant of a power of attorney over your property to someone you trust
- A designation of someone to make your health care decisions if you cannot make them yourself
- A living will stating whether you wish to be kept alive artificially if there is no hope of your recovery
- A designation of someone to act as the guardian of your person and property if necessary

Your attorney should give you options in planning the estate. He or she should explain the advantages and disadvantages of a variety of estate-planning tools and answer all your questions. Is a will or trust better suited to your needs? Are there beneficiaries with special needs to consider? All these elements require good communication between you and your prospective lawyer.

When I am asked to discuss estate planning with a client, the first thing my staff does is send the client a questionnaire. The questionnaire is confidential and is designed to assist the client as well as the lawyer. The client completes the questionnaire at home at their leisure. This allows the client time to give more accurate information and saves considerable time during our interview. The format causes the client to focus on the estate-planning task at hand, organize his or her thoughts, and give serious thought to important issues.

The information gathered in my questionnaire is the same information any estate-planning attorney needs, and which you should be ready to provide.

- The names and address of all persons involved and their relationships to each other
- A short family history regarding marriages, divorces, children, etc.
- Agreements or court orders that may affect the estate plan, such as prenuptial agreements, divorce decrees, or judgments

- Your plan of distribution and arrangements for special needs, such as a disabled child
- Concerns or worries you wish to share
- Names of people who need to be protected from others or from their own faults
- Your assets and how they are owned or held
- The people who will act on your behalf when you die to administer your estate
- Who you wish to name as your power of attorney during your life
- Whether you wish to make a living will
- Who you designate to make your health care decisions for you if you cannot act for your self, known as a health care surrogate
- Who you choose to be your guardian if you need supervision before your death
- Anything else you think your lawyer should know about you

When preparing for your first meeting with your lawyer, it's important to come prepared. The following is a list of questions you may want to ask your lawyer about your specific situation:

- Is a will or trust better for me and my beneficiaries? What are the advantages and disadvantages of both in my case?
- If I make a will, what must my beneficiaries do at my death to obtain their inheritance? How much will it cost and how long will it take?
- If I make a will or trust, how does it work and what must my beneficiaries do at my death to obtain their inheritance? How much will it cost and how long will it take?
- I am concerned that I may become ill and spend time in an expensive nursing home before my death. How does that situation affect my assets and my family? What government plans may help me in that situation?
- How are assets such as an Individual Retirement Account (IRA) or insurance policy handled at my death?
- Is my estate subject to estate or death taxes? If so, how do I legally avoid these taxes?
- Who has the legal right to challenge my will or trust and what are the chances they may be successful?

- Do you see that I may be especially vulnerable to an inheritance hijacker? How can I best protect myself against an inheritance hijacker?
- How often should I review my estate plan?
- Will you contact me if the laws change and affect my estate plan?
- Where should I store my estate-planning papers? Who should have copies?
- What is your fee to prepare my estate plan?
- (Anything else you care to ask)?

We've already discussed many of these questions. However, your individual circumstances will affect the answers.

Choosing the right administrator for your estate plan

One of the most important decisions a person makes when creating an estate plan is choosing an administrator. Administrators are called personal representatives, executors, trustees, surrogates, or conservators in different jurisdictions. An administrator of a probate estate or a trust is handed control of the assets and is perfectly positioned to hijack the estate if he or she is so inclined.

A beneficiary who has a personal investment in the other beneficiaries is often chosen to administer an estate or trust. This may be a child, sibling, or other relative. As you have read in chapters 1 through 6 and will read in the case studies, these are often the worst choices. The temptation is often too great to resist, and the trusted person becomes a hijacker.

> One of the most important decisions a person makes when creating an estate plan is choosing an administrator..

Probate estates are handled in the probate courts, where the courts can provide a remedy if the administrator hijacks the estate. However, the courts are not proactive and do not police the administration of a probate estate. The courts act only when a beneficiary complains about the alleged illegal actions of the administrator. The burden of bringing proof of wrongdoing to the court's attention is on the victim. The administrator is given ample opportunity to defend himself against the allegations of wrongdoing. The court simply sits in judgment and hands down a remedy if appropriate. Unfortunately, the remedies available may be neither swift nor adequate.

For example, let's assume the administrator of a probate estate collects all the assets of the estate and refuses to distribute the assets to the beneficiaries. Instead, he transfers the assets to his own bank account and then moves to a distant state. The beneficiaries petition the court for relief. After all, they tell the judge, their estate has been hijacked and they want justice. The judge agrees and orders the administrator to appear before him and explain himself. The administrator becomes defiant and refuses to appear before the judge. The matter then goes thorough several hearings. Finally, after several months and much legal expense, the judge enters an order in favor of the wronged beneficiaries for the amount due to them. What do they do with the order? Is it worth the paper it is written on? They must hire a lawyer in the state where the administrator fled with the inheritance to try and recover their inheritance. Several more months pass with more legal expense. In the end, the beneficiaries may never see their inheritance.

If the court required the administrator to post a bond, there may be an opportunity to get some relief. However, bonds are posted by insurance companies, which are notorious for refusing to pay claims until they are dragged into court. This means more expense with the prospect of an uncertain outcome.

The administrator of a trust, the trustee, is subject to even less oversight than the administrator in a probate proceeding. The law requires the trustee to initially give information concerning the trust and the trust assets to the beneficiaries. During administration, there is no direct supervision of the trustee. Beneficiaries must wait for the trustee to provide information and distribute assets. A reluctant trustee may refuse to give accurate information, distribute assets, or even answer simple questions. This leaves the beneficiaries with only the option of filing a lawsuit in hope of getting some relief from the court while the trustee uses the trust assets to defend his wrongdoing. Again, the beneficiaries are faced with expense, delay, and uncertainty. Many trustees are easily turned into hijackers by the temptations offered to them when they assume their duties and take control of the trust assets.

Revocable living trusts are all the rage in estate planning today, but they must be used with caution. A revocable living trust is a written document created by a person to manage their property during their life and efficiently pass the inheritance at their death. The maker creates the trust. A trustee, typically also the maker, manages the trust assets until the maker dies. At the maker's

> Revocable living trusts are all the rage in estate planning today, but they must be used with caution.

death, the assets are distributed to the beneficiaries of the trust. A revocable trust can be amended or voided by the maker at any time before death, when it becomes irrevocable and cannot be amended or voided.

These trusts are typically created by a single person or a married couple wishing to save their beneficiaries, usually their children, the trouble and expense of probate. The typical trust names a child as successor trustee to distribute the assets after the death of the makers or parents. The parents mean well when they create the trust and choose their successor trustee, but they often do not realize that they are creating a perfect situation for a hijacking child who assumes control as trustee.

A more dangerous situation is created when the maker of the trust names a person who is not a child to handle the trust. Typically, these third parties are chosen because the parents cannot trust the children to get along when the estate is to be divided. The third party is a trusted outsider such as an uncle or aunt. These people may have hidden motives to seek revenge for some long-held grudge. Or they may simply want the money so badly they will steal from their trusting family members. Again, the administrator is handed the tools and the temptation, which may turn them into a hijacker.

How does one choose an administrator who can be trusted?

A corporate administrator, such as a banking trust company, is often a good choice. The disadvantage to a corporate administrator is the fee he or she will charge. Most people would rather see this fee distributed as part of their estate to their beneficiaries. This makes corporate trustees a last resort choice to many people. Also, corporate trustees are not inclined to accept relatively small estates because the fees will not compensate them adequately.

Attorneys will sometimes be asked to act as administrators of probate or trust estates. Attorneys are honest, knowledgeable, and efficient. Over time I have learned to be very careful in agreeing to administer an estate. No fee can compensate for battling a beneficiary who insists on having things done their way, even if the law and good sense are contrary to their desires.

A wise choice often is to name two or more beneficiaries as the administrators. This provides a system of oversight and checks and balances. Each will review the acts of the others and keep them in check. The disadvantage is that every detail of the administration must be consented to and signed off by each administrator. Each administrator has veto power over every detail of the administration, such as distributing and selling assets, paying expenses, etc. In the end, if the administrators cannot get along well, there will be litigation among them.

Another alternative is to name all of the beneficiaries as co-administrators. This assures all the right to oversee the trust assets and each other. In the real world, this may work if there are two or three beneficiaries who get along well, but not with a larger number.

Many people recognize that their children do not get along as well as they would like. They appoint, out of frustration, the best in a bad bunch to do the job. This is asking for trouble and inviting a lawsuit among the beneficiaries, if not an outright hijacking.

The lesson to be learned here is that the choice of an administrator must be carefully considered. If there is any doubt, the best choice may be a corporate trustee or an attorney in spite of the accompanying fees. It will be money well spent if it avoids a lawsuit or a hijacking.

Communication: a key element

A donor who communicates well to his beneficiaries and makes his intentions clear to all concerned greatly reduces the opportunity for a hijacking. Making intentions known earlier in life rather than later improves the situation.

For example, if a donor in his fifties clearly states his intention to disinherit one of his three children, and maintains that position throughout his life, there is little chance his decision will be challenged and the estate hijacked. But if the same person has been closemouthed throughout his life and, at eighty years of age and in bad health, makes a will to disinherit that same child, there is certain to be a lawsuit by the disinherited child, who will feel his estate has been hijacked.

Unfortunately, communication between donors and beneficiaries is generally sorely lacking. Donors dislike revealing their assets and their intentions to their beneficiaries. Beneficiaries dislike bringing up the subject lest they appear greedy and offend someone. Whatever the reason, donors and beneficiaries do not communicate as much as they should. This increases the incidents of hijacking.

Tips on good communication

In my experience, risk is the greatest impediment to communication when estate planning is the subject. When I say risk, I mean the fear that the discussion may cause someone to be unhappy with the discussion. For example, parents will decline to discuss their estate plan if they feel there is a risk that one or more children will become unhappy. The fear may exist even if the parents are dividing their estate equally among their children if the parents know that one child expects more than just an equal share of the estate.

The best way to approach the fear of discussion is to remove the risk of making someone unhappy with the estate plan, even if the distribution favors some persons over others. How is the risk reduced or eliminated? There must be calm and frank discussion. This may sound like a catch-22. "Is he saying that the best way to remove the risk of discussion is through discussion?" Yes, that is correct. Overcoming the fear of discussion is by conducting a proper discussion.

The manner in which the discussion is conducted is the key to success. Discussing your estate plan with your beneficiaries is one of the most important discussions any of you will have in your lifetime. It should be treated by all with the respect it deserves. It should not be handled over a casual meal or while driving or during other situations where the parties can be easily distracted from the serious subject at hand. The parties should be told in advance that a discussion about inheritance will be conducted at a certain day and time. This will prepare all involved for the subject and allow some time to think about the subject beforehand.

The key word in this section is "discussion." A discussion is a calm discourse among people on a subject. It is not a meeting where a pronouncement is made in a take-it-or-leave-it fashion. If the parents are discussing their estate plan with their children, they should let the children know that they have given considerable thought to the subject, even anguished or prayed over the subject if appropriate. The children should participate in the discussion as equals. Their point of view should be treated with respect and not dismissed by the parents. The children should not feel they are just being dictated to by parents who have made an inflexible final decision. The parents should draw the children into the discussion as participants in the decision-making process. This will result in a decision being made by team effort among the children and parents.

> Discussing your estate plan with your beneficiaries is one of the most important discussions any of you will have in your lifetime. It should be treated by all with the respect it deserves.

The parents may have decided to favor one child over others or to treat all equally. Some children may not be entirely happy with the decision. Nevertheless, if the family group can buy in to the process, the chances of a hijacking are greatly diminished.

A frank discussion enlightens the family members to what others think. There may be some surprises that can change some minds and decisions. The parents may alter their plan after listening to their children's point of view.

I recently handled a probate estate where the father disinherited one of his sons, which is always a regrettable situation because it tears at the fabric of the family. The other four children disagreed with their father and agreed to divide the estate equally among the five children. Had the father discussed the subject with his children, he may not have disinherited his son and avoided the unpleasantness.

It is unfortunate that most families will never participate in a discussion about inheritance and come to a happy result. The risks involved in discussing inheritance issues are just too great for most families to chance. Prejudices, grudges, feelings of entitlement, a need for privacy and secrecy, and many other emotional issues are often too strong to overcome.

Safeguarding your documents

Do you remember the story I told about the son who destroyed his mother's will to disinherit his cousins? Because his mother died without a will, he inherited all of the estate as her only heir at law. Had his mother safeguarded her will, she would not have become a Target A victim for her son.

You should be certain your original documents are in safe storage. If you are uncertain about where to store your originals, leave them with your attorney and take copies for yourself.

Again, communication is important. You should distribute copies to the beneficiaries and administrator. This will allow the intended beneficiaries to guard against becoming a Target B victim. Many people decline to distribute copies lest they later change their plan of distribution and insult someone. If you decline to distribute copies to everyone involved, you should at a minimum give copies to people you trust.

The practice at our office is to scan all estate-planning documents to digital computer files after they are signed as a permanent record. The client is sent a copy by e-mail and is free to distribute the copies as he or she sees fit.

It is inevitable that some documents will be lost. This will not prevent the probate of the estate according to the lost will or trust. In these cases, a will or trust can be established through a court proceeding if a true and correct copy is available. However, the question of whether the will or trust was intentionally destroyed is raised when a document is lost, and a hijacker may take advantage of the situation.

If you make changes to your documents, you should make the changes known to all concerned. This will avoid conflict over the validity of contradictory documents.

Here are those four tips on how to safeguard your documents again:

1. Store the originals in a safe place
2. Make and distribute copies
3. Safeguard the copies by scanning the documents to digital computer files
4. If you change your documents, make those changes known to others and safeguard the new documents

Element 2: The inheritance itself

If we all knew with certainty the day we will die, the incidents of inheritance hijacking would be greatly reduced. We would all simply spend our last dollar on our last day on Earth. Fortunately, life does not provide such certainty, and we must all deal with the unknown.

Donors control the size of their estates. Beyond preparing a hijack-proof estate plan, the best way to protect an inheritance is to make it less tempting to steal. This means reducing the inheritance through gifting before death. But how much of a reduction is enough?

In some cases, a donor may believe the solution to avoiding a hijacking may be to choose not to have an estate at all. The donor may gift away all of his estate before death. This solves the problem of estate administration and potential hijacking. On the practical level, this solution is not available except in small estates where a parent will choose to live with a child during their last years. The parent does not need assets because the child cares for the parent in their home.

For the vast majority of people, divesting themselves of substantially all of their assets and then relying on a child for support is not an acceptable alternative. Most people need to feel they are independent in their later years, even if they are highly dependent on others. The need to retain control over assets is a key factor in maintaining independence.

Although making some pre-death gifts to beneficiaries has many advantages, many donors, even the wealthy, refuse to part with their assets before death. The most compelling reason is that the prospect of running out of money before death strikes terror in most people, even the very wealthy. It is a fact of life that most people will choose to retain control of their assets until death in spite of the risks of hijacking.

Element 3: Intended beneficiaries and unwitting victims

Beneficiaries are in a precarious position. They often feel uncomfortable pressing the donor about their inheritance lest they appear to be greedy. At the same time they want to ensure they receive their inheritance. If the donor is closemouthed, as many parents and elders are, the beneficiary can do little to help themselves. They often must wait and hope for the best.

Adequate communication between the donor and the beneficiaries brings the situation into the light and allows all involved to assess and protect their interests. Lack of communication works in favor of the hijackers, who prefer to operate in the shadows.

A beneficiary should do all he or she can to open communication and educate the donor to the great risk they are taking by not making their intentions known to all concerned. How should a beneficiary accomplish this? Give the donor a copy of this book. And let the donor know that the beneficiary is available to assist the donor if requested to do so.

In the best situations, beneficiaries should have a copy of the donor's will or trust and know where the original is located. A full inventory of the donor's accounts and assets is essential in helping a donor avoid a hijacking. Assets are not likely to be hijacked before the donor's death if they are watched over by the beneficiary as well as the donor. In addition, sharing this information during life avoids the tiresome and time-consuming task of locating assets after death.

Element 4: Hijackers can be identified early in many cases

It bears repeating that every hijacking is a surprise to the victims. Why is this always the case? Because the victims were unable or unwilling to identify the hijacker prior to the theft. In many cases, potential hijackers can be identified before the theft occurs. Some are easily spotted.

> It bears repeating that every hijacking is a surprise to the victims.

This is a list of the dozen most likely hijackers. This list is not intended to cause people to become suspicious of everyone and paranoid about their inheritance. All of the potential hijackers have legitimate reasons to have a relationship with the donor. No person should be asked to avoid other people because there may be a potential hijacker somewhere out there in the weeds. This list is offered as a tool to be used by the knowledgeable and vigilant person in defending against a possible hijacking.

1. The friendly neighbor who goes out of their way to assist the elderly widow or widower is a frequent hijacker, particularly if the friendly neighbor is considerably younger. These hijackers attempt to create a wedge between the elderly person and their family.

2. Health care workers should be carefully screened. They have been known to steal valuables, request loans that are never repaid, and to become surprise beneficiaries in revised and sometimes forged wills.

3. Extended family members, such as grandchildren and nieces or nephews, of elderly persons often identify their aging relation as a possible source of an inheritance. The typical tactic is to heap attention on the elderly person to gain their trust. They then convince their target to deed over real estate or change bank accounts, insurance policies, and wills to benefit them.

4. Family members who move in to take control during a person's last days. These folks are those who want things done their way or no way at all. They have not been heard from in some time, but now they are there to help—themselves, that is. No one else has the right idea about anything. They want a say in everything from who stands vigil at the bedside to the funeral arrangements. They want to know everything about the safe deposit box, finances, bank accounts, and where the will is kept. You can be sure that if the estate is not handled to their satisfaction, they will make everyone else miserable. The meek members of the family may succumb to their demands and lose all or a part of their inheritance. If granted control of the matter, everyone else may lose their inheritance.

5. New love interests, especially when disparate ages are a factor, have strong advantages as hijackers. If the potential victim is so smitten with their new partner that he or she is blind to the other's dishonest intentions, there is little an outsider can do if the victim is legally competent. The couple may even marry if they wish, further complicating the situation. I call marriage the "silver bullet" in the hijacker's tool box because it cannot be questioned by a beneficiary who loses his inheritance. There may be a serious downside to marriage for the hijacker, aside from being legally tied to someone for the love of money and not the person. I know several couples whose marriage late in life caused irreparable harm to their finances because of health costs. The best advice I can give to seniors is to live life to the fullest but do not

marry, even if both have the best intentions and a prenuptial agreement is in place to protect the beneficiaries of each partner. The fact that the couple marries puts their assets at risk in many ways, including health care costs, debts, taxes, and unforeseen liabilities.

6. Administrators of wills and trusts are vested with the power to hijack and are subject to little or no oversight except by the beneficiaries, who are typically inexperienced in such matters. A trust can be drained of assets in the blink of an eye, leaving the intended beneficiaries with the prospect of financing a lawsuit to recover their inheritance or suffer the loss without redress. Trust and verification is a good approach for all beneficiaries. The beneficiary has no choice but to trust the administrator, but the beneficiary can seek verification of the transactions to ensure proper administration.

7. Unscrupulous financial planners and advisors who court the senior market are a dime a dozen. They offer free meals and a sales pitch on how to solve all your financial problems. Their goal is not to help their customers but to make money for themselves. They have no obligation to their customers, whom they call "clients." The workings of most of the complicated financial products sold by these folks are impossible to fully understand. The advisors point out the advantages and avoid talking about the disadvantages. These folks can hijack an estate by selling a financial product that earns them a large commission but actually reduces or restricts the customer's assets. Regulation of this industry is designed to punish a hijacker rather than avoid a hijacking. There is no standard by which to measure the value of any of the products sold in the industry as a whole. The worst product can be sold by a huckster to the most gullible senior, and no one oversees the transaction. The best way to avoid this hijacker is to deal only with trusted financial advisors and to seek the advice of your attorney and accountant before making any commitments.

8. The trash talker is anyone close to Target A who never seems to have a nice word about the victim's intended beneficiaries. This hijacker uses the power of undue influence to control the victim, one of the most difficult tactics to combat. The hijacking is done in secret behind closed doors. The trash talker can double as one of a number of the other hijacker types we've already discussed, such as the distant relative, the new love interest, or the friendly neighbor. The key is that the trash talker has the victim's ear. This hijacker provides a constant flow of misleading information, which eventually becomes the truth in the mind of the victim. In some cases, the hijacker begins his campaign early, perhaps decades before the inheritance is hijacked. Sometimes, a

sibling may attempt to turn a parent against another sibling for reasons other than hijacking the inheritance, and later find that the result of their smear campaign is the hijacking of the inheritance. In many cases, the hijacker meets the donor late in the donor's life and seizes upon the opportunity to hijack the estate. Time is on the hijacker's side and will take its toll over months and years. As people age, small lies and half-truths have a large impact on their decision making. Those professionals who serve the older population encounter many cases where an aging frail person falls under the influence of another. Sometimes the intentions are honorable and no hijacking is contemplated. Other times the goal is a hijacking.

9. The embezzler is one who sees an opportunity to plunder an account owned by the victim and acts on that opportunity. Often the embezzler is the very person trusted to assist the victim in handling or reconciling his accounts. This trust affords the embezzler the opportunity to conceal the crime. This hijacking can take the form of simply forging a victim's name on a check. Or it may be as sophisticated as Internet bank fraud. In all cases, the victim is not protected by proper oversight of his finances. This type of hijacking leaves a clear paper trail and is sometimes prosecuted by the criminal justice system. Unfortunately, it goes undetected in many cases.

10. A child who moves close to an elderly parent often inherits a disproportionate share of the estate, leaving other children with less of an inheritance. The child may deserve the larger share or may have hijacked the inheritance of other children. A feeling of entitlement often motivates a hijacking in this situation.

11. The owner of a power of attorney. Giving a power of attorney to a trusted relation or friend is often a recipe for disaster. Giving control of your assets without proper controls is always dangerous.

12. The giver of misleading legal advice is last on this list but first on the list of devious hijackers. This hijacker intentionally and skillfully misleads the victim to gain an advantage. Here is a common example: The hijacker convinces his parent to deed real estate or transfer an account to the hijacker, who promises to distribute the asset as the parent instructs. The hijacker insists he is helping to avoid the expense of probate. When the victim dies, the hijacker owns the account by operation of law. If he chooses to disregard the parent's instruction regarding distribution to others, he has hijacked the estate.

Another example of misleading legal advice is in the making of a will. A will seems to be a simple and straightforward document. Yet it is filled with legal language with implications far beyond the plain meaning of the words on the page. A hijacker will often prepare a will for a victim that does not reflect the victim's last wishes but instead favors the hijacker. Once the victim dies, the hijacker probates the will and successfully hijacks the estate. How does one defend against this hijacker? Consultation with an independent attorney who serves only the donor is the only answer. Most people offer themselves up as victims because they are reluctant to consult a lawyer in what appears to them to be a simple, straightforward transaction. Elderly persons in particular, who are the most vulnerable, are reluctant to consult an independent attorney. They dislike disruption of their routine, traveling to the attorney's office, and paying the fee. Hijackers will discourage consultation with a lawyer. Nevertheless, independent legal advice is the best and often only defense against this type of hijacker.

This list is certainly not exhaustive. We must all be vigilant in our relationships.

Element 5: Those who receive the fruits of the hijacker's labors are sometimes also victims

Hijackers sometimes do their work not to benefit themselves but some other persons, such as their children or grandchildren. For example, a daughter may convince her mother to change her will to favor her children over her sister's children. If the daughter is successful, she has hijacked a portion of her mother's estate for her own children. This is not a direct benefit to the daughter.

When the daughter's children learn they have been favored by their grandmother over other grandchildren, they may be surprised. How will they react? Will they see through their mother's hijacking and attempt to right the wrong? Rarely will they attempt to reverse the gift. In almost all cases, the grandchildren will take the money and run even if they feel the distribution is unfair. Their mother has undoubtedly explained to them that their grandmother favored them over the other grandchildren. Whether they believe this with all their heart may be in doubt, but it is enough of a reason to keep the money.

> The hijacker will wonder if the money she hijacked for her children was worth the damage inflicted on the family relationships.

The grandchildren who have been cheated will do what they can to recover their rightful inheritance, and a family feud will develop. This leads to an unintended consequence. The hijacker may not have intended to destroy the relationship her children had with their first cousins, the other grandchildren, but she has driven a wedge between them that will never heal. The result is that the victimized grandchildren suffer a loss of money as well as their relationship with their first cousins. The hijacker's children gain some money but no longer have a relationship with their cousins. In the end of this family dispute, as in all inheritance disputes, the score must be tallied. The hijacker will wonder if the money she hijacked for her children was worth the damage inflicted on the family relationships.

The best defense to any hijacking is education and vigilance

Inheritance hijacking can be prevented. Understanding the law and how hijacking occurs is the best defense. Ignorance of these factors opens the door to a hijacker and invites him in to plunder the inheritance.

A person unschooled in inheritance matters is similar to an unarmed man being confronted by a robber with a gun in each hand. The first and best defense against hijacking is arming yourself with knowledge.

All lawyers are astounded by the general public's ignorance of the law. Even the most intelligent and educated person can be misled by bad legal advice. A person asking a friend for legal advice will almost always receive misleading and erroneous information. The friend does not mean to give erroneous or misleading legal advice. They just do not know any better. They may recall something that happened to someone they knew, possibly years ago and in a different state, and they relate that story to their friend in hopes of being helpful. Invariably, it is advice that will damage their friend rather than help solve a problem.

Often a hijacker will offer legal advice specifically designed to mislead a target. If the hijacker is a trusted relative or friend, the target usually accepts the advice and acts on it to the hijacker's advantage.

Knowledge of the law and how hijackers operate is the only defense against erroneous advice. A further word of caution is required here. Lawyers are trained to look for important issues in a particular situation. You may not fully appreciate or recognize all of the important issues in your personal situation. The knowledge you gain in this book is designed to alert you to danger signs and act against a potential hijacker. This book is not meant to substitute for a good lawyer's evaluation of your situation, which may be more complicated than you recognize. Seek out that good advice if you are confronted with a possible hijacking.

After gaining knowledge, you must be vigilant. For example, if you are the son of an elderly parent, look for people in their lives who have no good reason to befriend them other than their money. Is there someone who is taking your elderly mother to lunch? What are their motives? Has your parent joined a new church? Does the church ask for more money than you think appropriate? Has your parent made any "loans" to their caregivers? Do you review your elderly parents' finances from time to time? Are they sending large amounts of money to a television evangelist? Is that appropriate? Have they made large gifts to friends or family who recently befriended them? Does your elderly parent speak badly of someone? This may be a sign that someone is poisoning their mind against that person in hopes of placing a wedge between them.

These and a thousand other situations should throw up red flags for the vigilant observer. This will sound cynical, but if there is smoke there is usually a fire. If you see a red flag, you will probably find someone doing something they should not be doing. You must then act to remedy the situation before it spirals out of control.

What to do if you suspect a hijacking has occurred

In any legal situation, the facts dictate the outcome. It is absolutely essential that the facts be gathered and preserved. It is not enough to assume that because a bank account was hijacked the bank can provide all the records needed to prove the hijacking. You must act quickly to build the strongest possible case and recover the hijacked inheritance as quickly as possible. You should acquire the following information at the very least:

1. Learn your legal rights by visiting a lawyer. Your lawyer can help by filing documents that slow down or halt the hijacker's progress.

2. Contact the decedent's lawyer to obtain copies of estate-planning documents. Gather the documents from other places if necessary. These documents include wills, trusts, powers of attorney, health care surrogate designations, etc.

3. Gather all financial records at the decedent's home, office, and storage facilities, such as bank safe deposit boxes.

4. Gather deeds, titles to vehicles and boats, mortgage documents, and other documents evidencing ownership of real and personal property.

5. Forward the decedent's mail to yourself if possible. Banks and other

financial institutions send statements on a regular basis. This is often the best source of information in a hijacking.

6. Review credit card statements, checking accounts, and bank records for suspicious transactions.

7. Contact anyone who had a power of attorney or the power to sign on or manipulate the decedent's accounts to determine if they conducted any transactions. You may be asking a hijacker to confess his crime, so verify all you are told.

8. Make a list of names and contact information for the decedent's neighbors and social contacts.

9. Make a list of all doctors, health care workers, pharmacies, and other medical services or providers.

10. Carefully inspect the decedent's residence and vehicles to recover cash, jewelry, coin collections, stamp collections, documents, letters, and other items that may have value and that may bear on the case.

Top ten list to safeguard your inheritance

I know everything we've discussed so far is a lot to take in. So, here is a brief recap of everything we've learned in this chapter to safeguard your inheritance from hijackers:

1. Prepare an estate plan
2. Hire an attorney loyal only to you
3. Hire an experienced attorney
4. Do not rely on anyone other than your attorney for estate planning and legal advice
5. Create the plan *you* want
6. Appoint the right administrator for your will or trust
7. Communicate your estate plan to all concerned
8. Change your estate plan when necessary
9. Avoid dangerous shortcuts such as joint ownership with others
10. Do not procrastinate. Do it now!

A last bit of advice before the case studies

It is my sincere hope that you have enjoyed and been enlightened in some small way by part 1 of this book. It is my pleasure and privilege to bring this important information to you. I hope it will improve your life in some way, especially in your relationships with your family and friends. The ultimate goal of this book is to save all readers from the pain and suffering a hijacked inheritance brings down on all concerned.

Part 2 consists of case studies that bring to life the laws and theories discussed in part 1. These real cases will broaden your understanding of the complex and often confusing laws and human relationships involved in a hijacking.

Because the case studies examine relationships between human beings, you will see the good and bad in the characters. No hijacker is entirely evil, just as no victim is without fault. There are some redeeming qualities and some undesirable qualities in all of us. I hope you find the stories and characters as interesting as I do when I am confronted with them in daily life.

Part II

CASE STUDIES

LESSONS LEARNED FROM EXPERIENCE

Inheritance hijacking comes in many forms. These case studies illustrate how the legal theories explained in part 1, chapters 1 through 7, come to life in actual hijacking cases. The cases warrant close examination to illustrate, not only the crime, but more importantly the characteristics of the victims and the hijackers. A hijacking cannot occur without an opportune meeting of circumstances, victim, and hijacker.

The places and names have been changed to protect everyone involved and to avoid breaching the attorney-client privilege of confidentiality. Any reference or resemblance to any person, living or dead, is pure coincidence and unintentional. Some case studies are drawn from two or more actual cases to illustrate multiple points. Each hijacking and how it was accomplished or thwarted presents a real situation.

While the case studies are entertaining, they are designed to help the reader develop a sense of how, why, and when a hijacking opportunity can appear in their own family situation. Armed with that knowledge and sensitivity, the reader can better guard against a hijacking. If they do become the victim, they can better identify the problem and quickly seek to right the wrong.

I wish you good reading.

Case Study One

HIJACKING BY THE TRUSTED BUT CUNNING CHILD

The simplest hijacking is outright theft by a hijacker who has been given the power to steal by the victim. These cases warrant close examination, not only because of the crime, but because of the human relationships between the parties. Notice as you read the victims' naïveté to the risk of trusting a particular person. The victims have nothing to be sorry for except the trust the victims had in the hijacker. Once the hijacker is empowered to steal, the only obstacle to the hijacker's success is the hijacker's own conscience. While the trusting victims gave the hijacker the opportunity to strike, the hijacker would not have acted without the internal motivation provided by her relationship with her sister. When the hijacker rationalizes the theft to quiet her nagging conscience, there is no stopping her.

Private trusts are the most popular estate-planning tool. Thousands of private trusts are created every day to avoid the probate system and reduce estate taxes. Creating a trust is the beginning of a long and complex financial relationship among the participants, who are almost always family members with their own personal histories and relationships. Those relationships often change when the trust assets are thrown into the mix. This case study illustrates the dangers inherent in all private trusts.

Olivia and Brenda: Two sisters, two annuities and one trust, one hijacking

This is the story of two sisters, Olivia and Brenda, who were born in San Pablo, California. Their father, a newly discharged World War II Navy veteran with a genius for engineering, was attending the University of California at Berkeley on the GI Bill when they were born. Their mother, a tall, stunning blonde, worked as a bookkeeper at a local lumberyard to help support her husband and two girls.

111

The girls were born just thirteen months apart and were some of the first baby boomers. They had long blond hair like their mother, which was never fully under control. Their mother would have cut the often-tangled locks if she did not adore them so.

Their father, Brad Simmons, earned a bachelor of science degree in just three years. He then earned his master's degree in aeronautical electrical engineering in a mere fifteen months. Brad was driven to succeed in school in order to get on with living his life.

During Brad's last semester in school, the large corporations came calling on the best and the brightest at Berkeley, as they did every year. Brad was seduced by a large salary and a chance to work in Houston, Texas, on what was known as the Jet Propulsion Project, later known as the Rocket Project, and finally known as the Space Project. At the time, no one imagined that the Russians would launch Sputnik into orbit and send the United States into a full-bore race to the moon. Brad was unknowingly inducted into the group destined to put the first man on the moon.

One evening, Brad came home earlier than his usual eight or nine o'clock arrival time. After kissing his two girls and his wife, he casually asked, "How would you like to move to a tropical paradise?"

"What do you mean?" his wife, Sandra, asked.

"We have a chance to move to Cape Canaveral."

Sandra became excited. "Florida?" She had not been able to acclimate to Texas and was growing increasingly weary of Houston.

"That's the place."

"What is Florida?" Olivia asked.

"A place called the Sunshine State," her mother answered. "With beautiful water and everything else."

"I take it you're willing to discuss the matter?" Brad said.

"There is no discussion," Sandra answered. "If you want to go, we'll move tomorrow."

Brad laughed. "They offered me a project manager's slot. I don't know about tomorrow, but we'd probably be able to leave in about four weeks. I'll tell them we accept."

Sandra threw her arms around Brad's neck and kissed him. "Come here, girls," she said to Olivia and Brenda, hugging them. "You are going to be eating oranges before you know it."

Brenda said, "But we had orange juice today."

Brenda's answer struck Sandra in her funny bone. She burst out laughing and, in a rush of excitement, hugged both the girls and Brad until they insisted she stop.

The Sunshine State was good to Brad, Sandra, and the two girls. Sandra found a nice home a few blocks from the beach to raise her girls. The family settled in easily to the slow pace of Cocoa Beach. Life revolved around the space center, the largest employer on the east coast of Florida between Jacksonville and Miami. All of their friends and neighbors either worked at the space center or earned their livelihood from the people who worked there. When *I Dream of Jeannie* aired, the family identified with the characters as though they were neighbors down the block.

Seasons quickly slipped away almost unnoticed and folded into years. It didn't seem long before the family was attending Brenda's high school graduation at Cocoa Beach High School in 1961. Olivia had graduated a year earlier and had finished her freshman year at the University of Florida in Gainesville. Brenda would start Florida State University in Tallahassee, the arch rival to the University of Florida, in the fall. The two universities competed for superiority in Florida in every arena from sports to academics.

Brad and Sandra knew the advantages a good education can afford people who do not have family wealth or social connections. They insisted the girls apply themselves in school to ensure a bright future. The girls, wishing to please their parents, willingly complied. They graduated near but not at the top of their high school classes. Brenda edged out Olivia for the best GPA between the sisters, but only by a tenth of a point.

The choice to attend rival universities underscored a lifelong rivalry that existed between Olivia and Brenda. The girls had unconsciously competed with each other for their parents' affection from the time they could crawl onto their parents' laps. The competition for their father's affection and attention was especially keen. Brad loved working long hours at the space center and often missed their bedtime when they were young girls. He was sometimes away for days to work on launches or special problems. When Brad was accessible, the girls did all they could to please him. The competition guided the girls throughout their lives and forged their relationship.

Olivia became an accountant and later a CPA. Brenda became a high school English teacher. In the career competition, Olivia felt she had won because she earned more money than her sister. Brenda, on the other hand, felt she had won because she felt she was much happier with her career choice than her sister, who griped about tax season and working long hours.

Both of the girls met young men while in college and later married those young men. The spouse competition was something of a draw. Each married an engineer who took job at the space center.

Each girl had three children. Two girls and a boy for Olivia. Two boys and a girl for Brenda. Again, a draw for anyone counting.

Brad's career grew with the space program. He was recognized by his peers as an outstanding engineer. When Neil Armstrong stepped out of the space craft on to the Moon on July 21, 1969, Brad was justifiably proud of his own large contribution to the success of the project.

Brad retired in 1985 at the age of sixty-five. He hated to leave his work but was pushed out to make way for younger engineers with recent educations in the modern theories. Brad learned to enjoy his retirement and lived to enjoy the millennium. Even as he approached eighty years of age, his mind was sharp and his memory clear. He died peacefully in his sleep from heart failure in late 2000.

Sandra was confused by Brad's death. Unlike Brad, Sandra's memory had begun slipping in early 1997. She masked her memory loss for a time, but by the time of Brad's death her disability was well established.

Olivia and Brenda and their spouses met at Brenda's home after Brad's funeral to discuss Sandra's situation. They all recognized Sandra's disability and her inability to manage her monetary affairs.

Years before, Brad and Sandra had taken the good advice of their estate-planning attorney. They had created a revocable trust to manage their assets during their lifetimes and pass the assets to their daughters at their deaths. The lawyer was experienced and sensitive to the needs of his aging clientele. He knew that two of the worst fears people have as they age are losing control of their lives and outliving their savings. The lawyer told Brad and Sandra that if they became incompetent, their daughters had the ability to assume management of the trust. However, if their daughters assumed control, they could manage the trust only, the lawyer stressed, for the benefit of Brad and Sandra. Anyone who managed the trust while Brad and Sandra were alive had a fiduciary duty to Brad and Sandra, as well as to the beneficiaries of their trust estate at their deaths. The manager could not use the money for the benefit of anyone except Brad and Sandra. The lawyer made his point by saying that if anyone breached that fiduciary duty, they were committing theft and could be prosecuted as a common criminal, as well as sued by the victims.

The lawyer did a fine job with one exception. He failed to explore the relationship between Olivia and Brenda. Had he pressed his clients on this issue, he might have learned that the two girls were very competitive in almost every way throughout their lives. This should have alerted the lawyer to the possibility of competition between the daughters for their parents' inheritance. Brad and Sandra believed the competitive spirit between their daughters made them both better persons because they pushed each other to higher levels. They failed to recognize the darker side of the competitive spirit between the girls.

They chose Olivia to be the manager of their estate when they were no longer able to because of her career experience, with Brenda as an alternate.

Brad and Sandra felt very comfortable with their lawyer and followed his advice to the letter. The lawyer advised Brad and Sandra to give copies of the trust to Olivia and Brenda and talk about their desires with their daughters. Brad and Sandra did give copies to their daughters and explained that they intended to be fair with them and treat them equally. Olivia and Brenda knew that their parents' assets were to be divided equally between them at their parents' death. Until then the assets were to be used only to benefit Brad and Sandra. Brad made a point of telling his daughters that there might be nothing left for them. When the girls learned of the extent of their parent's estate, they were sure there would be something left unless catastrophe struck.

After Brad's funeral, the two sisters and their spouses met to map Sandra's future.

"I think we should let Mom stay here, in her own home, for now," Olivia told the others. "She can manage very well on her own."

Brenda agreed, "She'll need a cleaning lady once a week or so. Just about everything else she can do herself."

Liking the direction of the conversation, the husbands agreed without comment. Their fear was that Sandra would be taken into one of their homes by Olivia or Brenda. Although they professed to love their mother-in-law, they were not willing to disrupt their lives and become caregivers to her. They each harbored these concerns in silence and alone, afraid to voice them lest they be thought of as heartless and unloving.

"I think Mom can handle living by herself for now, but I think we should consider taking over her finances," Brenda said.

"I agree," answered Olivia.

"What do we need to do to accomplish that?" Brenda asked.

Olivia explained, "According to the trust, we can have Mom examined by her physician. If he agrees she is not capable, the trust names me as the first successor trustee, and you are second successor trustee, an alternate, if I cannot handle the job. I guess they did it that way because I'm a CPA."

The sisters and their spouses agreed the plan created by Brad and Sandra made life easier for all of them. They agreed to follow their plan until it required revision.

Olivia viewed her appointment as first successor trustee as a signal from her parents that she was the favored child. The truth was that the lawyer who drew the trust made the decision. He asked Brad and Sandra what their children did for a living. When they responded that Olivia was a CPA, he suggested she be the first successor trustee, with Sandra as the alternate. Brad and Sandra simply agreed with the lawyer's recommendation without thinking much about it. Favoring one daughter over the other never crossed their minds.

Olivia and Brenda visited Sandra to discuss change in control of the trust. To their surprise, Sandra willingly agreed to relinquish control. She was happy to be relieved of the burden and bother of worrying about money, which she had little need for at her age.

Olivia insisted the accounts held in the trust be transferred to her bank for her convenience and to consolidate the accounts. Seeing the advantages, Brenda agreed.

Brenda's husband, Charlie, a loan officer at the bank where Sandra and Brad banked, questioned moving the accounts. "You had better keep an eye on your sister," Charlie cautioned Brenda. "She needs watching."

Brenda said, "I'm not worried. She would never do anything to hurt Mom."

"It's not your mother I'm concerned about," Charlie told Brenda. "You are the one at risk."

Wishing to avoid the subject, Brenda did not reply to Charlie. She felt comfortable with the situation, at least for the time being. At that particular moment Brenda was preoccupied with much more serious concerns. Earlier that week Brenda performed a self-examination and discovered what she thought might be a lump in her breast. She did some research on the Internet and was deeply troubled by what she learned. She called her doctor to schedule an exam. Not wishing to cause concern where it may not be warranted, Brenda did not mention her discovery to Charlie. She chose to shoulder the burden alone for the time being.

The doctor confirmed Brenda's worst fears. Her breasts were riddled with cancer, and it had metastasized. She needed radical breast surgery and chemotherapy to slow the deadly growth.

Charlie and her children rallied around Brenda, as did Olivia and her family. Sandra was not told of her daughter's cancer. Brenda and Olivia decided

Sandra did not need to worry about her children at her age.

Brenda harbored a concern she was embarrassed to share with anyone, but as the surgery drew closer, the need to share her concern with her husband overcame her embarrassment. Brenda decided there was no tactful way to approach the subject, so she decided to just blurt it out.

"I need to ask you something," she said to Charlie. "This may sound foolish, but will you still love me without my breasts?"

Charlie thought Brenda was joking. "Why do you ask that? Your breasts are not all that important."

Brenda started to weep. "You love them so much," she whimpered. "I thought you loved me because of them."

Charlie laughed to brighten the mood. "Of course, I love your breasts," he said. "They are magnificent. I thank your mother's genes for them. But if they are gone, it is not a big deal. We'll still have the memories of them." Charlie took Brenda in his arms and held her. They were silent for a long moment.

Brenda began to weep uncontrollably. She managed to say between her sobs, "I am not crying about my breasts. I am crying about the cancer. I don't want to die."

"You are not going to die," Charlie whispered to his wife, who was now almost limp in his arms. "You are not going to die." Charlie began to weep, careful not to allow Brenda to see his tears. Brenda pressed against Charlie, wanting to crawl inside her strong husband for safety. Brenda felt Charlie's weeping from the sudden swell of his chest and his uneven breathing. She felt his heartbreak and wept for him as well.

Brenda's illness became the focus of the family. Charlie and Brenda's lives were centered on doctor's visits, lab tests, reactions to drugs, and worry. Her cancer had advanced beyond her breasts to her organs and bone marrow. The chemotherapy slowed the cancer's progress and had an unusual and dangerous side effect. The drug used to attack the cancer in the bone marrow also caused the bone marrow to shut down the manufacture of red blood cells. If Brenda continued to use the drug, she would die for lack of red blood cells. The doctors decided to attack the cancer in the bone marrow by other means. Unfortunately, the replacement drugs did little to slow the cancer's destructive progress.

During Brenda's ordeal, Olivia succeeded in taking total control of her mother's assets. The accounts were moved to Olivia's bank, where she had dealt with the bank personnel for years. The bankers trusted Olivia and cut corners when they could to please their longtime customer.

When Olivia opened the new checking accounts, she asked for an ATM and debit card. This allowed her to avoid writing checks when making purchases. Incidentally, it also left less of a paper trail and evidence of the purchases.

When Olivia opened the new accounts and ordered the ATM and debit card, she did not intend to use her mother's accounts for her own use. But as chance would have it, she was short of cash on one occasion and used her mother's debit card to pay for her personal purchases. After that first purchase, Olivia found it very convenient to pull out her mother's debit card when shopping. She knew her mother could not possibly use all her savings in her lifetime. Olivia considered use of her mother's money to be an advance on her inheritance. And, she reasoned, she was handling the trust and should be paid for her work, even if it was for her mother. Soon Olivia was using the card on a daily basis to finance her personal life.

Olivia and her husband, Harry, decided to take a cruise to the Western Caribbean from Miami. Olivia thought about the consequences of charging the expense to her mother's account. Eventually, she decided in favor of charging the cruise to the account. Olivia was on the edge of a slippery slope and sliding quickly to self-destruction.

Brad and Sandra were conservative savers during their earning years. They put their money in safe investments. Years before their death, they were sold annuities by a smooth annuity salesman. They were confident in their financial futures. The annuities allowed Brand and Sandra to name beneficiaries in the event of their deaths. They divided their annuity investment into two equal shares for their two daughters and named the daughters as beneficiaries of one-half each. Brad mentioned this to Olivia and Brenda years before his death.

"Your mother and I have money put aside for each of you," he told the two sisters. "Equal amounts. You will inherit it when we are both gone. You will not need to work again, I can tell you that," he said. The plan to treat the daughters equally was the heart of the plan. Olivia searched her parents' paperwork until she found the annuity policies. Her parents had purchased annuities to support themselves during their lives and named Brenda and her as the beneficiaries at death. The amount, hundreds of thousands of dollars for each sister, astounded Olivia. She was giddy about it for a few days. Becoming rich at her mother's death excited her. She decided to keep the discovery to herself for the time being to allow time to assess the situation.

Brenda's condition worsened by the month, then by the week. She was fighting a valiant battle, but she was losing. It was clear she would neither be cured nor go into a long remission. Neither Brenda nor Charlie gave any thought to Sandra's finances. They knew Sandra was receiving good care. Immersed in their own problems, they ignored the details.

During this time the financial industry was in an uproar about the annuities it had sold years earlier to people like Brad and Sandra. The same companies that had sold the annuities were now claiming they were bad investments in the present financial environment. They had created a market where none existed to churn the assets of their clients. They created products to replace the older annuities. Their salesmen, deceivingly titled Financial Advisors, seized the opportunity to sell their clients new financial products and combed the countryside for prospects. Brad and Sandra were two very attractive prospects. The hundreds of thousands of dollars in their annuities could be converted to a different investment while throwing off large fees to the lucky salesman who convinced them to switch.

The salesman who targeted Brad and Sandra found Olivia in charge of the annuities. After learning that Olivia was a CPA, he expected resistance to any change. He anticipated Olivia to work the numbers and find that a change would benefit the salesman but not the client. He was surprised when Olivia accepted his advice to cash in the older annuities in exchange for new and improved annuities. Olivia used the power of attorney her mother gave her to complete the transaction. While working the transaction, the salesman smelled a rat when Olivia changed the owner of the annuity from Sandra to herself. He studied the paperwork and discovered Brenda was being deprived of her share of the inheritance. Olivia explained the change was for estate tax planning. The salesman wondered if he was doing the right thing for Sandra and Brenda in allowing the change without their approval. It was plain that Olivia might be hijacking her sister's inheritance. He weighed the harm done to the family against the possible loss of a large commission. He decided the family situation was none of his business and collected his money.

Olivia did not hijack her sister's inheritance in cold blood. She thought about what she was doing and wondered if her conscience would let her live with herself. She reasoned that Brenda's illness changed the entire family dynamic. It was clear to Olivia that Brenda would not outlive Sandra. Olivia told herself that if her parents had known one of the daughters would not survive them both, they would have given that daughter's share to the surviving daughter. Never mind, she told herself, that her parents specifically provided that a deceased daughter's share would go to the daughter's children. Olivia told herself that language was just lawyer talk and not what her parents would have wanted for their daughters. Olivia's self-inflicted delusion eased her conscience and allowed her to live with the theft of her sister's inheritance.

When the papers were signed and the hijacking complete, Olivia was relieved. "It is done," she told herself. "This is what Dad and Mom would have wanted. Once Brenda dies, Charlie and his brood will drift away from the rest of us. They will not bother Mom or me for the money."

Olivia continued to use the ATM and debit card. She became infatuated with spending money on her family and arrogant about the spending, going so far as to buy her husband tickets to the Daytona 500 for his birthday.

Florida winter weather is balmy and clear when compared to weather anywhere else in the United States. The Sunshine State lives up to its name almost every day of the year. As pleasant as Florida is, there are times when a winter cold front passes through Florida on its way to the Bahamas. When a cold front presses down in February or March, it brings high winds and surf along with falling temperatures. The worst of the fronts endanger the winter orange crop, sometimes causing millions of dollars in damage. Rarely do the cold fronts linger. They race thorough to the Bahamas. Just such a cold front came through Cocoa Beach as February turned to March, bringing more changes than just the weather.

Olivia has vivid memories of that morning when the cold front killed the winter tomato plants Harry forgot to cover with a sheet the night before. She looked out at her backyard to see the succulent plants in the cold and knew they would turn yellow by the next day and then collapse where they once stood strong. She remembered the day not because of the tomato plants but because she received a call from the Cocoa Beach Police. Her mother had an emergency at home and managed to call 911. When the police arrived they found her unconscious on the floor. She had died before the paramedics arrived. With that call, Olivia's world collapsed like her tomato plants caught in the freeze.

Brenda struggled through her mother's funeral, not thinking much about money or an inheritance. She assumed everything would work out for the best.

Brenda remembered what her father had told her about her inheritance. She talked with her husband, Charlie, about the conversation. Brenda told Charlie, "If there is an inheritance, I want you to have it when I am gone. Spend it on education if you can, for the children and grandchildren. Don't let the children spend it foolishly."

"You're not going anywhere. You can spend it yourself," Charlie told Brenda in as reassuring a tone as he could muster, knowing he was trying to lie to both his wife and himself.

Three weeks after Sandra's funeral, Olivia visited Brenda. They exchanged pleasantries and sat down to a cup of tea. Brenda brought Olivia up-to-date on her treatment. Olivia tried to be as optimistic as possible, telling Brenda she looked as if she was getting stronger. When the conversation lagged, Olivia pulled an envelope from her purse and handed it to Brenda.

"This is half of what was left when Mom died. I paid all of the funeral expenses. There were no medical bills since she died so suddenly."

"I did not expect this so soon," Brenda said. "I expected a complicated mess, to tell you the truth."

"There wasn't much left," Olivia said as Brenda opened the envelope to find a check for forty-two thousand dollars made payable to her.

"This is all that was left?" Brenda asked. "What about the money Dad talked about?"

"I'll be damned if I can find any of that money," Olivia answered. "I don't know where it went, if it ever existed. Dad may have been telling us a story. I don't know."

"Dad was not like that," Brenda said. "Maybe it will turn up. Do you think so?"

"Believe me, I have looked everywhere for more money," Olivia answered. "I was afraid Mom would run out of money and we would have to support her."

Brenda returned the check to the envelope and pushed it aside. "If you don't mind, I am very tired," she said to Olivia. "I need to take a nap."

"Of course," Olivia answered, happy to be able to end the questions about the inheritance. "I'll visit again soon."

Olivia sighed in relief as she drove from Brenda's home to her own. Before visiting Brenda to hand her the check and lie to her about her inheritance, she imagined all sorts of bad scenes. She timed the visit to avoid Charlie and his questions. Olivia felt comfortable with the way she left it with Brenda. Olivia guessed that the forty-two thousand dollars would satisfy her sister. Olivia wondered what would happen if Brenda figured out the check should have been for the true amount of Brenda's inheritance, fifteen times that amount.

Later that day, Brenda gave the check to Charlie and asked him what he thought. Charlie studied the check, noticing something odd. "This check is from Olivia's personal account. Why is that? It should be from your mother's trust."

"Olivia says there is no more money. She can't find any more."

"I knew it," Charlie said. "I just knew it. I never trusted her. I tell you, she stole the money just as sure as I am sitting here."

Brenda looked at Charlie and looked at the check. She decided she was just too tired to deal with the matter on that day. "I need to take a nap."

"Let me help you," Charlie answered, rising to help Brenda to her bed.

Brenda was right not to concern herself about money and material things. Her condition had taken a turn for the worse. Charlie backed off the subject of her inheritance, but he did not forget. Charlie had observed the competition between his wife and her sister since he married Brenda. Each tried to outdo the other in subtle ways. Charlie believed the two sisters genuinely loved each other, but the lack of an accounting of funds from Olivia deeply bothered him. He did not like the smell of the entire situation. He knew that if something smells, it is probably rotten. He wondered if, in spite of their love for each other, Olivia would try to cheat Brenda out of her rightful inheritance. Would Olivia see this as the last arena in which the two sisters would have an opportunity to compete? Would Olivia cheat her sister and her sister's family out of an inheritance for the sake of winning this last competition? He did not know then that he would soon answer some of these questions.

The next seven weeks were not easy. Brenda quickly declined. The doctors offered little hope. Hospice served Brenda in her home until the end. Brenda died peacefully at home with her family and her sister's family at her bedside. All questions of money and inheritance were put aside during this period.

When the ordeal of the funeral was over, Charlie rented a small house in the Florida Keys and took his adult sons deep-sea fishing. The dolphinfish, known as mahi-mahi in Hawaii, were in season running up past the Keys to the Carolinas to spend the summer. Charlie chartered a big fishing boat to troll the Gulf Stream with his sons to clear his mind and refresh his body. They pulled in their fair share of the beautiful iridescent blue-green-yellow fish and renewed their spirits.

At dinner their last night in the Keys, Charlie brought up the possibility of Olivia hijacking Brenda's inheritance. The possibility gnawed at him. He could not bear the thought that his wife and children might have been cheated.

"If we go after this, it is not for me," he told them. "It is for your mother and you, her children. I am not entitled to any of it. And I do not want it. But I will pay a lawyer to make it right. I owe that to your mother."

Charlie's sons saw that he was angry and revenge was the only remedy. "Dad, if you need to do it, we're behind you," his sons said.

The next week Charlie sat with a lawyer recommended by one of his banking colleagues. During the interview the lawyer asked Charlie, "How old was your wife when she died?"

"Sixty-one years," Charlie answered.

"We may be able to charge her with a criminal act," the lawyer told Charlie.

"Embezzlement?" Charlie asked.

"No," the lawyer answered. "The state's attorney does not have the gumption to go after these cases to charge embezzlement. I mean abuse of the elderly. This Olivia person abused her mother by defrauding her, and she also abused your wife by stealing from her."

Charlie's ears perked up.

"This is something new. The laws in Florida have not been tested in this way, but they should be," the lawyer continued. "If you are willing to throw everything we can at her, I will see if the judges will support us."

"Let me tell you something," Charlie told the lawyer. "I loved my wife more than anything. And I love my children. They are all wronged by this. I want it made right. I don't care what we need to do. I want it done!"

The lawyer opened a probate estate with Charlie as the personal representative. This gave Charlie the right to act as Brenda's representative and sue Olivia. Charlie sued for breach of fiduciary duty, civil theft, and elderly abuse on Brenda's behalf. Following the paper trail took months. Olivia hired lawyers who obstructed Charlie's lawyer at every opportunity.

As the saying goes, you can run but not hide. Eventually, Charlie's lawyer followed the paper trail and found the money. He made veiled threats about insisting on criminal prosecution. With the trial date fast approaching, Olivia's lawyers began sending settlement proposals. At first they claimed Olivia had spent the money and was judgment proof. They said that Charlie might get a judgment, but he would never collect. When Charlie insisted on a trial to get his judgment, they changed their tactics and began offering money to settle the case. Charlie rejected every offer and would not compromise one inch. He insisted on recovering every penny due his wife and children. His motivation was to right the wrong that had been done. The money was a tool with which to punish Olivia.

Although Charlie had insisted on collecting every penny due his wife, he knew that trials can lead to unexpected and bad results. With the trial scheduled to begin the next morning, Charlie accepted a settlement he could live with. Even though he accepted a settlement for less than he wanted, Charlie knew it was killing Olivia to pay the money, and he luxuriated in her pain.

Comments on Olivia and Brenda

The lessons to be learned from this case study are straightforward. Had Olivia not been offered the opportunity to hijack her sister's inheritance, she would be an honest woman to this day. However, the temptation to continue the lifelong competition with Brenda overcame her loyalty to her family. She betrayed her parents as well as her only sister. The family was forever destroyed.

Olivia became a hijacker when she detected the weakness in her first victim and Target A, her parents. As the parents aged, the hijacker slowly gathered her courage. She struck when the Target A victims were too weak to defend themselves. Brenda, the hijacker's second victim and Target B, was a weak adversary from the start. Brenda's preliminary weakness was the trust she had in her sister and later her illness, which distracted her from overseeing her parents' wellbeing. At the critical time, Brenda was not available to help her parents or herself.

An important lesson to take away from this case study is that it is impossible to determine who may succumb to temptation. Brad and Sandra had good reason to trust both their daughters to do the right thing under any conditions. Unfortunately, trust in another is not a guarantee of loyalty or defense against a hijacking. Trust affords a hijacker the opportunity to be tempted to commit the crime.

It is true that it is better to be safe than sorry. Had Olivia and Brenda both been nominated to serve as administrators of the trust with equal powers, the girls would have kept an eye on each other. Olivia would never have been tempted to hijack her sister's share of the estate.

As well as illustrating how much power a person possesses when they are sole trustee of a trust, we see that power corrupted Olivia. Olivia substituted her judgment for her mother's judgment when she decided Brenda's children should not inherit Brenda's share of the estate because Brenda was dying of cancer. This change was clearly not her parents' wish, yet Olivia was allowed to make the change because she had the power to do so. Fortunately, it was reversed by Charlie, but only after a long legal battle.

The annuity salesman should also carry some of the blame. His only interest was his own selfish well-being. He could have alerted Brenda to the hijacking of her annuity, but he chose not to do so. The lesson here is that we should not rely on strangers to do the right thing and protect us from harm, even if they know we are in danger.

Case Study Two

HIJACKING BY FRAUD AND FORGERY

Fraud, while a powerful tool in the hijacker's arsenal, is often difficult to hide from an inquisitive and tenacious victim. As a consequence, outright fraud is rarely used by hijackers. However, there are instances where a desperate person stumbles on an opportunity to hijack an inheritance using fraud. In this case study, Herman, the desperate son, is such a person.

The word "forgery" evokes images of sinister men, experts in their field, in far off places creating false documents, perhaps to help smuggle a refugee across a dangerous border. Unfortunately, the art of forgery is practiced in every corner of the world, sometimes by *inheritance hijackers*. What sets the inheritance hijacker apart from the other forgers is the motivation behind the crime.

Herman turns a page

Herman O'Rilley pulled his brand-new silver Bentley GT coupe into his reserved parking space in the parking garage. Herman sat for a moment with the motor running to enjoy the odor of the beautiful leather interior of the powerful and beautiful high-tech automobile. "This is the best of the best," he told himself. "I am at the top of my game and no one is above me." Herman exited the automobile and enjoyed the sound of the closing door. "So solid," he thought, "the best of the best."

Herman stopped halfway to the elevator to turn and view the Bentley. "A work of art on wheels," he thought and smiled. "Wait until my friends see it. They will drool."

The unmistakable sound of a vintage, air-cooled Porsche Carrera and screeching tires echoing in the parking garage caused Herman to move to the side. Herman knew it was his business partner, Tulio Soto, who would be speeding past to his reserved parking space in a moment. Herman waited to show off his new Bentley to Tulio.

Tulio sped past and pulled his pristine red Porsche Carrera into the parking space next to Herman's Bentley. Herman was waiting by the Bentley with the door open for Tulio to climb out of the Porsche. "*Hola. Mucho bueno*," Tulio complimented Herman with a wide smile.

"The best there is," Herman said.

"Maybe so," Tulio said. "Smells wonderful. How much ching for this ride?"

"It's a lease. Three grand a month," Herman answered.

Tulio joked, "You can't drive this down Ocho Rios after dark without getting mugged," and the two men shared a laugh.

"How does your new wife like it?" Tulio asked. "What did you have to give her to get this?"

"She likes jewelry. Let's just leave it at that," Herman answered, and they laughed again. Herman recently married a beautiful young woman who was known for wanting the finer material things in life. Herman had dated her on and off for years and asked her to marry him many times. Only after Herman became rich overnight and offered her a three-karat engagement ring did she agree to marry him. He knew he was taking a chance with this woman, but he wanted her so badly that he would give up anything and do anything to get her.

Herman and Tulio had both grown up in Miami's Little Havana in Spanish-speaking homes. Both had managed to learn to speak English as well as anyone else in Florida, learn the mortgage brokerage business, and break out of Little Havana to affluent Coral Gables where they both owned their own homes. They both were living the dream of the Cuban immigrants. As children, they were taught the rule that hard work brought success in America. They were living proof that following the rule leads to success.

The two men, in their early twenties and full of themselves, rode the elevator to their offices on the eighth floor. The elevator door opened to reveal their office door with their business name, "O & S Mortgage Consultants, LLC." They chose the business name to avoid any ethnic slant. They had learned that the Cuban and Spanish community likes to deal with their own. They felt the world outside Miami does not like to deal with businessmen from Miami, and a strong ethnic slant would be a disadvantage.

Herman O'Rilley felt his surname was a great advantage in dealing with bankers in New York or Chicago, who were comfortable in dealing with an "O'Rilley type of guy," as Herman put it, over the telephone. He meant an Irish, white professional. Those same people would not have been comfortable trading millions of dollars in mortgages with a man named Rodriguez, his mother's name, in Miami.

Herman's mother, Maria, married John O'Rilley when Herman was two years old. His natural father died in an industrial accident. John O'Rilley loved Herman's mother so much that he moved into Little Havana where she wanted to live. He bought the best home on the street and adopted little Herman, whom he brought up as his own son. John O'Rilley could have afforded much better housing. He owned several auto body shops around Miami.

John was content to provide his wife and children with all they needed and more, and banked the excess. After Herman came his sister, Rose, and two brothers, John Jr. and James. Even though Herman was not a blood offspring of his adopted father, he was treated just like his siblings. His father taught Herman the ways of business, and Herman was successful at a young age. John thought so much of Herman, he named him to be the administrator of his trust and will when the need arose. Herman was proud of the faith his father placed in him. Herman knew there was a great deal of responsibility involved in the estate. His father was a wealthy yet modest man who never flaunted his wealth nor wasted his money.

When the children were grown, John and Maria planned on traveling and enjoying their grandchildren when they came. Their plans came to a sudden end when Maria died suddenly while driving home from Publix with groceries for the week. She slumped over the steering wheel of her SUV while traveling on a side street. Her heart had suffered a sudden change in electrical current, racing so fast that it could no longer pump blood, then it stopped beating altogether. Her SUV slowed and rolled off the road into a residential front yard, where it stopped. Had she received CPR or had there been a defibrillator immediately available, she might have been saved. No such help was available. John was devastated. His reason for living had left him without a good-bye. He never found closure.

Herman and Tulio entered the mortgage brokerage business at just the right time. The investment bankers at the big Wall Street firms decided to loosen their credit standards for residential lending. In the past, a borrower needed a substantial down payment and a steady income to purchase a residence. The big shots on Wall Street decided it was time to stimulate the economy and line their pockets with gold by lowering the standards for home lending. Their stated intention was to make housing available to more people at the lower end of the economic scale and stimulate the housing market.

The plan worked well for two years. Banks and mortgage brokers lent money to unsophisticated working folks who contracted with builders to build them a home. The investment bankers bought the mortgages in bulk and sold them in million-dollar bundles to big investment houses, who in turn made money by selling the bundled mortgages to other investors. As more people wanted to purchase their own home, the demand for homes grew and prices began to rise. As prices rose, sophisticated speculators saw an opportunity to make a profit by contracting to build homes and sell them when prices rose. These speculators increased demand for homes, and builders increased prices even more. As prices rose, inexperienced investors with little capital to invest wanted to get in on the real estate boom and make money. Unscrupulous real estate and mortgage professionals saw an opportunity to make a fast buck. The builders teamed with real estate brokers and mortgage brokers to target inexperienced, even naive and gullible, investors. As these investors came into the market, demand for housing skyrocketed. Homes were selling for two or three times what they sold for two years earlier. The builders, real estate brokers, and mortgage brokers were making tons of money. They were buying new homes and Bentleys and Porsches with their newfound wealth. They did not understand, nor wanted to understand, that the market was in for a deep dive.

The residential economic engine was driven by the easy ability to borrow money. As time went on, the truly qualified individuals who had invested in the residential market were becoming scarce. The local mortgage brokers such as Herman and Tulio turned to less-qualified individuals and offered loans to them. Herman and Tulio were increasingly astounded at how easy it was to make and sell loans. The investment bankers who were purchasing their loans were lending money to anyone who was breathing in Florida.

Herman received a telephone call one afternoon from a builder in Fort Myers, Florida. He was looking for buyers for his homes in Lehigh Acres where he owned thousands of empty lots ready to build on. He claimed to be the biggest builder in the Fort Myers area.

Herman and Tulio drove across Alligator Alley from Miami for their meeting in Fort Myers. They were impressed with the builder's operation, to say the least. He was in fact the biggest builder from Fort Myers to Naples, one of the hottest real estate markets in the nation. He had a huge model center where buyers chose the home and upgrades supplied by his company. He made an offer Herman and Tulio did not want to refuse. It seems this builder had found credit unions and small banks across the country that wanted to get in on the hot real estate market in Florida. He offered these relatively small lenders a chance to make some fast money. In the end, the lenders lost a lot of money fast.

Herman and Tulio were excited on the ride back to Miami. "That man knows how to make a lot of money, and we'll ride on his coattails," they agreed.

In Miami, Herman and Tulio connected with several real estate brokers. Together they developed a presentation for unsophisticated individuals in their particular Latin market. They lured people to "seminars" where they presented a "fail-safe, can't-lose, little-money-down" program they called "Strategy for Success." They knew they were competing with many others for the same pool of customers, so they created a very slick presentation.

They offered any investor who had $2,000 to put down the opportunity to purchase an investment home. The investor was told that the home would increase in value at as rapid a rate as homes have increased in the past two years. During construction, the home may be flipped for a profit or held for even greater profits in the future. They named their plan "The Money Machine." Their presentation was smooth and convincing. However, there was one major flaw in the presentation that would haunt them. The investors were told this was a "sure thing" and the return of 15 percent per year was "guaranteed," with expected profits in the 25 percent range.

The statement that returns were "guaranteed" seemed to be innocuous to the real estate agents and Herman and Tulio. They all believed the real estate market would continue to explode with profits as it had for the last two years.

The real estate salesmen were selling houses as fast as they could process the papers. Herman and Tulio were making loans and collecting fees as they had never dreamed. They hired more help and moved to an expensive office space overlooking downtown Miami.

When the sign "O & S Mortgage Consultants, LLC" was installed, Herman and Tulio celebrated with a hundred-dollar bottle of single-malt scotch. Herman raised his glass in a toast as they looked out over the Miami skyline across Biscayne Bay to Miami Beach. "We have arrived, my friend," he said.

The investors the "Strategy for Success" attracted were not well-off and could not afford to lose the money they had at risk. They put down their $2,000 and took out the mortgage, expecting a smooth transaction. The investors were working middle-level professionals in the Miami economy, who had families and children and not a lot of savings. Their mistake was not accurately assessing the risk. They believed their risk was the $2,000 down payment. Their actual risk was the $250,000 mortgage they were taking out to finance the project.

Buyers were encouraged to buy as much as they were able. Some buyers bought four or five homes, thinking their retirement was secure when the time came. Some buyers' only income was a monthly social security check. How were they able to get mortgages on such little income? they asked. "We just state the income and the lender approves the loan," they were told. In other words, the lenders, hungry and even desperate for loans, were not paying any attention or verifying any information.

The $250,000 mortgage paid for the land at an inflated price, the home at an inflated price, the real estate broker's commissions, the mortgage broker's commissions and fees, the interest on the construction loan, real estate taxes, and a lot of profit for the mastermind in Fort Myers. Before the boom, the same house sold for $125,000, including the land. The investors were starry-eyed and optimistic while being led down the garden path by the Strategy for Success team.

What happened next was as unexpected as the real estate boom—the market crashed. The entire system was built on the lenders' assumption that the people buying the homes and taking out the mortgages would be able to pay the mortgages when the homes were completed.

The lenders did not take the borrower's point of view into consideration. The borrowers did not intend to pay mortgages they could not afford. They intended to flip the homes for a profit. The borrowers' plan was to sell the home when it was completed and break even if need be. No borrower anticipated losing any money.

The borrowers could not pay the mortgage payments when the homes were completed, and the mortgages became the responsibility of the borrower rather than the builder. The borrowers tried to sell their investments. They found that they were competing with the builder, who wanted to sell more homes and all the thousands of other investors whose homes were being completed.

There was suddenly a glut on the housing market.

Smart borrowers who could take a loss saw the writing on the wall and dropped their prices just to make a sale. Other borrowers dropped prices lower to compete. Soon, there was a sudden drop in value in the Florida real estate market as had never been seen before. No one wanted to invest in housing.

All of the investors in The Money Machine were now upside down in their investments by tens of thousands of dollars. They were worried and frantic. None of them could absorb such losses.

Who does an investor blame when their investments turn sour?

Why, their investment advisors, of course.

Before the shine had worn off the Bentley, the first of the certified letters from the investors' lawyers arrived. Then the process servers started lining up. Home buyers were in default of their mortgages. Lenders sued to foreclose.

Realizing they faced great losses, the home buyers sued the real estate brokers and mortgage brokers who brought them into the deals. The phrase "guaranteed investment" and like phrases were the basis for the lawsuits. The home buyers insisted their guarantees be honored. The real estate litigation lawyers never had much respect for real estate agents and mortgage brokers. They had seen too much sleazy behavior. These lawyers were having a field day.

The process server was waiting in the reception area reading a magazine when Herman and Tulio entered the office. "You again?" Herman asked.

"Don't kill the messenger," the process server answered.

"Where do I sign?" Herman asked.

The process server took the signature without saying a word. He had heard it all before.

Herman carried the papers into his private office followed by Tulio.

"These legal bills are beginning to break my back," Herman said to Tulio.

Tulio read the papers delivered by the process server. "The same old thing," he said. "What a bunch of crybabies. They knew what they were getting into."

"Did you hear about the big man in Fort Myers?" Herman asked.

"You mean our house building friend?"

"Yes, he is out of all this mess, you know," Herman said.

"No way! How?"

"He sold the company at the height of the market. Got something like a hundred and fifty million for it," Herman explained.

"How did he do that?"

"Who knows. He is a lot smarter than we thought."

"Screw him and his millions," Tulio said. "He got us into this, and now he is off the hook. I guess we were just as stupid as the home buyers."

Herman looked out the window across the bay to Miami Beach. "We can't do anything about it now."

"I just don't want to lose everything. That's all," Tulio said.

Herman did not respond. He knew, after all the meetings with the lawyers and reading the newspapers, that he was going to lose it all to either the home buyers or the lawyers he hired. He had made a lot of money, but he had spent a lot of money and did not have much in reserve.

Herman worried most about his wife. How would he break the news that they were almost broke to her? He doubted she would tolerate a life without luxury. How long she would stick around once she heard the news?

Herman hated himself for letting his greed overwhelmed his good judgment. He was losing it all in the end.

Across town in Little Havana, a family crisis began. John had been suffering from lower back pain for some time. His family physician prescribed muscle relaxers, which gave little relief. A chiropractor made regular adjustments to his spine and lower body, blaming the pain on John's lack of good posture. A massage therapist blamed the pain on tightness in his leg muscles.

The pain became unbearable for John, who rarely complained. He called his son, John Jr., who lived nearby. At the hospital emergency room, doctors admitted John and ordered an MRI. John's children rushed to his bedside. A cancer specialist informed John's children that their father had aggressive pancreatic cancer, which had already decimated most of his pancreas and spread to his other organs. After considering the unattractive treatment alternatives, John chose not to accept treatment and let nature run its course. He felt that God had some purpose in ending his life at that time. Even though he was Catholic, he doubted there was an afterlife where he could meet his beloved Maria. But he hoped it was so.

John was admitted to inpatient care at a wonderful hospice facility. His most treasured personal possessions, photos of his wife and family, were brought to his private room. All the children were devastated and did all they could to comfort their father, who immediately began to receive an intravenous morphine drip and was soon drifting in and out of a lucid state.

The family visited daily. John Jr. and Herman left the hospice together one evening with their spouses. When they reached their vehicles in the parking lot, John Jr. asked Herman, "Where is the Bentley tonight?"

"That piece of shit," Herman answered. "One of the fuel pumps gave out, and they had to order another from Germany. The car sat in the shop for thirty days, and I called them on the Lemon Law. They had to take it back."

"What a surprise," John Jr. said. "Such a nice car."

"For a while it was," Herman said. In truth, the Bentley had been repossessed by the leasing company. He concealed the repossession from everyone, even his new wife, who was the last person Herman wanted to tell about financial woes. In the back of his mind, he worried that she would leave him if she knew he was about to go broke.

Herman, as the appointed administrator of his father's estate, realized his responsibility to inventory his father's assets and prepare for his father's death. The total was more than he had expected. It was a shame, Herman thought, that his father had accumulated wealth he never enjoyed. It was better to spend it and enjoy it than to die a wealthy man.

Herman was granted access to his father's bank safe deposit box, where he found his father and mother's last will, a power of attorney to him, and his father's living will.

Herman studied the will, which directed that his father's estate should be divided equally among his four children. The will was prepared by a Miami attorney who Herman did not recognize. Herman called the attorney's telephone number printed on the envelope containing the will. The telephone was disconnected. Herman called the Florida Bar Association's office in Tallahassee and found the attorney had retired two years earlier and was no longer an active member of the Bar. Herman attempted to find the attorney in the local telephone books and through the Internet with no success. He had disappeared. Herman assumed he had either died or retired to Costa Rica or Panama as many Floridians did.

Herman studied the will more closely. It was printed on quality paper that Herman recognized. He had seen it at the Office Depot when purchasing supplies for his office. The font was typical of legal documents, a Courier style. The individual pages were not initialed.

Herman did some figuring. He calculated that his share of his father's estate was about half of what he needed to solve his financial problems.

Herman's mortgage brokerage office was full of computers, printers, and paper-processing equipment. He decided to try an experiment. First, Herman typed out a page identical to the second page of his father's will, the page where his father directed the estate be divided equally among his four children. Herman experimented with fonts, page margins, and line spacing until the page was identical to the page in his father's will. Then Herman changed the disposition of the estate to say that he was to receive one-half of the estate with the balance to be divided equally among his siblings. Herman worked until the true page two could be replaced with his new page two without suspicion of forgery being raised. He then purchased paper identical to that in the will and staples the same size as those used in the original. Herman did not replace the page as yet. He waited to see what might happen.

John Sr. did not suffer, even though his innards were riddled with cancer. He lingered in hospice care for five weeks in a near-vegetative state brought on by the constant Morphine drip. His four children visited daily for the first week or so. When they realized their father was unable to communicate and their presence was unnoticed by him, they visited less often. When the nurse called to say the end was near, they all rushed to his bedside with their spouses. The priest said prayers while the gentle and generous man named John O'Rilley Sr. quietly slipped away. It was sad but comforting to the children.

All the children knew Herman was designated to be administrator of their father's estate. They were all anxious to learn what they were to inherit and when to expect the inheritance. They put their questions about the inheritance on hold in honor of their father's memory.

The lack of questions about their inheritances emboldened Herman in his plan to present the will he had forged. Herman set out to further put his siblings at ease with him to gain their confidence before he presented the forged will.

Herman arranged a meeting at his father's house to divide the furnishings, family photos, and other things of sentimental value. Herman offered to have all of the photos scanned for all to keep, and offered to be the last to choose when dividing personal items. Herman's three siblings and their spouses left the meeting impressed with Herman's generosity. They felt confident he would do the right thing in handling the estate.

Herman hired a probate attorney with offices in Coral Gables to handle his father's estate. The attorney commented that it was a shame that John Sr. had not created a revocable trust during his lifetime to transfer the estate at his death. He would have saved most of the probate fees, he told Herman. Herman replied that his father was a simple man who did things in simple ways. It passed through Herman's mind that if there had been a trust, many people would have copies. He would not have had the opportunity to forge the will.

The lawyer looked over the forged will and agreed to handle the estate without questioning the validity of the will. The will was "self-proving" and would be admitted to probate by the circuit judge without the need to call the witnesses to vouch for its validity. The lawyer explained he would give notice of the proceedings to Herman's siblings as required by law and send them copies of the will. Herman was relieved he would not be forced to face his brothers and sisters and look them directly in the eye when they learned of the will. He did not know if he would stand up to the pressure such a fraud would put on him.

When Herman's siblings received the notice of probate administration and copies of the will from the lawyer, they immediately met to discuss the situation.

"There is no way Daddy would have done this to us," Rose complained. "I just don't believe it. Herman is not even his blood."

James was livid with rage. "This is the biggest bunch of crap. I want to do something about this."

John Jr. suggested, "Let's get a lawyer of our own and see what can be done. I am Dad's namesake. Why would he do this to me, or you even?"

Herman's lawyer called and said, "Your brothers and sisters are challenging the will. Can you meet with me and my partner who handles cases like this?"

"On what grounds?" Herman asked.

"You name it, forgery, undue influence, insanity, the usual laundry list."

Herman met with the lawyer and his partner, an experienced probate litigator. The three men discussed the will and decided that there was little chance the challenge to the will would succeed. The will had been prepared by an attorney years before. John Sr. was free to change it any time during those years and he chose not to do so.

"Do you have a copy of your mother's will?" the litigator asked. "If her will is identical it will show both your parents were in agreement."

"I do not know," Herman said, knowing his mother's will was in his desk drawer.

The lawyer summed up his opinion at the conclusion of the meeting by saying, "Unless they pull some rabbit out of a hat, you have nothing to worry about, Herman."

Herman thanked the two lawyers and left, worried that he had overlooked the possibility that there might be copies of his mother's will and his father's will floating around somewhere waiting to be discovered or divulged. Did his brothers and sisters have copies of the true will? Herman considered agreeing to take only a fourth of the estate rather than one-half to end the lawsuit before the forgery was discovered. He wondered what the penalty for forgery is. Would he be sentenced to jail if it was proven? What would his wife say about all of this? Should he forge his mother's will as well to cover up his father's forged will?

Herman visited his father's home, determined to find copies of his parents' wills if they existed. It was common to keep a copy of a will at home when the original was kept in a bank safe deposit box, he knew. He went through every nook and cranny for hours without finding a thing. His futile search raised his anxiety to a higher level.

Herman drove home that evening to find his wife dressed in a sexy negligee, ready for a night of affection and intimacy. The next morning, Herman decided he could not risk losing his beautiful wife. He shut his mind to any compromise about his father's estate. The inheritance would solve all his financial problems and allow him to keep his wife.

Herman knew that he was trading his relationships with his brothers and sister for the inheritance. He knew they knew that their father would never treat them as anything but equals and that he had used some trick to change the wills. Herman simply hoped that they would never know the truth, as it would be the end of his life as he knew it.

Months went by and the lawsuit dragged on. There were depositions and document requests. Herman played the time card and refused to give his brothers and sister any part of their inheritance before the suit was settled. At the same time, he took his one-half of the estate as his inheritance and solved his legal and financial problems. Having had enough of the mortgage business, Herman took over his father's auto body shops, claiming them as part of his inheritance.

When John Jr., James, and Rose realized the suit to overturn the will was futile, they made sojourns to settle the case and obtain their inheritances. The case settled with Herman agreeing to waive any fee as personal representative of the estate and pay the attorney fees to defend the will from Herman's personal funds. Herman thought this was only fair since the will should not have been defended at all.

Herman's brothers and sister never spoke to him again. Herman and his wife were divorced three years later when the auto body business slumped during a broad economic recession. She took half of what Herman owned and moved on to bigger and better things.

Comments on John O'Rilley and his stepson, Herman

What went wrong with John O'Rilley's estate plan? After all, he visited a lawyer and took his advice. Is that not enough to ensure the estate plan will not be broken?

Hindsight is always twenty-twenty and usually reveals foreseeable reasons for the disaster that occurred. John became Herman's Target A because of his lack of communication with his children. Trusting Herman with the power to carry out the plan excluded the other children from overseeing the process and participating in the administration. Herman's exclusive possession of his father's will gave Herman the opportunity to amend the will and hijack a large part of his siblings' inheritances. Had John O'Rilley shared his will with his other children, the forgery would have been prevented and the family would not have been torn apart.

Herman's opportunity to become a successful hijacker presented itself as a result of his father's reluctance to communicate with his family. This unwillingness to share information was his father's weakness, rendering him an attractive Target A. Herman's siblings, his Target B, were attractive victims because they did not seek information from their father. This was more the fault of the father than the children. Nevertheless, the children became the Target B victims.

Herman's Target B, his siblings, were unaware of the hijacking until the deed was done. They were left with the prospect of challenging the will without the facts to support their suspicions. What could they have done to prevent the hijacking? Communication with and oversight of their father would have prevented the hijacking. However, their father's desire to be secretive about his finances may have caused disagreements, or he may have declined to cooperate with his children. Again, lack of communication played an important role in a hijacking.

Case Study Three

HIJACKING USING UNDUE INFLUENCE

"Undue influence" is a legal term of art with no precise meaning. It arises when a hijacker exerts influence over a victim to the degree that the victim loses his own free will to the hijacker. Deciding an undue influence case is more often than not a very close call. It is like beauty. You know it when you see it.

This complicated and powerful legal cause of action is used almost exclusively in the area of inheritance litigation. Victims use the claim of undue influence in attempts to overturn a will or trust, nullify a real property deed, recover money taken from a bank account, and right other alleged wrongs.

The distinction between legally influencing someone to do something and "unduly" influencing someone to do something is a dicey matter requiring the judge or jury to decide between what are often two seemingly rightful and lawful claims to the same inheritance.

Undue influence technically requires a victim to lose their free will to the hijacker. Although it may appear that recognizing the loss of a victim's free will is easily identified, it is almost never an easy call to make. In many cases, undue influence is found to exist when a person simply pushes too hard to get something for which he should not be entitled. The transaction smells rotten. Often small details tip the scales.

This case study is the story of Shelly and her sister, Barbara, and a desperate attempted hijacking at the eleventh hour. It was Shelly's last chance to right what she felt were the wrongs done her throughout her life.

Notice how Shelly attacks her mother, her Target A, when her victim is at her weakest. At the same time, Shelly's Target B is not able to defend their inheritance.

Shelly: Attempted theft on a deathbed

Shelly McCarthy and her twin, Barbara, grew up in the suburbs of Pittsburgh, Pennsylvania. Although the two girls were born from the same womb just minutes apart on June 7, 1949, under the sign of Gemini, they were twins in name only. Shelly was dark and slight, even spindly, with dark eyes and a narrow face with a large nose. As a teenager she remained slim with not much of a defined chest. Barbara, on the other hand, had a much fairer complexion and a pretty, round face. Her mother took great pleasure in combing and braiding her thick, straight, light brown hair when Barbara was young. Shelly was not much of a student and struggled through school. Barbara was serious about school and cruised through while taking a leadership role in her class. The sisters' differences were reflected in their friends. Shelly gravitated to the non-starters and drug users. Barbara was drawn to the movers and shakers who wanted and expected success in life.

Sibling rivalry is common in any normal family. Competition for a parent's love and affection is usually outgrown by the time children become adults, but there are many exceptions. Shelly was one of those exceptions; she never outgrew her need to better her sister, Barbara, to gain their mother's attention. The competition lasted even beyond Barbara's death, ending only with their mother's death.

The contrasts in the two girls played out throughout their lives. Shelly finished high school and went to work in a small factory outside Pittsburgh doing piece work on a screw machine. Barbara went to college and became an elementary school teacher. Shelly, desperate to move from her parent's home, met and moved in with Bud, a slightly built young man with shoulder-length hair whom she met at the screw machine shop. Bud had a nice smile and an old but still nice Camaro. Bud kept the machines running for the dozen women who operated the screw machines, which spit out thousands of small parts each day. Bud was preparing himself to live his life in a dead-end, low-level factory job. Bud had dropped out of high school. His father was a drunk who beat his mother and him until he was old enough to best his father in a fist fight. Bud's uncle on his mother's side had found the job for him. Bud was just what Shelly's parents did not want for her, which was the reason Shelly was drawn to him. Shelly and Bud took up housekeeping in a casual sort of way. Their apartment on the third floor of a rundown house was sparsely furnished with hand-me-down furniture. Her parents, Emily and Stanley, did not support Shelly's decision to move in with Bud. Consequently, they avoided Shelly's apartment, hoping she would return to their home. Shelly took this as another rejection.

Shelly and Bud filled their weekdays with work. Their evenings and weekends were filled with alcohol and recreational drugs.

Emily and Stanley knew Shelly could do better. "Shelly, honey, you need to go back to school, get a good education to secure your future," her mother told her.

Shelly, quick to be enraged when her buttons were pushed, shot back in anger, "For the last time, I do not want to be like Barbara. I can't stand it when you tell me to do like Barbara does. I am my own person. When will you learn that?"

"I just meant that you can do better for yourself," her mother pleaded.

"I do not want to do any better," Shelly shouted back in a rage. "I am happy. Don't you understand? I am not Barbara. Let me be myself." Shelly turned away, holding back a flood of tears. "Again," Shelly thought, "she rejects me for the wonderful and glorious and perfect Barbara."

Seeing how upset Shelly was, Emily chose not to continue the argument and quietly left the room.

"Another rejection," Shelly thought. "She can't stand to stay in the same room for two minutes to discuss it with me. Damn her. Damn Barbara."

Shelly had long ago reconciled herself to her notion that her parents did not love her as much as they loved her sister. The differences were shown to Shelly at every turn. Barbara was always the pretty one, the smart one whom their parents praised. Shelly was the underachiever whom their parents criticized for her shortcomings. Shelly hated that her parents did not see that not being as pretty or as smart was not her fault. She was just as worthy of love as her sister.

Shelly's perception of her parent's love for Barbara and her was fatally flawed. Emily and Stanley took great pains to love their daughters equally, in their actions and in their hearts. Shelly focused on the attention Barbara received from her parents for being Barbara. Shelly overlooked the attention she received for being Shelly.

The attention given to Barbara was praise and encouragement for her accomplishments. Emily and Stanley never worried much about Barbara. She almost always did what they would have recommended she do without being told.

The attention given to Shelly was directed toward correcting what Emily and Stanley viewed as bad choices on Shelly's part. When Shelly refused to join any clubs in high school, Emily and Stanley encouraged her to do so to broaden her social life. Shelly took the encouragement as criticism. She equated criticism with diminished love for her. After all, she reasoned, Barbara was never criticized by her parents. Therefore Barbara must be loved more than her.

Emily and Stanley saw Shelly make one bad choice after another. They encouraged her to read more when she spent her time watching television or hanging out with her friends. They encouraged her to wear makeup and style her hair differently when she took up wearing jeans and tee shirts all of the time. They demanded that she not stay out until after midnight when she began coming home in the wee hours of the morning smelling of alcohol and acting strangely. They criticized her choice in music when she chose Jimi Hendrix and The Doors to play loudly in her room. Emily and Stanley believed they were simply being good parents in their attempts to redirect their daughter to a better and safer path in life. Shelly read the advice as criticism and rejection of her in favor of her sister.

Shelly did what was the natural thing to do at the time. The music was telling everyone to rebel. The Vietnam War was raging, and protests on college campuses were resulting in death. Timothy Leary advised everyone to turn on and drop out.

Shelly could not overcome the pain she consciously and unconsciously felt because she had decided her parents had rejected her in favor of her sister. Shelly dropped out in her own way. Shelly and Bud parked the Camaro one afternoon and without notice or a good-bye to anyone hitchhiked from Pittsburgh to San Francisco to spend time in the Haight-Ashbury district. They intended to make a new life, perhaps find a commune to live on, and be free. Shelly intended to cut her old ties and get on with her life. Bud was less optimistic about their prospects in this strange place thousands of miles from home and familiar things. They mingled with all sorts of people, dropped acid in Golden Gate Park, took up residence in an abandoned tenement, and broadened their horizons.

In a few weeks their money ran out. Shelly and Bud found that panhandling for money and eating in soup kitchens was not what they wanted to do for the rest of their lives. They tried to find some sort of commune to join, but none were to be found. Reluctantly and without admitting defeat, Shelly called home for money. Emily and Stanley, thankful their daughter was safe, happily wired funds to the Western Union office in San Francisco. Shelly and Bud rode a Greyhound back to Pittsburgh, feeling defeated in their attempt to make a better life.

Back in Pittsburgh, Shelly and Bud found that things were about the same as they had left them. They went back to their former life of work during the week and wasting their time on the weekends. They moved back into their old apartment and went back to work at the same screw machine shop. Their landlord was happy to again collect rent for the rundown apartment. Their former employer was glad to take them back in spite of their poor work record because they did not need to be trained in the jobs.

"I guess the grass is not greener on the other side," Shelly thought one morning while setting up her screw machine for the day's run. "Damn it!"

Time and distance have a way of concealing wounds under layers of denial and forgetfulness. So it happened that Shelly, now living with Bud away from her parents and Barbara, made a new life for herself on the other side of Pittsburgh. Her memories of her parents slighting her in favor of her sister slowly faded to the rear of her consciousness and were replaced by more recent happy memories made during her life with Bud. To be sure, Bud was not Shelly's prince charming. He was not ambitious or even hardworking. But he was there every day and night for Shelly, and that was enough for her.

Shelly and Bud spent the holidays dividing their time between their respective families. The holiday gatherings permitted everyone to put aside their anger and hurt over past wrongs, real or imagined. The holidays, especially Christmas, gave everyone hope for a better future. Serious discussions never developed, and everyone parted in happy moods, guardedly assured by the lack of controversy that their family troubles were behind them and better times were ahead.

Each Thanksgiving, Bud and Shelly visited Emily and Stanley's home for an early lunch and then traveled to Bud's parents' for a late afternoon meal. Barbara was ever present, of course. Although Barbara was dating her longtime boyfriend, Dave, and worked as an elementary school teacher, she still lived at home. This subconsciously reinforced Shelly's assessment of the family relationships. Barbara was always the favored one, in Shelly's mind, and forever would be. Shelly put aside any hard feelings for her family and caught up with Barbara and her mother on people and gossip. Everyone went away pleased they had seen each other. Although the visit to Shelly's family was uneventful and festive, the visit to Bud's family was strained and difficult. Bud hated to visit his parents because he never knew what to expect from his father, who had ruined so many holidays in the past with his drunken rages.

Shelly always sensed the trepidation in Bud as they drove silently through Pittsburgh in the fading afternoon Autumn light to visit Bud's parents for Thanksgiving. "What's wrong?" Shelly always asked.

"Nothing. Why?" Bud always answered.

"We can always just leave if you want to. Or not even go," Shelly suggested.

"We can't disappoint my mother," Bud always said, and the conversation ended. What Bud wanted to say was that he desperately wanted to visit his father and put the past aside. Bud wanted to invite his father to a ball game or do something with him as a father and son. Maybe, Bud hoped, things would change. It never turned out as Bud hoped.

That Thanksgiving, by the time Bud and Shelly arrived, Bud's father had been drinking for the afternoon seated in front of the television watching football. Bud's mother greeted them warmly. His father wished them a happy Thanksgiving. The food was put out shortly after they arrived. They ate and left for home with no opportunity for an argument. Everyone liked it that way. Nothing had or would ever change, Bud decided each year as they left the house. By the time they left, Bud's father was well on his way to a drunken night's sleep. He was getting older, Bud noticed each year. He had slowed down quite a bit over the last year or so.

Life continued in this uneasy but unchanging way until Shelly became pregnant. Both Shelly and Bud swore it was a mistake. The United States Supreme Court had decided *Roe v. Wade* a year earlier, in January, 1973, legalizing abortion. Shelly and Bud had the option of aborting the fetus. Instead they decided being pregnant was not such a bad mistake and announced their wedding plans for June, two months away.

Shelly and Bud visited each of their parents to announced their engagement. Their mothers were excited but, with no real prospects for the future, were very wary of the union. Bud's father predictably congratulated Shelly and Bud and offered no assistance in the celebration. Stanley overcame his misgivings and made efforts to welcome Bud to the family. Although Bud desperately longed for a warm welcome to Shelly's family, he was not accustomed to unconditional acceptance. Bud handled Stanley's overtures to friendship awkwardly and with suspicion. Stanley felt he had overstepped some imaginary line drawn by Bud and backed off from the relationship. This left Bud confused about his relationship with his new in-laws.

Shelly became overwhelmed with excitement in the weeks leading up to her wedding. It slowly dawned on her that this was a milestone in the history of the family. She was to be not only the first daughter in the family to marry, but also the mother of the first grandchild. The family dynamics would change forever. Surely and finally, Shelly thought and hoped and wished, she would outshine Barbara to be the first daughter.

Barbara was happy and excited for Shelly. Barbara pitched in and, with her mother, planned the wedding with Shelly.

Everyone was happy Shelly was finally settling down, and hoped for the best. "I am guardedly optimistic," was the way Stanley put it to Emily in the privacy of their bedroom. What else could they do? they concluded. It went without saying among the family that Bud was not much of a catch. But then, Shelly was not much in the way of bait.

Shelly solicited her mother's help in reserving the Irish American Club banquet hall for the reception, planning the menu, choosing the dress, and handling the details. There never seemed to be enough time to handle all the details. Shelly was always on edge it seemed to Emily and Barbara. Often the smallest unimportant detail set her off. The people around Shelly learned to avoid confrontation with her. They attributed her hair-trigger temper to the pressure of planning the wedding and her early pregnancy changes.

One afternoon, Shelly handed her list of her attendants to her mother for review.

"I don't understand," Emily said to Shelly. "Why is Barbara not your maid of honor? Who is Sandra? Do I know her?"

"Sandy is my friend. You may not know her. We have been friends for a long time, maybe a year or so."

Emily was cautious, not wanting to trigger an outburst. In a measured tone she said, "Friends come and go, but family is forever."

Shelly thought for a moment before responding. Her response was sharp and to the point. Her tone was icy cold yet pleading for understanding. "Mom, this is my day. Can't I have one thing in my life the way I want it to be without you forcing Barbara on me?" Shelly fixed her eyes on her mother in a steady stare, waiting for a reply she perhaps did not want to hear. The last thing she wanted to hear was a demand that Barbara be named the maid of honor. This would confirm what Shelly had known all of her life but was afraid to speak of, that Barbara was the favored one, the more-loved daughter.

At that moment, Emily had an epiphany about her daughters' relationship to each other. Emily had assumed that her daughters loved each other as much as she loved them. She was shocked to realize that she had misunderstood them all of their lives.

Emily sat stunned, holding her tongue lest she say something she would always regret. Emily desired to give Shelly her big day and make it her own. At the same time she wished Barbara could share in the experience and help make it a wonderful day for the entire family.

Shelly's words cut through the last twenty-five years as cleanly and precisely as a scalpel in a skilled surgeon's hand. With one skillful move, the image of tenderness was replaced with a dark image of division and conflict with little of the love Emily had previously imagined.

Emily felt her chest tighten, and she suddenly became short of breath. Slowly, she slumped in her chair and forced herself to relax her tense muscles. Emily sat silent, feeling Shelly's stare upon her, afraid to look Shelly directly in the eye.

Shelly waited patiently. She had prepared herself to hear her mother demand that Barbara be named as maid of honor. At the same time she desperately hoped her mother would simply bless her right to make her own choices. Shelly steeled herself against the words and waited. Her mother said nothing. What was she waiting for? Why wouldn't she speak?

Emily sat silently and calculated the possibilities in her mind. Would it do any good, she pondered, to talk about this any longer? She felt Shelly's expectant stare upon her. No, Emily decided, it would not do any good for anyone to make this an issue. She would bless Shelly's choice and hope for the best in the future. Emily prepared herself to speak, not quite able to muster the strength to say the words that she knew would be her admission to herself that her girls were not who she thought them to be. It would be a condemnation of her parenting. Where had she failed her two beautiful girls? This was not the time to attempt repair of something that took so long to break. Emily was ready to speak, but she pondered the question and stood silent for an instant too long. Just as she was about to speak, Shelly reacted.

Shelly could not stand the suspense any longer. She knew how her mother felt and what she was going to say. Her mother would try to change Shelly's mind to favor the precious Barbara over her own wishes. This would be the last straw to break her back. Barbara would be chosen over her yet again. Shelly burst into tears, sobbing uncontrollably from the very first. Shelly felt all the tension she endured during the past years rush to her chest and exit her body in loud sobs of pain. She let it happen without trying to control herself. She knew it was good to finally unmask her emotions. These were the tears she should have cried all those times she felt rejected by her parents who favored her sister. "Listen to my sobs, Mother," she said to herself. "What do you think now?"

Later that day, Emily confided in Stanley, "I honestly do not know how to deal with Shelly and her feelings. How can she say we do not love her as much as we love Barbara? It does not make *any* sense."

Stanley held his tongue. He had witnessed the acts that gave birth to Shelly's suspicions of being second best. Emily fawned over Barbara from time to time. He had hoped Shelly did not sense Emily's favoritism, but apparently she did. It was probably too late in the game to repair the damage, Stanley surmised. So he held his tongue and chose not to enlighten Emily to the favoritism he had witnessed. "Perhaps we should be more sensitive to Shelly's feelings," Stanley offered as advice.

Emily fell silent. In her heart she knew she favored Barbara over Shelly ever so slightly. "Yes," she answered after a long pause. "I will be more sensitive." The parents left it at that. What was done was done. The future was the important time.

When Barbara heard of Shelly's choice, she was devastated. Barbara went to her mother. "I knew she doesn't like me very much. I can sense it. I have sensed it, especially the past few years."

Emily felt the pain her daughter was feeling and knew she was the cause. Emily began to weep softly.

"Don't be upset," Barbara consoled her mother. "This is not your fault. Why should you be so upset?"

Emily did not say a word. She felt that by favoring Barbara she had let down Shelly and caused Shelly to dislike both Barbara and herself. Now she felt she had let down Barbara and caused her pain because she did not love Shelly as much as she should have.

The complicated mess she had caused was just too much for Emily to bear or articulate to Barbara or even understand fully. She certainly could not repair it because she did not know what to do. "Let's just get through the wedding," she offered as a compromise. "Shelly is upset about her pregnancy and all of that. Can you please just live with it? I know you can."

Barbara decided to just roll with the punches. Why should she become upset and ruin her own day or week or life over something she could not change? "No problem, Mom," Barbara said in her no-nonsense tone. "Let's just get through it, shall we?"

The wedding did go smoothly enough. The small church was filled with friends and family. Shelly did not show her pregnancy at all. Bud asked Barbara's steady boyfriend, Brad, to act as a groomsman to pair him up with Barbara.

Maybe that was the catalyst that drew Barbara and Brad to the altar because Brad popped the question that Christmas. Barbara and Brad were married the following June. Barbara taught second grade at the elementary school across town where poorer students attended school. She had the opportunity to teach at a school in the upper-class neighborhood, but declined. She considered teaching at that particular school a personal sacrifice and her contribution to bettering society. Brad was just a few years out of school and getting started in his career as a civil engineer.

Barbara taught school for only one year after being married. Then she began popping out babies, three in three years, two boys and then a girl. She named them Kevin, Richard, and Rebecca. Brad and Barbara moved their family to the best school district and set about raising their three children.

All went well for four years until Barbara discovered a lump in her breast while conducting a self-examination. There had to be some mistake, she told herself, it could not be a dangerous lump. It had to be a cyst or something like that. Barbara put off calling her OBGYN for an appointment, hoping the lump would disappear. When it did not disappear or shrink, she reluctantly called to schedule an exam.

The news could not have been worse. Not only was it a lump, it had metastasized and spread to her bone and organs.

Everyone was in shock when they heard the bad news. Everyone grieved when Barbara died six months later, leaving behind her husband and three small children.

Emily and Stanley pitched in to help Brad where they were able to pick up the slack. Emily felt somehow responsible for her daughter's death. As Barbara's mother, Emily suffered a vague but gnawing guilt for giving Barbara the gene that led to the cancer. Emily knew the link could not be proven, but she believed it to be true much the same as someone who has faith in God. It cannot be proven, but it is as true as if it had been proven beyond any doubt. Emily vowed she would see that the three motherless children would not suffer because of her faulty genes.

Emily's attention to her three grandchildren brought an unintended result. All of the attention lavished by Emily and Stanley on Barbara's children did not go unnoticed by Shelly and Bud, who were paying close attention. Shelly and Bud had three children of their own by this time. Times were a little harder for them because they did not have the level of education or self-discipline that Barbara and Brad possessed. Consequently, Bud and Shelly came to rely on Emily and Stanley for help from time to time. The borrowing was for important emergencies at first. Over time the flow of small sums of money from Stanley and Emily became a steady stream. Bud and Shelly came to rely on Stanley and Emily's generosity. Bud, especially, kept his eye on the new relationship Emily and Stanley were forging with Barbara's children. Bud did not want that relationship to change what he had come to rely on.

Stanley was secretly pleased that Emily was turning her attention to the three motherless children rather than focusing on Bud and Shelly. Stanley was uneasy with the amount of money he was donating to support their family.

The money Emily and he gave to Bud and Shelly was not a large amount. That did not bother Stanley. What irked Stanley was Shelly's sense of entitlement and Bud's lack of gratitude for the gifts. Stanley had worked hard for his money. He felt he earned his money by spending his time toiling at something he disliked when he could have been doing something more to his liking if he did not work. Stanley kept it simple. He knew that the money was given to him in exchange for his time spent working. So, he reasoned, when he gave someone some of his money, he was in truth giving them some of his time. He had sacrificed a part of his life doing work to give them the money. If the recipient of the gift was not grateful for the time Stanley had spent earning the money, it was a great insult to Stanley.

Bud visited Stanley one afternoon to ask for another "loan," which they both knew would not be repaid. Stanley turned him down. "I just don't have it to spare right now, Bud. I would like to help you out, but I just don't have it to give."

Bud kept his cool and left without showing his anger. "Do you know what that old fart told me?" he asked Shelly later as he popped open a beer. "He said he didn't have the money. What a damn lie. Everybody knows he has a fat bank account. He is just too damn tight to let any of it go before he dies. Well, I never saw an armored car in a funeral procession. You can't take it with you."

Shelly did not respond. She had her own concerns. Now Barbara was reaching beyond the grave to deprive her of her parent's favor. Now the money was going to Barbara's children, those three brats. What did they ever do to deserve it? They didn't even need it. Their father had a good job.

During the next decade the family fell into a strained equilibrium. Brad and his children visited Shelly's family on holidays and important events. They did not socialize otherwise because they had little in common. Bud and Shelly partied and smoked pot for recreation. Bud was sometimes out of work for weeks at a time when the factory was slow or he had walked out on his job in anger over something trivial. Their children's behavior reflected the parents' inattention to self-discipline. They were unruly and always in some sort of trouble at school. Bud Jr. dropped out of school in the eleventh grade to work beside his father and begin a lifestyle filled with alcohol and drugs. It was just a matter of time before he committed a major indiscretion. He was out one night with his friends and managed to get arrested for driving while under the influence. Shelly called her mother in tears to borrow the bail money and the fee for the attorney. When Bud Jr. walked into the house after being released on bail, Bud gave him some fatherly advice. "Don't get caught again. We won't bail you out the next time." And so it went for Shelly and Bud's family and children.

Brad insisted his children attend preschool, and he closely watched their progress in school. He was the mother hen brooding over his children and the strong father. It paid off for him and his children. Each one of them enrolled in college right after high school and became serious students.

When Stanley compared the two families, he was astounded that his genes could produce such diverse daughters and sets of grandchildren. Emily doted on Rebecca, whom she openly admitted to herself and Stanley was her favorite among all her grandchildren. Rebecca became Emily's surrogate for Barbara from the time Barbara died. Although she never admitted her favoritism to other family members, it was plain to all who observed the family.

Shelly and Bud took notice of Emily's favoritism, but they were powerless to change things. So they suppressed their frustration and left things alone.

After a few years, Stanley relented and gave Bud and Shelly some small "loans" as Bud called them. Stanley called them "gifts" when he spoke to Emily. The unspoken threat that Stanley could end his lending practices at any time kept Bud and Shelly from complaining about Emily's favoritism toward Rebecca and her brothers. Shelly felt that in some way the money made up for the lack of affection and love.

Rebecca finished college with honors and was accepted to the University of Miami College of Medicine to attend medical school. Miami was her first choice of medical schools because it was her first choice of places to live. Rebecca had fantasized about living in Miami since she visited Disney World with her father and brothers. They drove from Orlando to Key West. Rebecca, then ten years old, found the clear ocean water, palm trees, and sunshine to be her idea of heaven. The contrasts with Pittsburgh's nasty weather and dirty, tired city amazed her young eyes. She vowed that some day she would live in Miami. This was her first real chance to do so. Rebecca was one happy young lady.

When Rebecca announced her plans, Emily asked, "How long is medical school?"

"Four years," Rebecca answered.

"Do they give you vacations and the like, to come and visit us?"

"I think so. But it is very, very time consuming and difficult. I may not be home much."

Emily's mind was filled with thoughts of having to bear the loss of her daughter for a second time. Barbara had died. Now Rebecca was going away.

It would not be the same. Even if she visited, they would never see each other as much as Emily would like.

As soon as Emily and Stanley were alone at home, Emily began working on him. "I am going to miss Emily very much," she said.

Half-joking and half-serious, Stanley asked, "So what do you want to do? Move to Florida?"

"Yes. As a matter of fact, I do. It is about time we really retired."

Emily and Stanley visited Brad and the children the next day. "Guess what?" Emily said, giggling with excitement. Before anyone could answer she said, "We are retiring to Florida!"

Emily did not know just how Shelly and Bud would take the news of their leaving. She decided to telephone them to make the announcement rather than visit in person. Shelly was shocked and wished them all the best during the telephone conversation. But she wept as soon as she hung up the telephone. "She just does not understand how it makes me feel when she rejects me," Shelly whispered to herself.

Emily and Stanley found the perfect little house for themselves in Coral Gables, not far from the University Medical School, with a small garage that was converted to a guest house for Rebecca. The family moved into their new digs and everything was just perfect, as far as Emily was concerned.

Rebecca soaked up the international Miami culture like a sponge. After twenty-one years of Pittsburgh's harsh winters, the sunshine, new foods, and new culture fascinated her. She began learning Spanish to assimilate herself into the community. Her fellow students came from fifteen different countries. The common experience of being students in a strange place bonded them together.

Emily and Stanley followed Rebecca's lead in meeting new people and making new friends. Their world broadened, and they loved it.

Four years goes by in the blink of an eye, even faster when you are busy. Before Emily knew it, Rebecca had finished medical school and accepted an internship at the University of Miami/Jackson Memorial Medical Center in Miami. Emily and Stanley breathed a sign of relief when they learned Rebecca decided to remain in Miami.

Before moving to Miami, Emily and Stanley had contacted their lawyer in Pittsburgh to ask about their wills. Should they be updated or changed to conform to Florida's laws? The lawyer advised them to contact a lawyer in Florida after their move. They found an estate-planning attorney in the yellow pages and made an appointment. As luck would have it, the attorney, Dennis Kulinowski, had migrated to Florida from eastern Pennsylvania just after finishing law school. Emily and Stanley formed a fast bond with the attorney, and he served them well.

Their estate, they told him, was to be divided into two parts. One part goes to Shelly. The second part is to be divided among the children of their deceased daughter, Barbara. The lawyer explained that their plan was the same as the law would provide had they died without a will, and that most people do the same sort of division in their wills. It is the fair way of dividing the estate, he told them. Emily and Stanley were encouraged to hear they were doing the right thing.

"Who will be personal representative to administer the estate?" he asked.

Emily was filled with pride when she answered, "Our granddaughter, the doctor."

"I have a question," Stanley said. "My son-in-law will not have anything to do with this, will he? He likes to borrow money, and I don't trust him."

"The spouses have nothing at all to do with this," the lawyer answered. Stanley was pleased.

The lawyer drew up the will to read as they desired, prepared a power of attorney, living will, health care surrogate designation, and pre-need guardian document. Everything was set in stone as far as Emily and Stanley were concerned. The will was fair and square with the children. They rented a safety deposit box at the bank with Rebecca as a co-owner to allow her access. They deposited the original will in the box and put a copy in their dresser drawer at home. They were done with it and need not worry.

Stanley began showing signs of advanced age soon after Rebecca received her license to practice medicine. Although Rebecca thought about continuing her advanced medical training at another school, she chose to stay in Miami to care for her grandparents.

Stanley died quietly of natural causes in his sleep one balmy night with a beautiful full moon above. His heart gave out, the medical examiner decided.

Shelly and Bud flew down to Miami for the funeral. As much as their children loved Stanley, they could not afford to fly their children down, they explained to Emily. Emily understood. She remembered that Stanley was never close to Shelly's children. They never visited Stanley and her while they lived in Pittsburgh, she recalled. They never visited in Florida. Emily knew perfectly well why they did not travel to Florida for the funeral. They did not care.

Shelly and Bud stayed at Emily's home for a week after the funeral. Bud "borrowed" money from Emily to drive to Key West, and for the plane fare for the funeral. At the end of the visit, Emily was happy to see Rebecca drive them to the airport.

Late that week, Emily and Rebecca shared a meal Emily prepared for them. "You know," Emily said, "I have the feeling Shelly and Bud went through all my things. Everything is just a little out of place."

"What do you mean," Rebecca asked.

"I think they were looking for what they could find."

Rebecca did not answer her grandmother and wrote the remark off to the stress of Stanley's death and the funeral.

Emily dropped the subject, not wanting to sound paranoid or senile. As strange as it may seem, however, Emily was absolutely correct. Shelly and Bud had gone through all of Emily's cabinets, drawers, and potential hiding places. They looked under her mattress. They considered searching Rebecca's little guest house, but decided it was too much of a risk.

Shelly and Bud decided to search the home as soon as they heard of Stanley's death. They suspected Stanley and Emily had been influenced by Rebecca or Brad to cut them out of their inheritance. They would certainly have attempted to convince Stanley and Emily to cut Barbara's children out of their inheritance if they had the opportunity. They were certain that Rebecca had worked on her grandparents all those years in Florida to gain the advantage.

When Shelly and Bud came across the copies of Stanley and Emily's wills, they were pleasantly surprised to see the equal division of the estate. Their inheritance was safe, for now at least, they concluded. But who knew what Rebecca might do now that Stanley was gone. Now was the time to strike if Rebecca wanted to do so. What would Rebecca do? they wondered.

Shelly and Bud had realized some years ago that they would never have the earning power they desired. It was just not in the cards, they told themselves. It was fate that put them here, but an inheritance could change their lives, to be sure.

For her part, Rebecca could have cared less about cheating someone out of an inheritance. She had some idea of what her grandparents were worth, and knew she would soon be earning much greater sums of money. To be sure, she would not stand for being cheated out of her share as a matter of principle, but she did not plan her future on what she may or may not inherit. To Rebecca, that was a loser's game. She planned to make it on her own, if she was able.

While on the airplane from Miami to Pittsburgh, Bud had what he thought was a stroke of genius. He sat up in his seat and leaned to Shelly. "You know how the will gives half of the estate to the grandchildren?" he asked Shelly to gain her attention. "Now it goes just to those three brats."

"Right. So?"

"What if that half went to *all* of the grandchildren? Barbara's kids *and* our kids?"

"What if it did go that way?"

"Don't you see? You would get your half. Then our three kids would get half of the other half. And the three brats would get only half of the other half."

"Right."

Bud was getting excited about his idea. "It is only fair. Don't you think? You, as a daughter, get half. And the grandkids split the other half. They're only grandkids, not a daughter like you. Our kids have much less that those three brats, and it's not their fault."

"Fair or not," Shelly said. "That is not what the will says. And we cannot change it. It is what it is."

His enthusiasm deflated, Bud sank back into his seat. "Damn it."

. . .

Emily's health declined at a steady pace to the point where she needed more care than Rebecca could provide on her own. Rebecca hired a companion to watch Emily during the day. Rebecca looked after Emily at other times.

Emily had been complaining of lower back pain for the last year. Her primary care physician referred her to a foot care specialist, who recommended support shoes to relieve the pain. The shoes were not helpful. Rebecca asked a colleague at Jackson Memorial who specializes in geriatric care to give her grandmother a thorough examination. A scan showed cancer was present in her liver, spleen, and pancreas and was affecting her spine. Surgery might help, the specialist explained. However, the surgery would certainly reduce her quality of life and could hasten her death. Emily and Rebecca discussed the options with the surgeon and with each other. They cried and prayed together. Emily decided to let nature take its course. "If God wants me now, I am ready to meet him," she bravely told the specialist. Rebecca arranged for hospice care in Emily's home until she would need inpatient care. They solemnly accepted Emily's fate and steeled themselves for the challenges ahead.

Emily and Rebecca called Shelly on a conference call to tell her the bad news and inform her of Emily's decision. Shelly spoke to Bud that evening and made airline reservations to visit and care for her mother.

When Shelly arrived in Coral Gables, she moved into Emily's guestroom with full intentions of taking over Emily's care. After all, she was her mother's only child and felt she certainly knew what was good for her mother.

The population of south Florida is Latin in large part. Many people are from foreign countries and have not yet been assimilated fully into the American mainstream. There are still parts of Miami where Spanish is the only language spoken. English speakers are foreigners in those enclaves. The health care professionals in south Florida are drawn in part from this population. Many do not speak English very well, especially in the less-skilled jobs. Emily's caregivers did not speak English very well. Emily did not care at all. She was accustomed to Miami and communicating with the general population.

The first time Shelly met Emily's Latin caregivers, there was a small problem in communication. Shelly was not accustomed to dealing with people who did not speak English well and looked down on them as being unintelligent or unwilling to act as she thought Americans should act. Shelly overreacted and insisted that Emily's hospice caregivers speak English as their primary language. The director of services for hospice was insulted because she spoke Spanish as her primary language. The director called Rebecca for advice. Should she take orders from this daughter? she asked. Rebecca consulted her grandmother, who had developed a friendship with the caregivers and did not care what language they spoke. Rebecca then had a talk with Shelly and explained that Emily had given Rebecca the power to make health care decisions for Emily, and Rebecca was overruling Shelly in this case. Rebecca told Shelly in no uncertain terms that "My grandmother does not need this sort of drama in her life at this point. You need to back off of this or go home to Pittsburgh."

Shelly went off the deep end. She called and complained to Bud. "Who does Rebecca think she is? I'm the daughter here. I know how to take care of my mother."

Bud's responded, "I told you so. Rebecca and the other brats don't have any respect for you. You should do something about this, to put them in their place."

With that dispute ended, Shelly stayed with her mother for the next three weeks. Rebecca was grateful to be relieved by Shelly in the evenings. Emily's health seemed to have stabilized. Her prognosis was that she could remain in her present condition for an indefinite period. Shelly returned to Bud and Pittsburgh.

Bud greeted Shelly with enthusiasm. "I put the plan into motion," he told Shelly.

"What plan?"

"The plan to change the will. I went to a lawyer here. The same one who handled the DUI for me, Matt Cocker. You remember him. I asked him about your mother's will. He read it and said, yes, it can be changed by a 'codicil' to the will. I looked into it all. I know what I'm talking about."

"Do you really want to do this?" Shelly asked Bud. "It will be a lot of trouble. It may cause a lot of problems. What if my mother does not want to change her will?"

"I asked Matt Cocker about it. The change is legal and binding if she signs the change in front of two witnesses. You don't need a notary or anything. But that would help, to have a notary there."

"Doesn't my mother need to know what she is signing? What are you trying to do here?"

"All I am saying is that we need her signature. That's all. She does not have to be able to recite the Gettysburg Address from memory or anything. She just needs to be awake."

Shelly was beginning to get the drift of Bud's plan. "So you want to wait until she is under drugs or something? Is that what you're saying?"

"Only if she won't make the change on her own. Only then."

"Well," Shelly told Bud, "I know she will not make the change as long as Rebecca has anything to say about it. She's the big shot down in Florida."

Bud moved close to Shelly and stared into her eyes to emphasize his next statement. "I know your mother would want to make this change if she was not being influenced by Rebecca. That is called undue influence and is not legal. I know we cannot prove it in a court of law. But I do know Rebecca is controlling your mother. Just look at how Rebecca took over from you with that hospice thing. That is proof enough that your mother is under her control."

Shelly felt a rush of anger toward Rebecca at just the sound of her name. "So how do we help my mother do this?"

"I don't know, yet. We just have to see what happens. You know, we shouldn't even mention it to Rebecca or your mother. That'd cause problems."

The next day, Bud called Dennis Kulinowski, the attorney in Coral Gables who drew up Emily and Stanley's wills. Bud explained that Emily had been planning for a long time to change her will, but never got around to it. Now Emily was seriously ill and needed his help. The lawyer agreed to make any changes Emily wanted and to visit her at her home if need be to oversee her signing. Bud told the lawyer he was grateful and he would call him as soon as Emily was able to see him. When Bud hung up the telephone, he felt pretty good about himself. He had made a plan, and he was beginning to put the pieces into place. He would show them all that he was just as good, if not better, than any of them.

Emily's condition took a sudden turn for the worse. Rebecca had been steadfast in allowing her grandmother to remain in her home until it was not possible to maintain her there. Now was the time to move Emily to a residential hospice.

Emily's condition had deteriorated quickly to the point where she was in constant need of morphine to dull the pain. She was also given twelve other medications for various reasons having to do with her impending death. Emily was conscious and lucid most of the time during her first few days at hospice care. She understood why she was there and reluctantly resigned herself to her own death.

Rebecca did what she thought was the right thing to do and called Shelly to inform her of Emily's move. Shelly and Bud knew what the move meant for Emily. Bud realized he must act now or not at all if he was to change Emily's will.

Shelly and Bud flew to Miami as soon as they were able to find a cheap airfare. They moved into Emily's home knowing that soon they would be owners of the home. Bud was excited. Although he had accumulated no savings to speak of, let alone any wealth, during his life, he was on the brink of being a man of some means. Bud surveyed the home with all the pride of ownership an undeserving beneficiary of an inheritance can possess.

It crossed Bud's mind that he would benefit from this inheritance only because he had married Shelly. He knew that she would be the legal owner of her mother's inheritance. He wondered if divorcing him had ever crossed Shelly's mind. Chances were that with her newfound riches she would not need him any longer. He knew for damn sure that he would think about divorcing Shelly if he was the lucky beneficiary. Shelly had not shown any signs of planning on divorcing him. Still, he thought, you never know about people. She could have something on her mind. They had come close to divorce several times in the past. Bud decided to consciously make an effort not to give Shelly any serious reason to divorce him.

Bud made an appointment with Attorney Kulinowski to talk over the changes to Emily's will. Shelly and Bud explained how they were certain that Emily planned to change her will, but she had just put it off a little too long. Her illness had been sudden, and she needed help now. They skillfully avoided mentioning that Emily had never talked about the change they proposed, nor had she attempted to change her will although she had been ill for some time and had plenty of opportunity to do so.

Attorney Kulinowski agreed to prepare the codicil to Emily's will and visit her at the hospice for the signing. He had been preparing wills and trusts for many years. He understood that Emily was his client, not Shelly or Bud. And the change in the will to benefit Shelly's children to the detriment of Barbara's children was an unusual change to make just before death. He was savvy enough to suspect Shelly's motives and take precautions to protect Emily from Shelly and Bud. He decided to be thorough in his pre-signing interview with Emily to ensure she was protected.

Shelly had arranged the lawyer's appointment at Emily's bedside for ten in the morning. Shelly and Bud knew that Emily was at her best at ten in the morning. If she was to pass any tests the lawyer was planning on putting to her, she would most likely pass them at that time.

The lawyer had planned on meeting Emily at ten that morning. Shelly had given him the address of the facility, but she had mistakenly given him the address of another hospice facility on the other side of Miami International Airport. The lawyer allowed himself plenty of time for travel, but he arrived at the wrong facility. It took some time to figure out what had gone wrong, and the lawyer arrived at Emily's bedside just after eleven in that morning. By that time Emily had fallen asleep and could not be awakened.

The lawyer did not need to speak to Emily to suspect she would never be competent enough again to make a valid will. What the lawyer saw was a very frail old woman on the threshold of death. She was asleep, and in her mouth was a sponge on the end of a stick to moisten her mouth. She was unable to drink liquids. Attorney Kulinowski made an attempt to speak to Emily, but she did not respond. His suspicions were confirmed. This lady was incapable of making any changes to her will that particular morning and any following morning, in all likelihood.

"Mom was bright eyed at ten o'clock," Bud told the lawyer. Shelly nodded in agreement. Attorney Kulinowski did not respond. He knew what was going on and did not like it one bit. Not only were these two trying to make changes to benefit their own children to the disadvantage of some innocent beneficiaries, but they thought he was a dummy and would go along with their plan.

Attorney Kulinowski wondered, "How can I best protect this lady?"

He suggested to Bud and Shelly, "Perhaps if I come back tomorrow at ten she can sign it then." The lawyer knew that if something was to come of this and a lawsuit ensued, he would probably be called as a witness. He wanted every opportunity to observe Emily and protect her if he was able.

"Yes, yes," Bud said. "Come back then. She'll be awake."

"Will you leave the documents you prepared here with us?" Shelly asked.

"No, I'm afraid I cannot do that," Attorney Kulinowski answered. He was not going to leave documents he had prepared with these two characters to be misused in some way, perhaps a forgery.

"Can I read the changes?" Bud asked.

Attorney Kulinowski reluctantly handed the document to Bud, who studied it for a long moment without speaking before handing it back to the lawyer. "That looks all right."

"In any event, I will return at ten tomorrow for the signing," the lawyer said and left the room.

Bud rushed to find a clean sheet of paper and a pen. He wrote what he thought was a proper codicil to Emily's will modeled after the attorney's work.

> *I, Emily McCarthy, being of sound mind desire to change my will to provide that my estate and assets shall be divided as follows:*
> *One half to my daughter, Shelly Dormer, and*
> *One half to be divided among all of my grandchildren.*
> *Sworn by me, Emily McCarthy.*

Bud drew a line where Emily was to sign and two lines where witnesses must sign. "Here is all we need," he told Shelly. "Now let me tell you what we need to do."

Shelly followed Bud's instructions and went to the executive director of the hospice facility with her tale of woe and asked for help. Shelly told the director that the lawyer had been late and missed her mother's good time of the morning for signing the will. The changes, Shelly explained, were requested by her mother, and the lawyer was just now getting around to preparing the documents. Would she please help her mother sign the document if her mother woke up during the afternoon? Shelly pleaded.

Always wanting to help the client, the executive director called the social worker in charge of Emily's case and instructed her to make a notary public available for Emily if the need arose. The social worker was a notary public, as chance would have it. Always wanting to please the executive director, the social worker agreed to notarize the document if asked to do so. "Was there anything else?" the social worker asked.

"Yes, make witnesses available if needed," answered Bud.

Later that day, around four in the afternoon, Emily awoke and opened her eyes. She laid on her right side as she slept and did not move when she awakened. Shelly sat in a chair directly in her mother's line of sight. "Rebecca?" she asked.

Shelly winced at the sound of Rebecca's name. "No, Mom, it is me, Shelly. You need your glasses."

"Shelly," Emily spoke.

Bud, who had been napping in a chair in the corner of the room lest he miss his chance to complete his plan, awoke with a start. "Huh?" Bud asked, "Is she awake?"

"Yes, Bud," Shelly answered. "Look, Mom," she said and took Emily's cold hand. "Bud has been in the room at your bedside all day. Bud, come here so Mom can see you."

Bud walked around the bed and stood in front of Emily, who looked at him without speaking.

"You need to sit up, Mom," Shelly said and began to roll Emily from her side onto her back. Bud, repulsed at the thought of handling an old woman riddled with cancer on her deathbed, did not offer help. Shelly managed to roll Emily onto her back. "Bud," Shelly instructed, "adjust the bed so Mom is sitting up." Bud dutifully adjusted Emily into a sitting position. "Mom, we need you to sign a document, if you will." Emily did not speak a word during this ordeal.

"Remember, Mom," Shelly said. "You do not want to be *unfair* to your grandchildren. Isn't that right?"

"Unfair?" Emily asked in a daze.

"*Unfair* to your grandchildren. You are being *unfair*, and you need to change your will. Isn't that so?"

Emily gave no verbal response, but Shelly saw her mother was listening and ready to follow her instructions.

"Bud," Shelly instructed again, "call the social worker and two witnesses."

Bud silently followed Shelly's instructions. Shelly placed Emily's eyeglasses on her face and adjusted Emily to allow her to sign her name if she was able. Bud returned with the social worker and two nurse's aides to act as witnesses. Shelly and Bud nervously eyeballed the three women who would be unwitting accomplices in their plan.

"Mom is doing so good this afternoon," Shelly said. "We explained that you are coming in to help her sign her change to her will as she wants to do. She said she is ready."

The social worker and two aides looked over Emily in the bed. She appeared to be frail, and they suspected she was out of touch with reality at that moment. The social worker wondered what she should do. She weighed refusing to cooperate in the signing. The two aides wondered why they were in the room and looked to the social worker for instruction.

"Does she know what she is signing?" one of the aides asked.

"Mom," Shelly said to her mother, "you want to change you will, don't you, to be *fair* to your grandchildren."

Emily did not respond. Shelly's heart sank into her stomach. Bud shuffled nervously, wishing the old lady would just sign the paper and get it over with.

Emily then looked up at Shelly and said, "I want to be fair. Yes, I need to be fair."

"She just read the change to her will," Bud told the three unwitting accomplices. "She needed her glasses to read."

That comment took the edge off the situation. Although the social worker had serious misgivings, she took comfort in the fact that Emily had read the document. If she was capable of reading the document, the social worker reasoned, she was capable of understanding the document. Therefore, this was probably something she should cooperate in. After all, her executive director had instructed her to do so.

Shelly put the document on a hard surface and a pen in Emily's hand. Emily's hand did not move. "This is where you should sign," Shelly told Emily. Emily was still.

The social worker spoke up. "I have seen people help other people sign their name if necessary."

"Oh," said Bud. "Is that legal?"

"Apparently so," the social worker answered.

"Try that, honey," Bud told Shelly.

Shelly took Emily's hand in her own and wrote her signature as best she could. "I guess this is the same as her signing it herself," she told the assembled onlookers. Shelly handed the document to the two witnesses, who signed their names in silence. They had their suspicions about a lady who was all but deceased signing important papers, but they figured that the social worker knew best, and it was not their place to question. The social worker signed the acknowledgment and affixed her notary seal.

The social worker was correct. Persons signing documents can be assisted in the signing. Documents can also be signed by others if a person is unable to sign on their own. However, the person must be fully aware that their signature is being made on a document and consent to the act. The social worker was ignorant of the awareness issues.

Bud thought, "Signed, sealed, and delivered. Just like that."

The next morning, at ten o'clock, Attorney Kulinowski appeared at the door to Emily's room, just as he had promised. Bud met him as he entered the room.

"Mom is sleeping again this morning," Bud told the lawyer, who looked in to see Emily in the same state she had been when he visited the day before.

"Can I do anything for Mrs. McCarthy?" the lawyer asked.

"I think it is best that we call you when Mom improves to the point where she can see you and sign the document. Is that all right?"

"Of course," Attorney Kulinowski said. He said his farewells and left the room. Not until later did he learn that Emily had signed the document Bud had prepared the previous afternoon.

Rebecca visited her grandmother each evening at the hospice residence. She attempted to sit quietly with Emily to say her personal good-byes. Rebecca's sister and brother asked if they should visit. Rebecca told them to wait until the funeral because seeing Emily in her present state was not productive. Rebecca knew as a physician that Emily did not have long to live. Two days later, and three days after Bud and Shelly procured the signed change to the will, Emily died quietly in her sleep. Rebecca and Shelly were at her bedside. Bud was contacting a real estate agent to see what the house might be worth in a quick sale.

Following the funeral, Rebecca visited Attorney Kulinowski to discuss probating her grandmother's estate. To avoid the problems that families can have when inheritances are the issue, Rebecca asked Bud and Shelly to join her. After all, Rebecca reasoned, Shelly was inheriting one-half of the estate and should be aware of the proceeding.

The lawyer explained the process, which appeared to be straightforward enough. "We need to file a petition for administration and admit the will to probate. The division of the estate is clearly stated in the will, and there should be no serious complications."

Bud spoke up, "There is the matter of this codicil that Mom made just before she died." Bud pulled the document from his pocket. "She changed her way of distributing the assets."

Rebecca read the document and asked the lawyer. "She signed this three days before she died? Is that legal? If it is, so be it."

The lawyer caught on to what had happened to Emily without being told any more. "When I visited Mrs. McCarthy, she was clearly not competent. Why did you not tell me of this when I visited her at the hospice?"

Bud and Shelly did not answer.

"I have serious doubts about this document being valid," Attorney Kulinowski told the three of them seated before him. "Before we go on, I need to inform you again that only Rebecca, as personal representative of the estate, is my client."

"We are beneficiaries," Bud answered. "We are also your clients."

"I am sorry," the lawyer told Bud and Shelly. "I cannot represent you in this at all. I must follow my client's instruction."

"Well, then we should get out of here. Thanks for nothing," Bud said and left in a huff with Shelly tagging behind.

Outside in the hot Miami sun with the traffic speeding by, Bud and Shelly stopped to talk. "What do you think?" Shelly asked. "What should we do?"

"Talk to another lawyer," Bud answered. "This is going to work out for us, one way or the other. We worked too hard for this."

Bud turned and walked down the street, oblivious to leaving Shelly standing alone. He was a man on a mission to see his plan through.

Bud and Shelly did visit another lawyer, who was very experienced in will contests. The lawyer explained that their case was riddled with problems. Bud had prepared the document Emily signed that day. The document did not read properly. It said that Emily intended to change her will, not that she was actually changing the will. Shelly and Bud were present when the document was signed. Shelly had actually signed for her mother. There was no independent determination of competency from an unbiased person such as a doctor. There was no independent witness to Emily expressing her desire to make a change. He would not take the case unless Bud and Shelly could answer at least some of his concerns. Bud did not like that lawyer's opinion, so he sought another.

The second lawyer Bud and Shelly visited was not so pessimistic about their case. He said that the issues brought up by the other lawyer could be explained away. After all, he opined, Emily did sign the document in front of two witnesses and a notary, all independent persons. That should be enough to make a good case, he told Bud and Shelly. After Bud and Shelly talked over the assets of the estate, the lawyer was confident that he would be paid his fee from Shelly's share of the estate even if he was not successful in proving the codicil was legal and binding. Bud and Shelly signed a retainer agreement to start the litigation.

Rebecca was absolutely devastated that her aunt and uncle would try to steal from her siblings and her. The situation was depressing and disheartening for all of Barbara's children. They knew their grandmother and grandfather loved their mother and them as much as they loved Shelly and her children.

When Rebecca was served with the court papers from Shelly's attorney, she saw in black and white the words attacking the love she felt her grandparents gave to her throughout her life. To surrender to Shelly's claims would be to admit that her grandparents did not love their mother as much as she knew they did. Surrender would mean her grandparents did not love them as much as she knew they did.

Rebecca had no choice but to fight. And fight she did. The estate was worth several hundred thousand dollars. She was the personal representative with the power to spend every last penny if necessary to prove Shelly wrong. Rebecca asked her siblings, Richard and Kevin, for advice.

"I don't give a damn if you spend all of the money in the estate to prove this is a ton of bullshit," Kevin told Rebecca. "They are not going to cheat us. It is just not right." Richard added, "That piece of shit, Bud, is behind this. I know it. And Shelly is a piece of shit for going along with him. Spend it all. I don't care."

Rebecca hired Attorney Rob Andrews, a top litigator recommended by Attorney Kulinowski, who would have been happy to handle the case, but was disqualified because he would be a material witness.

The case ground on through discovery and depositions. Everyone involved with Emily at the hospice was deposed under oath. A pattern emerged during those depositions. The hospice employees lacked any training in how to handle the signing of important documents by patients. These patients, almost always on heavy medication and pain killers, are terminally ill and should not be asked to make important decisions on their deathbed. The employees should not be asked to determine if they are competent to make decisions and if they are free of undue influence from others. Attorney Andrews knew he had a winning case after interviewing the employees. They placed Shelly and Bud in the room when the document was signed and confirmed that Emily was all but unresponsive when she signed the document. Attorney Kulinowski's testimony about Bud and Shelly's visit to his office put the icing on the cake, as Attorney Andrews put it.

Bud and Shelly consented to hiring a geriatric psychiatrist as an expert witness. Although he had never met Emily, he reviewed her medical records and was prepared to testify that Emily had the capacity to know what she was doing at the time she signed the document. Attorney Andrews commented on the psychiatrist, "This guy must be a total whore to testify that she was competent. Some people will do anything for money, even sell their reputation."

The trial was finally scheduled by the court. Judge McMannis, an experienced jurist, sat on the case. Rob Andrews was satisfied with Judge McMannis sitting on this case. The judge had been through many personal problems and therefore had some real-life experience to draw on.

What happened during the trial was unusual and could not have happened if the case was being tried by a jury. The first witness was the psychiatrist, who the judge seemed to give little credibility. "At least the judge knows this guy is a whore," Rob Andrews thought. Next witness up was the social worker who notarized the document. Everything seemed to click for Rob Andrews when he cross-examined her. The questions and answers fell into a fluid progression that gave everyone in the courtroom a clear picture of what happened in that hospice room that day. Shelly and Bud had called the social worker and witnesses into the room to witness a signature by a lady who was all but dead. There was no indication that she was competent or even lucid. This was exactly what Rod Andrews wanted to show the judge.

The testimony concluded just before noon. When the social worker left the witness stand, she did not make eye contact with anyone and quickly left the courtroom, knowing she had done a wrong to Emily.

Judge McMannis called the lawyers into his chamber. Not one to mince words, the judge asked Shelly's attorney, "How to you expect to overcome this testimony? Shelly was in the room. She procured the document and the witnesses. The lady was close to death. And this is *your* witness. How do you expect to overcome these facts?"

"We have other witnesses, your honor," was the response.

"And other facts showing she was competent?" asked the judge.

"The other witnesses will testify to the same facts," was the response.

"Well, I can't tell you now how I will rule because the trial is not concluded," the judge told the two lawyers. "But I will tell you that without other facts showing she was competent, I am going to rule that this so-called codicil is not valid. I am telling you this," the judge continued, "to allow you time to settle this over lunch if you wish."

The case did not settle over lunch because the only thing Shelly and Bud had to offer was full surrender. To admit defeat would be to admit they attempted to steal part of the inheritance rightfully due to Barbara's children. To admit they were capable of such a despicable act would forever brand them cheats and liars. Despite that Bud had been a petty cheat and liar all his life, he would not admit it in such a public forum. Bud and Shelly believed that allowing the judge to rule against them was more attractive than admitting wrongdoing. Bud and Shelly could always accuse the judge of being stupid or corrupt or on the take from Rebecca's attorney. There were all sorts of excuses Bud and Shelly could assert for their loss if the judge made the decision. They just could not admit they were the wrongdoers.

The trial concluded at noon the following day. The judge did precisely what he said he would do and declared the so-called codicil to be void. He ruled directly from the bench at the end of the short closing arguments rather than issue a decision after mulling over the facts. The facts were clear. He did not want to waste any more time on the case.

Rebecca did get a bit of revenge. Rod Andrews applied to Judge McMannis to charge Shelly's share of the estate with his attorney fees, a sum well into five figures. The judge happily granted the request. So in the end, Shelly and Bud paid not only their own attorney fees but also the fees Rebecca incurred in defending the suit.

Years later, Rebecca, while showing photos of her grandparents to her own children, thought about how life might have been different had this case never come about. She and her siblings never heard from Shelly and Bud and their children after the suit ended. She sent a card at Christmas for a few years after the trial, but stopped after receiving no response. She wondered how her cousins had turned out. There was only the tiniest bit of sadness, and she put the thoughts aside to answer a question from her own young daughter. "Do you have anything to remember your grandma by?"

"Many things," Rebecca told her daughter. "But most of all I know she loved me."

Comments on Shelly

This case is a textbook example of attempted but unsuccessful undue influence. Seldom is a case of undue influence as clear cut. Chapter 4 explains the tort in detail. Shelly did everything wrong, and the decision against her was easily reached by the court. It is also important that Shelly's mother probably also lacked testamentary capacity to make a change to her trust. The possible lack of capacity also made her more vulnerable to Shelly's undue influence.

This case also demonstrates how a hijacker can wait too long for their victim to weaken before they strike. Shelly, the hijacker, chose her mother as Target A. But she failed to act until her mother went beyond weak to totally unable to act even if she wanted to do so. Shelly missed her chance.

This begs the question, why did Shelly wait until Emily was on her deathbed? Did Shelly believe she had no chance while her mother was in good health?

Shelly may have been successful if she had browbeaten her mother for years before her death. Under intense pressure from Shelly to influence her decision, Emily may have been convinced that changing the will was the right thing to do. Still, if Shelly was successful in that fashion, she would have been subject to a claim of undue influence upon her mother. But her chances of success would have been much greater.

Shelly's story illustrates the intense and compelling motivation typical in a family inheritance dispute. Shelly desperately sought revenge for what she perceived to be the slights and wrongs done against her by her family throughout her life. These insults may have been real or they may have existed only in Shelly's mind.

The end result, a family torn apart never to come together again, is unfortunate but inevitable. The hijacking never heals the underlying wounds that motivated the hijacker. The dispute only tears a family with problem relationships further apart.

How could have this been prevented? Nothing short of posting a guard could have prevented Shelly from attempting the hijacking while her mother was lying on her deathbed. The root of the dispute goes too deep into the family relationships. Only family therapy years before Emily's death may have prevented Shelly's desperate acts.

Serial Hijacking in Cold Blood

As we age, it is inevitable that we will become attractive as a Target A victim. We become dependent on others for our care and eventually our survival.

In a perfect world, if we live long enough, we change roles with our children. When once our children were dependent on us, we become dependent on them. As our dependence on others increases, our ability to make decisions and carry out those decisions decreases. We naturally surrender our decision-making ability to others. These are some simple facts of life.

As the aging parent becomes more like the child, he becomes more attractive as a potential Target A victim. As the child becomes more like the parent, he should fulfill the parental role and protect the parent. In protecting the parent, the child also avoids becoming a Target B victim. Imagine, if you can, a playground seesaw with the parent on one end and the child on the other. They rise and fall in concert. If this balance can be maintained throughout their lives, each will protect the other at different life stages. Hijackers and other predators will be kept at bay.

If the child does not protect the parent, as happens in this case study, a vacuum exists. Hijackers can seize an opportunity, and the family members become Target A and Target B victims.

Cindy, the subject of this case study, understood the increasing needs of an aging population, and she endeavored to fill that need to serve herself.

Helpful Cindy scores, again and again

O-kee-cho-bee is the Seminole word meaning "big water." Lake Okeechobee is the heart of southern Florida's water wilderness, the headwater of the vast Everglades. No more than twelve feet deep, the fertile waters of the lake breed fish and birds in astonishing abundance. Stand on any shore and the opposite shore is beyond the horizon. Located equidistant from both of Florida's overly populated saltwater coasts, the lake waters are controlled by a dike running around the entire lake. The shores are almost devoid of waterfront homes so common elsewhere. The lake appears as wild and pristine as it was a thousand years ago. The wilderness surrounding the "Lake O" extends from the lake shore out thirty miles in any direction, interrupted only by a few small towns and huge sugarcane plantations.

Early in the twentieth century, a few small towns grew up around the lake. The early residents earned a livelihood from what the lake provided. These slow-moving towns, now populated by agricultural workers and their families, remain unchanged from decade to decade. Sugar is king south of the lake. Vast green sugarcane fields thrive in the rich muck irrigated by the lake with only an isolated sugar mill, as large as any oil refinery, to break the landscape.

The town of Okeechobee sits on the north shore of the lake, not far from where the Kissimmee River terminates and spills its precious fresh water gathered from north central Florida into the lake. The lake in turn distributes the water to the populations of Fort Myers on the Gulf Coast and Palm Beach and Miami on the Atlantic Coast. The balance flows to the south to the sugar plantations and Everglades, eventually flowing past the Ten Thousand Islands into the salty Bay of Florida just north of the Florida Keys. This central spine of Florida is a wide untamed wilderness from Orlando to the Bay of Florida with Lake O as the centerpiece.

When civilization came to Florida in the late nineteenth century, fish camps sprang up around the lake. When the Okeechobee Hurricane of 1928 flooded the lake and killed thousands of people and livestock, President Herbert Hoover ordered that the land around the lake be reclaimed and the lake waters tamed. A flood-control dike system was built around the entire lake. Boat access to the lake was restricted to a rim canal behind the dike, and a few canals allowing access to the lake. The fish camps relocated to the banks of the rim canal. Enterprising fish camp owners built small motels and trailer parks to accommodate the fishing tourists drawn to the fisherman's paradise unspoiled by the excesses of Florida's tourist industry.

Ed Mahoney fell in love with the "Lake O" and the laid-back lifestyle around the lake on his first visit. He and a few friends, all avid bass fishermen in Michigan, took a men-only vacation to fish the great Okeechobee waters. The first trip was spent in the town of Clewiston on the southwest shore of the lake where lake access is easy. The small group fished with guides and returned year after year. Later they explored other fishing spots along the lake, eventually settling on the town of Okeechobee on the north shore as their center of operations. Each year they fished, drank too much, and blew off steam built up during their year of labor at uninteresting jobs in Michigan. Their choice of accommodations was a single-wide mobile home rented from a local couple. Had they desired more luxurious housing, they would be hard-pressed to find it in Okeechobee, where a home that does not arrive on wheels is a luxury home.

Ed vowed to retire on the shores of his beloved Okeechobee after he put in the required years at his job. Ed and his wife, Marion, gave up dreams of bigger and greater things to raise their four children. Ed clung to the dream that he could have been an artist of some sort, perhaps a painter, had his life been different. Instead he took a job in the plating department at the small parts-manufacturing company when he returned from Vietnam in 1969, already thirty years old. Marion took a job as a screw machine operator at the same company. They traveled to work together, managing to earn enough to buy a small house and give their children a good religious upbringing. They counted themselves lucky that they avoided the problems other parents faced with drug addiction and illness. Ed and Marion measured their success in life by how their children were doing. "A parent is only as happy as their least happy child," they often said in jest, knowing it was true.

Marion died in the year 1998 from heart disease. "I was sure I would be the first to go," Ed told his friends and family. "Especially after all those years breathing in arsenic and who knows what else in that plating department."

Ed was a lost soul after all his years of marriage and companionship with Marion. His two sons traveled to Okeechobee to fish with him in an attempt to lift his spirits. The trip did the trick. Okeechobee was a happy place for Ed. Marion had never visited Okeechobee with Ed, and there were no memories and sense of loss to overcome. His sons, once worried about their father's mental state, were surprised how much the fishing trip changed Ed's demeanor for the better.

When Ed announced he was retiring from his job and renting a place in Okeechobee for the winter, his children were pleased. With his retirement funds and Marion's life insurance proceeds, Ed could get along quite well for himself. He decided to live a little, and maybe learn to paint watercolors of the great Lake Okeechobee he loved to visit.

Ed's first winter was a success. He made new friends in the park and joined the VFW, where he could drink for almost nothing and socialize. The new environment was good for Ed's mental health.

The second year, Ed decided Okeechobee was the place he wanted to be most of the year. Real estate prices were rising. Ed decided to buy a place while he could afford to do so. He placed an offer on an almost new double-wide mobile home in a quiet street in the park where he was renting. Ed was low-balling the offer, expecting a counteroffer. To his surprise, the counteroffer was only slightly higher, and Ed had bought himself a Florida retirement home. There were two bedrooms and plenty of room for his children and grandchildren to spend time during visits.

Ed's children and grandchildren visited for the next few years. They fished and toured the area around Ed's home, taking day trips as far as Sanibel Island and Naples on the Gulf Coast. With nothing much to do except fish or sit on the porch and watch the sky grow dark in the evening, the children and grandchildren became bored with Ed's Florida home. They wanted the excitement of Orlando or Miami, both out of reach on a day trip from Ed's home. Their visits to Ed became limited to an overnight or two if they visited Florida at all. Winter vacations were simply an extravagance they were not able to afford each year.

Ed's life in Florida became a routine of sleeping late, fishing when the weather was good and the fish were biting, and socializing at the VFW where he took his evening meals. It would be fair to say that Ed had evolved into a high-functioning alcoholic. Most mornings he was feeling the effects of the night before and his energy was drained. He puttered around his home until it was time for happy hour at the VFW, where he spent the evening.

Ed's neighbors were much the same as he, older folks who retired to Florida as the last big pleasure they allowed themselves in life, their gift to themselves for a life of hard work. They too lived a life of routine and habit as they grew old.

When he was a younger man, Ed had wondered if old folks thought about their own death much as they neared the inevitable end of their lives. He now knew they did. Every day they worried, but not too much lest they become severely depressed, about the end and whether they would be a burden on others before they died. Ed did not like to think about the end of his life or to wonder about how much time he had left. It depressed him. But he did think and worry a little every day.

Ed's personal hygiene began to slip. His home was not being well kept. Ed delayed emptying the ashtrays until the cigarette butts overflowed. One morning Ed took a good look at himself in the mirror. "You need a change," he told himself. "Marion would be ashamed of you."

Ed asked his friends at the VFW if they knew of anyone who would help him with cleaning his house from time to time. A friend recommended he talk to Cindy Manchester. Ed telephoned up Cindy, who agreed to come over to Ed's home to discuss his needs. When Cindy arrived at the door of Ed's double-wide, Ed's life changed for the better.

Cindy offered her hand when Ed answered the door. "Hello, Ed," she said in her honeyed southern drawl. "What can I do for you?" Ed fixated for a moment on Cindy's eyes, which were as wide and bright and blue as Marion's had been. For the first time since Marion's death, Ed felt a rush when meeting a woman.

"Come in, please," Ed said when he composed himself.

Cindy had learned when she was a pretty teenager with a ready smile that an outgoing personality can take you a long way in life. She cultivated her assets and prospered.

With that introduction, Cindy became an important player in Ed's life. Cindy was an independent woman. She had been divorced for many years and created a business around the needs of senior citizens to support herself. She provided maids, caregivers, chauffeurs, shoppers, landscapers, handymen, nurses, and any other helper a senior needed. She carried the business cards of doctors, dentists, hairdressers, barbers, and lawyers—what she called her "network." If you needed it, Cindy knew where to get it or who could get it for you. Cindy had made herself indispensable to many seniors in the Okeechobee area, who came to rely on her for many of the essential necessities.

To many of her older single male clients, Cindy became a surrogate for their deceased wives. Cindy was quick with the joke or comeback to a wise-crack. She loved to flirt with the old men and talk with the old women. Easily twenty years the junior of any of her clients, Cindy was never seriously considered as a mate by any of the men. "If I was twenty years younger and single," all of them to a man thought, "Cindy would be mine."

Four months later, Ed was a new man. Just the expectation of Cindy's visit every Wednesday to talk with Ed about his needs was enough to encourage Ed to clean up his act.

Ed's older son visited during a business trip to Tampa and was very happily surprised by Ed's healthy appearance and the cleanliness of his home. "Florida seems to agree with you," he said to Ed. "I was a little concerned."

"I like it here," Ed told his son. "I belong here. I just wish your mother was here to enjoy it with me."

Cindy also provided plenty of advice to her clients. She insisted they should have a will and put their financial affairs in order. Of course, she was available for financial counseling if needed.

On one of Cindy's visits to Ed's home, she brought up the subject. "Ed, do you have a will?"

"Yes, I do," Ed answered. Then, wanting to please Cindy, he added, "Would you like to see it?"

"No," Cindy answered. "But is it old? Did you make it up North?"

"Yes, before Marion died," Ed answered.

"Then here is the card of a good lawyer. You need a Florida will. Call him and tell him I sent you," Cindy directed. "Those wills from up North are not good here in Florida."

"Well, if the will is not good, I will call the lawyer as soon as you leave," Ed promised.

A small town like Okeechobee, where most people are struggling to make ends meet, is not a place where a lawyer is overwhelmed with wealthy clients. Rich clients are few and far between in the small town. The rich folks, what few there are, generally use the large law firms in Tampa or West Palm Beach where the expertise is thicker. Or they use the oldest good-old-boy lawyer in town, who has the rich clients all to himself.

Cindy referred Ed to Attorney Bruce Hutchinson, a member of her network. Attorney Hutchinson had made an awful business decision when he opened his practice. His first bad decision was hanging out his shingle in such a small town. He had grown up in Okeechobee, but his family was comprised of poor working folks with no connections. He was a nobody who went to college and law school on the GI Bill. He returned to Okeechobee because his wife insisted they return to their hometown where her large family of farm laborers resided. The second, and worse, decision was specializing in real estate and estate law. What juicy, large real estate deals there were around Okeechobee went to the old lawyers in town or to lawyers out of town. The people who were dying did not have any money to pass to their children. Their estates were small or nonexistent. Hutchinson's legal practice struggled. His wife ran his office as receptionist, secretary, and bookkeeper.

There is no proof that can be brought forward to prove Hutchinson's unspoken arrangement with Cindy. Only circumstantial evidence exists. But there is plenty of evidence if one digs into the public records. The evidence points to an arrangement where Hutchinson rewarded Cindy for referrals by suggesting to the client that Cindy be named personal representative of the client's estate. Cindy earned a fee for her work as administrator. In turn, Cindy hired Hutchinson to represent her as personal representative of the estate. Hutchinson earned a fee for representing Cindy.

The arrangement worked well for Hutchinson, who was able to earn a living, and also for Cindy, who made a better living than Hutchinson.

Ed visited Hutchinson one afternoon, learned Hutchinson was a military veteran, and immediately bonded with the lawyer. The interview went smoothly. Hutchinson suggested that Ed name Cindy as his personal representative since Ed's family was up North.

"You don't want to put the burden of handling your estate on your children, do you?" Hutchinson asked Ed. "The travel expenses will eat into the estate."

"I guess not," Ed answered, not knowing his options. "What do you suggest?" With that, the deal was done. Hutchinson named Cindy as personal representative and expected another probate case with Cindy as the personal representative and his client.

Ed was eager to please Cindy and happy to name Cindy as his personal representative. The arrangement gave him a reason to talk to Cindy about his life and finances as he had done with Marion. Ed believed the interest Cindy showed in his personal matters to be a show of genuine affection for him on some level.

The next few years passed without much change in the town of Okeechobee. Ed passed the time on the lake shore casting for bass and his evenings at the VFW. Cindy continued providing services to Ed and others. As the needs of her aging clientele increased, Cindy's influence grew. For some of her clients, including Ed, Cindy was their connection to the world. As Ed aged, he became increasingly immobile and decreased his social contacts. His evenings at the VFW were less frequent. Some days he did not venture out of his home, choosing to watch television and sleep. "It is just too hot to go out of doors," he would answer if asked by his drinking buddies at the VFW why he had not been coming around.

Ed decided that the drinks at the VFW were becoming too expensive, even though the price was less than a dollar for a mixed drink or a beer. Instead, he chose to drink alone at home. His drinking increased along with his seclusion.

Cindy noticed during her weekly visit that Ed's personal hygiene was deteriorating and there were too many empty whiskey bottles around the house. Ed's breath smelled of whiskey in the middle of the day. He was increasingly irritable.

"Ed, you need to get out more," Cindy told him. "You should not be cooped up in the house all of the time."

"Where is there to go?" Ed asked sarcastically. "It's too damn hot."

"You can go to church this Sunday. I can send someone by to pick you up," Cindy suggested.

"I have had enough of churches," Ed barked at Cindy.

"Okay, have it your way. I am just trying to help," Cindy answered, hoping to settle Ed down. "It's not like Ed to be aggressive," Cindy thought. "The alcohol must be getting to him."

Changing the subject, Cindy asked, "Have you heard from your children?"

"Not since Christmas," Ed barked at Cindy again. "They don't call me. Maybe once a month." Ed was quiet for a moment before he added, "Too busy with their own lives," as his voice trailed off and his mind drifted away from the conversation with Cindy.

Cindy detected a sadness in Ed, quietly concluded her business, and left Ed's home.

Cindy visited the next week and found Ed was in a much better mood. He explained he visited the VFW the night before and played cards with some of his friends.

"Getting out is good for you, Ed," Cindy told him. "You need to get out more often."

"I have been thinking," Ed said. "Can I ask you something?"

Cindy had dreaded this moment since she first detected Ed's attraction to her. She had given him the perfect lead in to asking her to go out with him. She knew she would have to refuse him and feared what that refusal might do to their business arrangement. Cindy did not want to lose the income Ed provided for her.

Ed looked Cindy in the eye and asked, "Can you help me pay my bills? I mean, if I am not able to pay them myself. Will you write the checks and pay the bills?"

Cindy was relieved. She smiled. "Of course, Ed. I will do all I can for you."

That afternoon, Ed and Cindy visited the Wachovia Bank branch in Okeechobee. They sat at the desk of a young, pretty female customer service representative and added Cindy as a signer on Ed's checking account. The banker was trained to be skeptical of transactions between elderly people and non-family members such as Cindy. "I don't want to be a burden on my children," Ed told the banker when she asked why Cindy was being added to the account. He added, "Cindy handles accounts for people. It's her business."

Cindy gave the banker one of her business cards to prove her legitimacy. Detecting the banker's skepticism, Cindy attempted to ingratiate herself with the banker. "Do you have online banking?"

"Yes, we do," the banker answered.

Cindy turned to Ed and said, "This bank will be easy to work with. I'll recommend more of my customers to bank here."

Cindy took control of Ed's monetary affairs without further encouragement. The bank's online banking system allowed Cindy access to all of Ed's checking and savings accounts and his credit cards. Soon Cindy was paying Ed's bills by direct withdrawal and transferring funds between accounts as she wished.

Ed was happy to be relieved of his financial responsibilities. Prior to Cindy taking control, Ed paid his bills only after receiving a second and third past-due notice. His habit was to throw the utility bills in the wastebasket if they were not threats to immediately cut off service. "Screw 'em," was his comment when discarding the bills.

Ed's drinking cronies at the VFW noticed Ed had become critical and cynical rather than easygoing as he had been.

"You don't look well, Ed. Do you have something on your mind?" one of the men asked him one evening.

"Everything is on my mind," Ed answered, abruptly ending the conversation and returning to his drink.

For the last few years, Ed had been drifting ever closer to old age depression brought on by years of abusing alcohol and cigarettes. There are limits to the abuse the mind and body can withstand before the aging process begins to rapidly accelerate. Ed's mind and body had reached that point.

Could Ed have helped himself to live longer if he quit drinking and smoking? Probably. But Ed did not have the motivation necessary to quit either drinking or smoking. To do so would destroy his quality of life, in his eyes. "And for what?" he asked himself. "I've lived my life as best I knew how. Why worry about it?"

Cindy's weekly visits to Ed became no more than social visits after a few months. Ed and Cindy sat on Ed's screened porch if the weather was tolerable and did no more than chat. Cindy picked up any of Ed's bills that had arrived during the past week and was gone. Ed never asked about what Cindy was doing with his money. He did not care. He was happy to be relieved of the hassle of bill paying.

Cindy studied Ed's telephone bills for any calls to or from his children. There were no calls from Ed to his children on the bill. She could not detect if the children had contacted Ed. He did not talk about them during her visits.

One afternoon as Ed and Cindy sat on the screened porch, Ed brought up the subject of his death. "I don't want to be cremated. You know that," he said to Cindy.

"Yes. You want to be buried beside Marion," she answered.

"I want you to have my furniture," he told Cindy.

"Why?" she asked. "What about your children? That was Marion's furniture. They may want it."

"They don't want anything, any furniture anyway," Ed answered. "What would they do with it?"

"Well, it is up to you," Cindy said. "I will do what you want."

"I know you will," Ed said with a deep regret in his voice. "I know you will help me when I need it. You are the only one I have here."

"I'll help, Ed," Cindy answered. "You know I will." Cindy took Ed's hand in her own and squeezed it to emphasize her concern to Ed.

Ed did not say a word. He looked at Cindy with the saddest eyes Cindy had seen in a long time.

Cindy felt uneasy with Ed's sullen mood. To cheer him, she kindly said, "Everything will be all right in the end. It always is."

Cindy left Ed alone with his sad and depressed mood. Had Cindy known what to do to help Ed, she would have seen he visit a doctor or psychiatrist to help him out of his depression. Instead, Cindy left Ed's home that afternoon with her game plan clear in her mind.

Cindy's mind was always devising ways to make money. She was not restrained by a moral compass in her business dealings. Cindy's network of service providers included two empty corporations that Cindy created but was not identified with in any way. She used her children and her maiden name in forming the corporations to cover her tracks. Each corporation had a professional-sounding name to garner credibility. One corporation allegedly provided home health services. The other allegedly provided transportation services to seniors.

Cindy planned to use her two shell corporations to drain money from her clients. She had not been presented with an opportunity to do so as yet. She was growing impatient. Ed offered Cindy just such an opportunity. The corporations issued false invoices for services not rendered on a regular basis. Cindy paid the invoices as she would any other legitimate expense. To the unwary, the expenses appeared to be legitimate. The invoices were vague in describing the services provided. If a child of a senior reviewed the invoices, always buried within the other ordinary bills, no red flags were readily visible. If Cindy's theft was discovered, she planned to fold the corporations to distance herself from the situation and cover her tracks.

Cindy started small with Ed's bank account. She wrote small checks to her two corporations for a few months. When she gained confidence, she wrote larger and larger checks. Soon she was draining a few thousand dollars each month from Ed.

Ed had slipped deeper into his depression and alcoholism. Cindy saw to it that Ed's home was as clean and respectable as possible. She did not want his hygiene and appearance to deteriorate further, lest outsiders start to probe into Ed's well-being. When Ed visited the VFW, he was always clean and well dressed. No one had reason to question his well-being.

Ed was in a rare good mood one afternoon when Cindy visited. "My grandson is visiting tomorrow," Ed blurted out, unable to contain himself.

Cindy's heart sank. Questions raced through her mind. Who was this grandson? How long would he be staying? What did he want with Ed? Cindy feared this family visit could be a serious threat to her plans for Ed's assets. She decided to closely monitor the visit.

"Can I help you in any way, Ed?"

"Always the helper," Ed answered. "I don't know. I'll just play it by ear."

The next day, Ed's grandson, Eric, arrived with his girlfriend, Lora. They were traveling to Fort Lauderdale for spring break. Ed was overjoyed to see his grandson. Cindy dropped in to visit Ed as Eric and Lora were just arriving. After a little small talk, Cindy offered to take them all out to enjoy some good Southern Bar-B-Q at Sonny's. Cindy's goal was to keep a close eye on what was happening between Ed and Eric.

Eric and Lora wondered what relationship Cindy, a good thirty years younger than Ed, had to Ed. Lora commented how strange it was that Cindy was so attentive to Ed, who appeared to be just Ed's friend. "Why would that woman want to spend time with your grandfather?" Lora asked. "It is kind of creepy when you think about it. What is really going on?"

If Eric had suspected Cindy's hidden motives, he would have thought about strangling Cindy. But he was just a naive college kid who never suspected the truth because it was beyond his young imagination.

Eric reported to his father that Ed seemed to be doing well. Ed's home was clean, and Ed was in good health. Eric did note that Ed appeared to be drinking more than he should be. Eric's father was relieved to hear his father was doing well in Florida. He had worried. Eric did report that, "This strange lady took us out to eat and was hanging around all the time, like she was Grandpop's girlfriend or something."

"Maybe she is," Eric's father said and wished his father well.

. . .

Ed had been noticing a strange color to his stool for some time. Not having any medical training and not recognizing the danger, Ed ignored the warnings.

One morning in July, with the sun beating down in a cloudless sky and the temperature already above eighty degrees, Ed awoke to find his underwear and bed soaked in his own blood. Instinctively, Ed called 911.

Cindy panicked when she learned Ed was taken to the hospital. She feared her income stream from Ed was ended. Cindy rushed to the hospital with the power of attorney for both financial and health care decisions that Ed had given her at Attorney Hutchinson's office.

Ed was in the operating room when Cindy arrived at the hospital. The doctor later explained to her that Ed had a perforated colon caused by cancer and was close to kidney failure.

"That explains the strange skin color," Cindy told the doctor. "What can we expect?"

Ed had three to six months to live. The cancer had spread and was inoperable. A kidney transplant was out of the question. Around-the-clock care or a hospice were the only options.

Cindy pondered the options. Around-the-clock care was out of the question. Ed could not afford it. Even if he could, Cindy wanted to dip deeper into Ed's bank account. Hospice care seemed to be the only choice.

Cindy called Ed's eldest son and broke the news about his dad. All of Ed's children made plans to travel to visit within the week.

Cindy was again panicked. What was going to happen now? Would they want to take over Ed's finances? Would they move him back up North? Would her financial gymnastics be discovered?

Ed's children arrived within the week and spent time at Ed's bedside in the Okeechobee hospital. Ed's eldest son took control. He asked for and later demanded copies of Ed's will and financial records from Cindy.

Cindy resisted turning over Ed's will and financial records. She knew that if Ed had been asked about the bogus charges for home care and transportation, she might be caught with her hand in Ed's cookie jar.

Ed's prognosis was for several months of bed care while being filled with drugs to fight the cancer and reduce his pain. Kidney dialysis was mandatory. Ed's withdrawal from alcohol and nicotine addiction would cause complications and pain.

The quality of Ed's life had been severely reduced. His children discussed the options available. Should they move their father back to his northern home? What level of care did he need? Where were the best doctors? How would the bills be paid?

Cindy became so anxious she could not sleep. She was certain she would be found out. In Florida, embezzling money from a senior is a felony. Would she be arrested? Why had she done this? Would she be sentenced to prison? How could she be so stupid? Should she confess and somehow make it right for Ed and his family?

God intervened while Ed's family was visiting him just before traveling back home up North. Ed's four children were at his bedside and had said their tearful good-byes for the trip back home. Ed smiled at his children as best he could. He slowly laid his head back on his pillow, closed his eyes, and stopped breathing. His heart was weak before his sudden illness and had given out under the strain. The doctors were called and made an attempt to revive Ed. After several minutes, Ed's children discussed the options and instructed the doctors not to resuscitate Ed. They had decided that forcing their father to continue his life was not in his best interest. They comforted themselves with the thought that their father was ready to meet their mother in heaven.

Ed's eldest son, Richard, and his daughter, Virginia, extended their stay in Florida to make arrangements to transport Ed to their home to be buried with their mother. They visited a lawyer in LaBelle, Florida, to discuss their father's will. They did not like the idea that Cindy, a stranger, would be the administrator of their father's estate. "What can we do about it?" Richard asked the lawyer. "After all, we are the beneficiaries, and we want to handle it ourselves."

The lawyer agreed to represent them in their father's estate. He explained that the person nominated to act as personal representative had an almost absolute right to serve unless they were disqualified because they were a convicted felon. The lawyer wrote to Cindy asking if she would waive her right to act as administrator.

Attorney Hutchinson responded on Cindy's behalf to the lawyer's request. He explained that Ed had told Cindy that Ed believed his children would not get along in handling his estate and he wanted a neutral third party to handle the estate. Ed had never told Cindy anything of the sort. Cindy manufactured the excuse to appear as if she was carrying out Ed's last wishes. Ed's children knew it was a lie, as well. Actually, Cindy knew that if she acted as personal representative of the estate, she could hide her theft.

Cindy signed the petition for administration of Ed's estate on the day she obtained his death certificate. Hutchinson filed the estate papers in the circuit court for Okeechobee County the same afternoon. Ed's children received the required notice by certified mail a week later.

Ed's children pleaded with their lawyer to find some way to block Cindy's attempts to administer their father's estate. They were ready to go to court if necessary, but they did not want to waste money if there was no chance of success. The lawyer explained again that the person nominated in the will had preference to serve. He also explained that the will might be invalid because Ed was incompetent at the time he signed his will or because of some fraud or undue influence.

Ed's children knew little or nothing about Ed's life in Florida and had no evidence to give the lawyer. They were angry but grudgingly acquiesced to Cindy's administration of the estate. Their lawyer fired off letters demanding information and an inventory of the estate. Hutchinson complied with the bare-minimum requirements of law in providing information to Ed's children.

Within a week of receiving her authority to administer the estate in the form of letters of administration from the probate court, Cindy had cleared out Ed's furniture and personal property. She gave the furniture to her family and friends. She packed Ed's family photographs and mementoes in a box and placed the box in storage as leverage against the children. She knew they would be asking for these items sooner rather than later. She held them as a chip to gain an advantage if necessary. Cindy was correct. Ed's children telephoned their lawyer, who sent a letter demanding the personal items and some pieces of furniture with sentimental value. When no reply came after two weeks, the children called Cindy and Hutchinson directly. Although Cindy never intended to comply with their requests, she promised to ship the items to the children as soon as possible.

The children and their lawyer demanded their father's financial records. The demands went unanswered except for the estate inventory Cindy was required to file by law. Ed's children were astonished to read how little money their father had left them. They were certain something was wrong but were unwilling to spend money on lawyer's fees to perform an investigation. They wanted proof of wrongdoing before filing a suit to right the wrong. Unfortunately, they were unable to obtain the bank records without filing suit, which they declined to do without proof. Had they asked their lawyer to file suit and conduct a thorough investigation, they would have uncovered the fraudulent checks Cindy wrote to her shell corporations. The checks were written to what appeared to be legitimate care providers to their father. Would they have then instructed their lawyer to investigate whether the expenses were legitimate? If they declined to do so, the thefts would have remained undetected anyway. However, if they did investigate, they may have found the truth.

As time passed, Cindy's anxiety about stealing from Ed subsided. She was confident the thefts would go undetected. Cindy collected Ed's cash from his accounts at Wachovia Bank. She deposited the money is a new account at SunTrust to distance the estate from the accounts where the theft occurred and further cover her tracks.

Cindy became worried while the children were making threats of legal action. She questioned whether she had done the right thing. Soon Cindy convinced herself that Ed's children got what they deserved. They had all but abandoned their father. She cared for him when he needed care. These thoughts convinced her she had done the right thing and eased her conscience.

Eventually the estate was settled and closed. Cindy and Hutchinson both took grossly inflated fees for their services. Ed's children were so frustrated with the situation that they were happy to finally receive their father's personal effects and the small inheritance Cindy mailed to them with the final accounting. The notice mailed with the final accounting informed Ed's children that they had the right to contest the accounting if they wished. Ed's son called his Florida lawyer. At the end of the conversation, he decided it was not wise to throw good money away without some evidence to justify the expense. The matter ended there.

Ed's family had no means of telling their side of the story to anyone in Florida except their lawyer. Back home they told their friends not to trust anyone in Florida with their own parents' well-being.

Among the folks at the VFW, Cindy's reputation as a trustworthy person was growing. Cindy's handling of Ed's estate appeared to be on the up and up. She told everyone she was doing a service to Ed and his family. This brought more clients to Cindy. One client in particular, an elderly lady whose husband had recently died, interested Cindy a great deal. The elderly lady had no children and her other family members were distant. She needed help with her daily needs and her finances. A friend of her late husband, who frequented the VFW, gave Cindy a glowing recommendation as a person to look to for help and support. Cindy was more than happy to add the lady to her weekly schedule to fill the time slot Ed had left.

Comments on Cindy, the serial hijacker

As I pointed out in the prologue to this case study, children must protect their parents to avoid becoming targets of an unknown hijacker. In this case, the children all but abandoned their father, allowing the hijacker in the door to prey on their father's estate.

Cindy convinced herself that Ed's children got what they deserved as a result of neglecting Ed when he needed them most of all. She believes she deserves the inheritance because she was there for him. Do you recall the section in chapter 3 about hijackers and how they justify their crimes? They rationalize all their crimes to ease their conscience, just as Cindy does here.

How is a hijacker like Cindy thwarted and brought to justice? Cindy is a mix of coward and clever planner. One of Cindy's secrets to success is to not take too big a bite of the apple at one time. She is content to slowly nibble away until nothing but the core remains for the beneficiaries of her victim's estates. This tactic, not taking too much at a time, is a common tactic for many hijackers who prefer to stay below the radar. Cindy believes that small thefts will go unnoticed and unpunished while a large theft is always noticed and the thief is always pursued.

This story is not an unusual tale that occurs only in rural communities. This brand of hijacking is widespread and increasing as families drift apart in our transient society.

Case Study Five

HIJACKING WITH THE SILVER BULLET: MARRIAGE

It is true that you can marry more money in five minutes than you can earn in a lifetime. Marriage—I call it the "silver bullet"—is a powerful and foolproof hijacking tool. Once a couple marries, each spouse instantly receives special rights under the inheritance laws. Of course, everyone marries for love or passion rather than money. It is when the love and passion wane that the spouses' legal rights become more important and prominent in the relationship.

In our final case study, we examine the relationship between Marilyn and Harvey. There is no doubt that Marilyn married Harvey for his money, and that he was happy she did. He begged her to do so. Marilyn needed support, and Harvey needed love. Harvey is Marilyn's Target A victim, yet he was a willing victim. Does Marilyn's gift of happiness to Harvey mitigate Marilyn's successful hijacking of her large share of Harvey's estate? Harvey's children certainly do not think so. You can be the judge.

Marilyn uses the silver bullet.

December 7, 1941, is one of the most memorable dates in modern American history. The world gasped as the news of the Japanese attack on Pearl Harbor was spread by radio and newspaper. Everyone knew a new uncharted world was coming. But inside the maternity ward at Tampa General Hospital, the turbulent outside world was a distant distraction for the moment. A newborn baby girl brought gasps to her parents. "She's so beautiful," her father, Jesse, said as he held the tiny baby in his large calloused hands for the first time, tears in his eyes, at his wife's bedside. "What shall we call her, Mama?" Jesse asked his wife.

"I decided on Marilyn," her mother, Theresa, said.

"It's a beautiful name for a beautiful girl," Jesse said. "Marilyn Brennan. That sounds good to me."

Jesse gently laid his new daughter in Theresa's arms. The new parents gazed at their daughter and silently wondered what cards life would deal her. They hoped life would be good to her and spare her any unnecessary pain. They did not hope for fame or fortune for their new daughter any more than they wished fame and fortune on themselves. Life had taught them that fame and fortune was not their destiny, and they accepted that.

Marilyn spent her youth in Ruskin, a farming community at that time. The war years were good to her father and mother. Both had plenty of work on the farms owned by their neighbors. Jesse was a jack of all trades and master of none. His strong hands and back were always in demand where hard work needed to be done. Theresa did cleaning and laundry for the farmers' wives who needed help in their homes.

After Marilyn came her twin brothers, Darrell and Hiram, in 1947. Born only six years apart, Marilyn and her brothers were born into different generations. Darrell and Hiram were the first of the baby boomers. As impressionable young men in the later 1960s, they were caught up in the Beatles, Rolling Stones, and drugs generation. Through television, the news of hope for a new and better world through the new self-awareness induced by new drugs reached the farms of Ruskin, Florida. The twins listened to the new prophets of the new generation. Timothy Leary told them to turn on and drop out.

The boys compared their lives in Ruskin with what was offered in the outside world. They looked to the future and saw it in a place other than Ruskin. One Saturday morning, they broke the news to their parents and drove off in their Ford pickup for greener pastures.

Marilyn was just enough older than her twin brothers that she wasn't caught up in the wave of the new generation. By the time the Beatles' first hit began to usher in the era of rock and roll, Marilyn was married with two children. She did not have time to change her lifestyle, or even time to think about it. Marilyn thought of herself as an old-fashioned girl when she compared herself to her younger brothers.

Marilyn was something of a Ruskin farm girl version of Marilyn Monroe, who had burst on the popular culture scene in 1957. She was blond and sexy and knew it. Just below the surface of her demure natural innocence, Marilyn radiated a rare form of animal magnetism that attracted men and women alike.

When Marilyn graduated high school in 1959, she decided Tampa was as far away from home as she wanted to go for college. Marilyn walked into Plant Hall at the University of Tampa one Tuesday morning to apply for admission to the teaching college. She had purposefully dressed as conservatively as possible to make a good impression on the admissions staff. Her conservative appearance heightened her innocent appeal and made her even more attractive.

On her first day of classes, Marilyn saw Brad, literally across a crowded room. "There is a man I would like to meet," she thought. Brad had seen Marilyn earlier in the day. "There is a girl I have to meet," he thought.

Brad tracked Marilyn down as she was walking to the cafeteria that afternoon and politely introduced himself. Marilyn liked his confident, easy manner. Most men either made fools of themselves trying to impress Marilyn or fell all over themselves in her presence. Marilyn never felt that men were comfortable in her company. Therefore, she was not comfortable in the company of men. Brad's confidence was a welcome change. Marilyn felt she met a friend when she met Brad, someone she could trust.

Brad graduated two years later with a bachelor's degree in engineering. Marilyn finished her associate's degree the same year. That summer they were married in Ruskin with their families and friends. Jesse and Theresa had been saving for Marilyn's wedding for some time. They threw the best wedding party they could afford. Brad's parents, who were moneyed people with some social standing in Tampa Bay, secretly wished Brad had married better than a local farm girl. But they could not begrudge him the pleasure of marrying the best girl he would ever meet in his entire life. They understood why he loved Marilyn as much as he did.

Jesse and Theresa watched as Marilyn and Brad gleefully drove away from the reception with "Just Married" written on the rear window of their car. They thought back to that day in the hospital when they wondered what life had in store for Marilyn. Jesse and Theresa thanked God that afternoon that God was treating Marilyn very well in their view.

Brad went into the contracting business with a loan from his parents. The couple settled down in Ruskin because Marilyn wanted to raise her children where she had been raised. They both worked hard at building their lives when the Vietnam War came into the American consciousness. The war and social upheaval during the 1960s and 1970s did not change their lives in Ruskin much. Work was plentiful for Brad during those years. The two children, Margaret and Sean, were strong and healthy.

Throughout their marriage, Brad considered himself to be the luckiest man alive. He had married the most beautiful girl in the world in his eyes. They had two wonderful children. Life was good for Brad, and he appreciated it.

Marilyn's world was expanding as she approached her thirties. She became sensitive to the issues raised by the so-called women's libbers. Marilyn had never been totally comfortable in her role as an attractive woman. She always felt people never looked beyond her beauty to her other qualities. Doors were opened for her by her beauty, and she was grateful for that advantage, but she felt deprived of further opportunities. Early in life Marilyn chose not to exploit her beauty. She could easily have been a model or perhaps an actress and lived off her good looks, but she didn't want that lifestyle for herself.

"People treat me as nothing more than a dumb blonde," she told her friends. "I want more than that out of life."

Marilyn desperately wanted out of her stereotyped image as a blond bombshell. She saw the women's movement as a path to her liberation. Marilyn joined a chapter of the National Organization for Women in Tampa and flourished with her peers. All were trying to find their identities in what was a man's world. The chapter sponsored a party for the Billie Jean King vs. Bobby Riggs tennis match in 1973. The event drew a large crowd. There was plenty of taunting and betting on the match. When Billie Jean King bested Bobby Riggs, the victory lifted the hopes of women everywhere. Women knew they were the intellectual equals of men. Now they were physically equal.

As Marilyn aged though her twenties, thirties, and forties she became even more attractive. Her girlish innocence evolved into an elegant womanly presence that men found even more attractive.

Marilyn took a job in public relations with a small Tampa firm. She relished the independence her own small paycheck provided. In spite of Marilyn's independent ways, or maybe to overcome her independence and make her his subservient wife, Brad took pride in being the bread winner and paying all of the bills. He showered Marilyn with all she wanted. He believed his role in life was to be the sole provider for his household, and he took that job seriously.

Brad's business flourished and declined with the Florida business cycles. Brad attempted to expand his business several times, but his timing was never good. His strategy was to expand during a growth business cycle. He inevitably chose the peak of the cycle, just before business opportunities contracted. Brad lost money on each attempt.

Brad's last attempt to expand the business came at the height of the residential building boom in 2005. Land prices were escalating daily. Homes that sold for one hundred thousand dollars in 2003 were now selling for two hundred thousand dollars in 2005.

Brad was about to celebrate his sixty-fifth birthday. The housing business had taken its toll on Brad. He was frustrated because his dreams of becoming a major player in the housing industry remained unrealized. He lost money on each attempt.

In 2005, at the height of the housing boom, two young men approached Brad to buy his business. They promised a small down payment and a lifetime of income for Brad and Marilyn. Brad thought it was wonderful and almost too good to be true.

Brad had thirty-five homes under construction. The buyers promised to immediately take over the business, pay Brad a healthy part of the profits on each home under construction, and pay a commission to Brad for each home they built in the future. Brad loved the finances. He would be set for life.

There was one stumbling block to the plan. Neither of the buyers possessed a contractor's license. The buyers needed Brad's license to operate the business until they obtained their own license. They promised it would not be long. Brad fully understood the risk he was taking. As contractor of record, he was personally responsible for each home. If any financial problems developed, his personal assets would take the hit. Brad had his eye on the profits and overlooked the financial risks.

At the height of the construction boom of 2005, the banks were lending money to anyone who walked through the door. The bank's construction departments were overworked and undermanned. They could not possibly supervise the draws taken by contractors on construction loans adequately. Brad had built an excellent reputation for honesty with the local banks over the decades, so the bankers did not worry about Brad's projects. At the height of construction, they did not even bother to inspect Brad's jobs. They knew that if Brad was the contractor, all was well.

The two buyers took advantage of Brad's hard-earned reputation. As soon as they gained control of the bank accounts, they put a freeze on paying subcontractors. The subcontractors did not worry because they believed Brad would pay them as soon as he was able. The two buyers told the subcontractors that the banks were so busy they were behind in paying the construction draws to the company.

"Keep working," they told the subcontractors. "All is well."

The subcontractors kept working. The banks continued paying draws to the company for the completed work. The subcontractors were not being paid. Soon the sophisticated subcontractors placed construction liens on the homes for payment. The home owners received lien notices in the mail. The banks received lien notices as well. The law requires banks to obtain a release of the lien before paying a draw to the contractor. However, the banks ignored the notices.

The math was simple, the two buyers thought. There are thirty-five houses under construction. They planned to embezzle one hundred thousand dollars in construction money from each house for a total of three and a half million dollars. They would then disappear. Their plan yielded slightly less than they had planned, but three million dollars is a lot of money.

The subcontractors began calling Brad at home, politely asking him for their money. Brad called his two buyers, who blamed the late payments on a new bookkeeping system. Brad did his best to reassure his subcontractors, some of whom had worked for Brad for decades. The demands increased. The subcontractors hired lawyers, who filed lien foreclosure suits. The home buyers became frantic and hired their own lawyers. The banks realized what was happening and alerted their lawyers. The home buyers contacted the news media and the state attorney, looking for help. Brad refused to be interviewed by the television stations. The state attorney began asking for information about the construction problems. Brad hired a lawyer, who told him there are severe criminal penalties for diverting construction funds, and that he, as contractor of record, was personally responsible.

Brad was frantic. He could not sleep. His buyers refused to return his telephone calls. Then the telephone at Brad's office went out of service because the bill had not been paid. The landlord began eviction proceedings for non-payment of rent. The new buyers had disappeared. The business bank account had less than one hundred dollars on deposit.

Brad reviewed his situation. Here he was at sixty-five years of age, broke because he had been swindled. He saw no possibility of starting over. The state would undoubtedly revoke his contractor's license. He wondered, "How will I tell Marilyn we have only our social security to live on? And we must sell our beautiful home?" Brad drove to his office one last time and parked in front of the locked and dark office. He prayed for mercy on his soul and that God would help his family. He pulled his Colt thirty-eight caliber revolver from under the seat where he had placed it that morning. Brad cocked the hammer and put the barrel into his mouth. He wondered if he should close his mouth or keep it open. He closed his mouth on the cold barrel, tasting the gun oil. Fully conscious that he did not want to pull the trigger, and knowing that he would regret pulling the trigger of the pistol as soon as he heard the blast, yet knowing that life was no longer liveable, Brad pulled the trigger.

Six months after Brad's death, Marilyn found herself in dire financial straits. The tragedy and feelings of self-guilt had overwhelmed her. She used her faith in God and personal strength to persevere. Brad's business practices left her with nothing but his social security survivor's benefits as an inheritance. Their beautiful home had been heavily mortgaged to finance his business. His estate was bankrupt. She considered herself fortunate to have her job at the public relations firm, although she wondered how long she could keep the job with all of the young people wanting to break into the business at any level.

Marilyn moved from her large home in Ruskin into a rented condominium in one of Tampa's best resort living subdivisions. Her strategy was to mingle with the affluent and hope for the best. Marilyn fit into the social scene among her neighbors and was soon going to parties and playing bridge and tennis on a regular basis.

Not yet over the loss of Brad, Marilyn kept her distance from the men she met. She was not yet ready to begin another relationship, even on a casual basis.

Although Marilyn had aged, she still retained the magnetism she possessed when she was a teenager. That magnetism was now mixed with a tasteful mature style, which was admired by the women and men she met. Among the widows in her social circle, Marilyn was a standout.

Marilyn caught the attention of Harvey Cohen during her first winter at the condo. Harvey spent the summers in New York near his children and wintered in Tampa. He had been widowed for three years and was lonely. Although he loved his wife, he decided it was time to move on. Harvey was retired and approaching his seventieth birthday. He was not at all attracted to the widows around his own age, yet he was fearful of approaching younger women lest he be thought of as a dirty old man. Harvey wished to retain his dignity in his late years. His problems were solved when he met Marilyn. Harvey fell head over heels for her. Here was a woman worthy of any man.

Harvey, intending to impress Marilyn, invited her to dinner at Bern's Steak House, the best restaurant he knew in Tampa. Knowing that he was risking a lot, Harvey made his intentions known to Marilyn on that first date.

"I am not a young man," Harvey told Marilyn over coffee in the third-floor Dessert Room. "When I see something I want, I lose no time in pursuing it. Marilyn, I want you. I hope you will consider me worthy."

Marilyn picked up her cup and sipped her coffee, looking at Harvey over the rim of the cup. She considered her options in life, put down the cup, and said, "I like you too, Harvey."

"That's a start." Harvey smiled his broad smile that Marilyn would learn to love.

...

"She's a gold digger," Harvey's daughter, Sara, told him. "I would not trust her. She is not at all like Mom. She looks like a floozy to me."

"You just met her," Harvey answered. "You do not know her. She is a wonderful woman."

"I call them like I see them," Sara answered. "She will never take Mom's place. I can tell you that."

Harvey began to get angry. "You need to be more tolerant," Harvey said.

"I am not going to let some stranger walk into our family and disrupt everything," Sara said. "If you do anything foolish, I don't know what I will do."

Harvey changed the subject. "Nice weather today, isn't it?"

Sara took a more conciliatory tack. "I am just looking out for you, Daddy."

Harvey hugged his daughter, "I know, honey."

...

Sara telephoned her brother, Seth. "I don't trust this woman," she said. "Marilyn is her name. She looks like an old Marilyn Monroe. She isn't even Jewish. Dad should know better."

"Calm down," Seth said. "I am sure there is nothing to worry about. Dad is a smart man. Daughters always dislike their father's new lady friends. Relax."

"Maybe we can have him declared incompetent so he can't marry her. She will walk away without our inheritance."

Seth answered, "I'm sure Dad is smart enough to do a prenuptial agreement with her. He wouldn't throw everything away on her."

"I don't know," Sara said. "Old people do funny things."

"If you are worried about the money, talk to Dad," Seth said.

"Oh, sure. Then I will look like the gold digger. No thanks."

"Then you just have to leave it as it is," Seth said.

...

Harvey wined and dined Marilyn and knocked her off her feet. He showered her with gifts. Harvey skipped spending the summer in New York with his children. He and Marilyn vacationed in Italy that summer.

Harvey, wishing to be a gentleman, asked Marilyn to marry him in front of the Trevi Fountain in Rome.

"Will you marry me, please," Harvey asked. "You will be my trophy bride." Harvey slipped a two-karat diamond on Marilyn's finger, and they kissed in the middle of the crowded Italian square.

. . .

When Sara heard of the engagement, she was beside herself. She called her father. "Dad, Seth and I have been talking. You need a prenuptial agreement before you get married."

"Why would I need that?" Harvey asked.

Sara tried to sound as diplomatic as possible. She took a deep breath before speaking. "Because you need to protect your money," she said.

Harvey was quiet for a moment.

"Dad, did you hear me?" Sara asked.

Harvey spoke in the measured tone he used with his children at those times he wanted to make it perfectly clear to them that he was having the last word and the conversation was ending. "I will talk to my lawyer," he said to Sara.

Sara understood her father's tone and meaning. "Okay, Daddy, I love you."

. . .

Harvey wondered how Marilyn would react to a suggestion that they enter into a prenuptial agreement. Harvey's understanding of a prenuptial agreement was limited to what he picked up in conversations with his social contacts. Harvey's friends were people with money on both sides of the relationship. They each owned substantial assets and worried about protecting those assets from their new spouse and their new spouse's children. In cases where both the husband and wife were wealthy, they simply agreed not to make any claim on the other's assets.

Harvey did not know that a prenuptial agreement can provide for a surviving spouse such as Marilyn, who had no assets of her own. He assumed that if he suggested a prenuptial agreement, Marilyn would receive nothing at his death. Harvey did not want Marilyn to be destitute, so Harvey chose not to deal with the issue. He did not want to do anything to taint his relationship with his fiancée, whom he adored more each day. However, he was afraid to marry until he had resolved the questions his daughter raised. He did not wish to disinherit his children. Since he did not know what to do, he decided to do nothing. When he was in New York next, he would visit his lawyer and work things out. Until then, he decided, he would do nothing to change the status quo. Harvey did not talk of the wedding date and changed the subject when it did come up. Marilyn grew uneasy with Harvey's unwillingness to talk about their wedding.

Soon after meeting Harvey and learning of his intense interest in her, Marilyn began researching the inheritance laws. She learned that a prenuptial agreement may leave her with nothing at Harvey's death. She also learned that if they married, she would be entitled to an elective share of 30 percent of his estate if he tried to disinherit her. If she and Harvey never married, she would be entitled to nothing at his death. She had been through that scenario with Brad and did not wish a repeat performance. Marilyn decided that if she was to devote her time to Harvey, she should be entitled to inherit some part of his estate if she survived him. It was only fair, she decided. She was confused and did not know how to proceed. She had no idea of Harvey's financial situation. She just knew he did not worry about money. Should she demand they marry immediately? Was the engagement a ruse on Harvey's part to use her until he no longer wanted her? Were Harvey's children working on him?

Harvey surprised Marilyn with a trip to Las Vegas for her birthday. "Is this a set up for a wedding?" Marilyn wondered. She hoped so. After all, Las Vegas is the marriage capital of the world.

Marilyn was almost giddy with anticipation when they flew into Las Vegas. Their suite at the Wynn Resort was exquisite. Marilyn did her best to please Harvey and make him feel like the luckiest man in the world to be with her. Marilyn was full of expectation and was painfully disappointed. Harvey did not say a word about marriage.

The day before their scheduled departure for home in Tampa, Marilyn was frustrated with not having a wedding ceremony. She planned drastic action.

At dinner, she announced to Harvey, "I want to get married before we leave Las Vegas."

Harvey did not know what to say. He had not planned for Marilyn's untimely demand. Harvey thought about what to say next. He had not spoken to his lawyer about a prenuptial agreement. He decided to stall.

"I would also like to get married before we leave Las Vegas, but I need to talk to my lawyer," Harvey told Marilyn.

"Talk to your lawyer about what?"

"About our marriage. You know, a marriage contract."

"A prenuptial agreement?" Marilyn asked.

"I guess so," Harvey said.

The only thing Marilyn knew for sure about prenuptial agreements was that she might be totally disinherited if she agreed. She did not know that a husband and wife can make other arrangements, such as an adequate income for life to the wife, rather than totally disinheriting the survivor.

Marilyn slipped her engagement ring off of her finger and slid it across the table to Harvey. Tears came to her eyes. "If you do not love me enough to take care of me, I do not want to be with you anymore," she told Harvey, who was stunned by her words.

Harvey quickly took stock of his situation. He saw that he was on the verge of losing the last woman he would love and adore in his entire life. He too believed a prenuptial agreement would leave Marilyn with nothing if he died. "Is this how I want to end my life?" he asked himself. "Do I always want to regret losing this woman because I wasn't willing to provide for her after I'm gone? Is this the kind of man I am? Will I give up happiness with her to hoard my money for my children? Do I want to die lonely and alone?"

Harvey decided to let his heart control his actions rather than his pocketbook. He reached across the table for Marilyn's hand and slipped the ring back on to her finger. He signaled for the waiter to come to the table and asked, "How does one get married around here?"

. . .

The wedding ceremony was performed the next day. Harvey and Marilyn boarded their flight back home to Tampa as husband and wife.

When Sara heard of the wedding, she cried for a week. Seth assessed the situation and decided there was nothing to be done but to hope for the best, which was the death of Marilyn before his father.

Two months later, Harvey was on the golf course with his regular foursome. Marilyn was watching her television when she heard the siren as the emergency vehicle drove into the subdivision. The telephone rang. Marilyn picked it up and learned that Harvey had suffered a massive heart attack on the golf course.

A week later Marilyn met with her lawyer to discuss Harvey's estate and her future. She learned that because she was what is called a pretermitted spouse, she was entitled to half of Harvey's estate, and she was entitled to act as the administrator of his estate.

The lawyer had done some preliminary investigation into Harvey's assets. He informed Marilyn that she was now a wealthy woman.

Sara and Seth visited their own lawyer and learned there was nothing they could do about the loss of one-half of their inheritance.

Sara asked the lawyer, "But they were married for only a few months. I know she is a gold digger. I can't prove it. But I know she tricked him into marrying her. Doesn't this count for something?"

"Unfortunately, no," the lawyer said. "Marriage is one of those things that can rarely be attacked. And the law is the law."

"Well, this law isn't fair," Sara said.

. . .

Marilyn became a regular with the bridge and tennis groups at the club where she and Harvey met. During one long afternoon while she was playing bridge with her lady friends, the conversation turned to the European cruise Marilyn had planned for the coming summer.

One of the ladies thoughtfully said, "We are a fortunate group of ladies, to live in such luxury."

Marilyn nodded in agreement and said nothing. Her friend had said it all in Marilyn's opinion.

Comments on Marilyn and the silver bullet

This case demonstrates again that several legitimate but different points of view are possible when an inheritance is at stake.

Although Marilyn married for the money, there are mitigating factors. Harvey was in love with and pursued Marilyn until she relented and married him. Therefore, she brought him happiness. It may have been a fair exchange. Marilyn was asked to be a hijacker, although Harvey's children will not agree. Harvey's children see this as a clear-cut case of marrying for the money and stealing a large part of their inheritance.

Contrast this with the case of the spouse who tricks the other into marrying with false promises of undying love and affection. There is no mitigation in such cases. The estate is hijacked in cold blood.

There is not much more to say about the effect of marriage on an inheritance that is not revealed in this case study. Once married, the surviving spouse will inherit a large portion of the deceased spouse's estate without fear of attack by others. This is true even if the surviving spouse used undue influence, deceit, and fraud to coax the deceased spouse into marriage. What two people whisper to each other is between the two of them. Once dead, a person cannot testify he was tricked into marrying someone. Even if trickery can be proven in court, it is not reason under the law to deprive the surviving spouse of his or her inheritance. Of course, marrying someone for money is always risky business. There is no guarantee on just how long they will live.

Parting Comments

As the author of *Inheritance Hijackers*, I would like to thank you for reading this book. I hope reading the book has been as pleasurable for you as writing it was for me. Most of all, I hope you have learned to protect your family and your inheritance.

One last word of advice. Please do not become overly concerned and look for hijackers under every rock. My goal is not to panic you. Now that you know the telltale signs of hijacking, just keep your eyes and ears open and communicate to those involved. Remember to consult professionals before doing anything. Plan early and often and all will be well.

GLOSSARY

accounting. A list of transactions and explanations of those transactions.

administrator. A person who manages a probate estate or a trust, otherwise known as a personal representative, executor, trustee, surrogate, or conservator.

annuity. Payment of a fixed sum on a regular basis. Typically an insurance policy providing for monthly payments to begin on a fixed date and continue until death or a fixed number of years.

beneficiary. One who receives a gift or is entitled to an inheritance or other benefits such as income from a probate or trust estate.

codicil. An amendment to a will that does not revoke the earlier will but usually makes minor additions or changes.

competency. Possessing the minimum legal capacity to perform an act such as making a will.

conservator. See **administrator**.

decedent. Deceased person.

descendant. One who is born of another, such as a son, grandson, etc.

donee. One who receives a gift; one who is empowered to act in a power of attorney.

donor. One who voluntarily makes a gift either during their life or after death in a will or trust; one who gives the power to act in a power of attorney.

due execution. The signing of a will with the formalities required by law. In most states, the law requires a will to be signed in the presence of witnesses, who must sign evidencing their presence.

duress. Threats of unlawful activity to force a person to commit an act. A threat to do any lawful act, such as threatening to collect a lawful debt, is not considered unlawful duress.

elective share. The share of an estate that the decedent's surviving spouse can demand if the spouse is disinherited or dissatisfied with the gift otherwise made to them. In Florida and other states, the elective share is typically 30 percent of the entire estate, including assets that are not part of the probate proceedings.

estate. The whole of a person's property and wealth; the assets being administered in a probate proceeding, called the "probate estate;" the assets being administered under a trust, called a "trust estate."

estate tax. The tax imposed by federal and state governments on a decedent's estate.

executor. See **administrator**.

expectancy. The reasonable belief that one will receive an inheritance.

family trust. A trust made by an individual or couple that is designed to manage assets during life and transfer the estate to beneficiaries within the family at death.

fiduciary. One who is trusted and relied upon by another person and who owes a duty of loyalty under the law to the other person. This includes administrators of probate estates and trusts, and guardians of persons and property among others.

fiduciary relationship. The connection between a fiduciary and the person who is owed the duty of loyalty from the fiduciary.

fraud. The use of deceit to obtain anything of value, or the use of deceit to cause a person to act.

generation skipping tax. An estate tax imposed on gifts or inheritances when the gift skips a generation. An example is an inheritance given to a grandchild rather than a child. This tax is in addition to ordinary estate tax. Currently, approximately $1,060,000 can be given before incurring the tax.

grantor. One who makes a trust, sometimes known as a "settlor," or who conveys real or personal property to another, who is known as a "grantee."

hijack an inheritance. To unlawfully divert an inheritance from an intended recipient to another by unlawful means.

hijacker. One who hijacks an inheritance.

health care surrogate. A person empowered to make health care decisions for another who is unable to make those decisions for him or herself.

homestead property. The real estate on which a person resides. In some states this has been extended to mobile homes, boats, and motor homes.

incompetency. Lacking the minimum legal capacity to perform an act.

inherit. To receive by will, trust, or operation of law.

inheritance. That which is inherited.

insurance trust. A trust created to own an insurance policy on the life of a person. At the death of the insured person, the insurance proceeds go the beneficiaries free of estate tax. This trust is used in larger estates to avoid estate taxation.

irrevocable trust. A trust that cannot be amended or voided either when made or on the happening of some act, such as the death of the maker. See **revocable trust**.

insane delusion. A form of incapacity resulting from the contention that a person has a diseased mind and has reached a conclusion that has no basis in fact.

intestate. To die without a will. In such cases, state law controls distribution of assets and appointment of an administrator of the estate.

joint tenancy. Ownership of an asset by two or more people in equal shares with the stipulation that if any owner dies, the survivor owns the asset by operation of law. See and contrast with **tenancy in common**.

letters of administration. The document issued by a probate court judge to the administrator giving them the power to act on behalf of the decedent of a probate estate.

life estate. The right in an individual to use an asset until their death, commonly used in real estate matters.

lineal descendant. A person of the same blood line who is born later, such as a child, grandchild, etc.

lineal ascendant. A person of the same blood line who is born earlier, such a father, grandfather, etc.

litigant. Party to litigation.

litigation. The commencement and maintenance of a lawsuit to settle legal issues in dispute.

living will. A written document stating an unwillingness to be artificially kept alive when death is eminent.

lucid moment. A short, temporary period where an otherwise incompetent person regains their legal mental capacity to sign a will.

maker. One who creates a will or trust, also known as testator (male) or testatrix (female), settlor, or grantor.

minor. A person who has not reached the age of majority, typically eighteen years.

mistake in execution. The act of signing a document believing it to be a different document, thereby rendering the executed document void.

oral will. A spoken will, not valid in most states, including Florida.

personal representative. See **administrator**.

petition to the court. A document telling the court why you are entitled to the court's assistance and what you want the court to do for you.

pour-over will. A will used in conjunction with a trust in estate planning to ensure all the assets of the maker of the trust are placed under the authority of the administrator of the trust. A pour-over will states that all assets of the maker that are not already under the jurisdiction of the trustee of the trust are transferred to the trustee.

power of attorney. A written document that gives the donee the power to do legally binding acts the donor of the power can do. The person who gives the power is the donor. The person receiving the power is the donee. The power may be broad, known as a general power, or restricted to a few acts, known as a limited power.

pre-need guardian. A person nominated in advance to act as a court appointed guardian if the need arises.

prenuptial agreement. A written agreement before marriage that controls the distribution of the couple's assets in the event of divorce or death. This agreement can be made after the marriage ceremony as well.

presumption. A legal conclusion that is reached if certain facts are present, or a fact that is assumed to exist when circumstantial evidence is presented to the court.

private trust. A trust made by an individual that is designed to manage his or her personal estate during life and transfer the estate to beneficiaries at death. See **revocable living trust**.

probate. The legal system that administers both testate and intestate estates. "To probate a will" means to ask the probate court to recognize the will. In both testate and intestate estates, the court grants legal authority to the administrator of the estate.

probate estate. An estate administered under the jurisdiction of the probate court.

remainderman. One who succeeds to ownership at the end of a life estate. See **life estate**.

revocable living trust. A written document created by a person to manage their property during their life and efficiently pass the inheritance at their death. A revocable trust can be amended or voided by the maker at any time before death, when it becomes irrevocable and cannot be amended or voided. This is the most common estate-planning tool after the will. See **trust**, **irrevocable trust**, **testamentary trust**, **insurance trust**.

settlor. One who makes a trust, sometimes called a "grantor" or "maker."

statute. A law enacted by the state legislature.

surrogate. One who acts for another. See **administrator**.

Target A. The hijacker's first victim, the donor of an inheritance.

Target B. The hijacker's second victim, the intended recipient of an inheritance.

tenancy by the entireties. Joint ownership between only a husband and wife.

tenancy in common. Ownership of an asset by two or more people in equal or unequal shares. Should an owner die, his share is inherited by his beneficiaries. Contrast with **joint tenancy**.

testamentary trust. A trust created in a will, which is effective at death rather than during life. See **revocable living trust**.

testate. To die with a will.

testatrix. Female who makes a will.

testator. Male who makes a will.

tortious interference. Unlawfully interfering with the right of a person to inherit an asset, a cause of action aside from other probate- or trust-related causes of action.

trust. A written document created by a person, the "maker," to manage property. The maker appoints an administrator, called a "trustee," who takes control of the property held in the trust and manages the property as directed by the trust to benefit the beneficiaries of the trust. The trustee has a fiduciary duty to the beneficiaries and the maker. See **revocable trust, irrevocable trust, testamentary trust, insurance trust**.

trust contest. A court proceeding to determine the validity of a trust.

trust estate. The property held in a trust under the jurisdiction of the trust. See **estate**.

trustee. The administrator of a trust. See **administrator**.

undue influence. The use of deceit, threats, or other underhanded means that cause an impact upon a person, such that the person is under the control of the influencer and their acts are considered not to be of their own free will. The control need not be over all aspects of the person's life. A will or trust procured by undue influence is void.

will. A written document that directs the distribution of the maker's estate and appoints the administrator of the estate among other things. Wills can be revoked at any time and are of no legal significance until death.

will contest. A court proceeding to determine the validity of a will.